Cannibals
&
Philosophers

CANNIBALS

&

PHILOSOPHERS

Bodies of Enlightenment

Daniel Cottom

The Johns Hopkins University Press
Baltimore and London

© 2001 The Johns Hopkins University Press
All rights reserved. Published 2001
Printed in the United States of America on acid-free paper
9 8 7 6 5 4 3 2 1

The Johns Hopkins University Press
2715 North Charles Street
Baltimore, Maryland 21218-4363
www.press.jhu.edu

Library of Congress Cataloging-in-Publication Data
Cottom, Daniel.
    Cannibals and philosophers : bodies of Enlightenment
/ Daniel Cottom.
        p.   cm.
    Includes bibliographical references and index.
    ISBN 0-8018-6551-4 (alk. paper)
        1. Body, Human (Philosophy)   2. Enlightenment.
    I. Title.
    B105.B64 C68   2001
    128'.6'09033—dc21   00-040562

A catalog record for this book is available
from the British Library.

This book is for you, Shug

Contents

ILLUSTRATIONS

PREFACE

*A*T FIRST glance the examples of cultural forms to which I devote my attention in this book might seem to have been chosen in an idiosyncratic manner. In a cultural study of the eighteenth century focused especially on matters related to the Enlightenment, why would one be confronted with a painting of a ray fish, with androids, with a resort city, with voyages in the South Seas, and finally with deathbed kisses? What are these things doing here, and what can they possibly have in common?

It is true that across a wide range of studies, including art, philosophy, anthropology, social history, and literary theory, few topics have attracted more attention in recent years than that of corporeality, which is at the forefront of my concerns here. Notable scholars in this area include Norbert Elias, Mikhail Bakhtin, Michel Foucault, Julia Kristeva, Ludmilla Jordanova, Evelyn Fox Keller, Steven Shapin, Barbara Maria Stafford, Thomas Laqueur, Kathleen Wellman, Anne C. Vila, Mary Ann Doane, Susan Meld Shell, Arthur C. Danto, Judith Butler, Mary Jacobus, Roy Porter, and Susan Bordo. Even readers predisposed to be interested in this topic, however, might be puzzled by my decision to consider together these particular tokens of eighteenth-century culture. Accounts of the Enlightenment do not usually direct us to dwell upon things such as these, or at least do not grant them the importance they are accorded here.

If these examples seem eccentric, I argue, it is because we need to revise our sense of what is central to eighteenth-century European culture. I hasten to acknowledge that many others have preceded me in challenging what was once considered to be the canonical fare in eighteenth-century studies, encouraging inclusion of the sorts of texts, events, and histories that I address. For example, a widely read book by Peter Stallybrass and Allon White, *The Politics and Poetics of Transgression,* remains an important precursor to studies of the sort that I am pursuing.

In this book I argue that the artifact known as the Enlightenment was defined from the beginning through an obsession with guts and disgust as much as through the mind and reason. Indeed, I contend that we falsify history when we fail to recognize the visceral turn that binds together the former and the latter terms. The thinking that led me to choose the examples of cultural forms I study here was guided, in part, by my concern to show the ways in which what I call the visceral turn in this era manifested itself in virtually every aspect of cultural life. Whether we attend to intimate and ancient bodily rituals or modern social ceremonies, to practices of art or science, to technological invention or imperial exploration, or to cannibals or philosophers, we find this turn playing a crucial and constitutive role. Moreover, we find that this role was widely recognized and debated at the time, despite the fact that it has generally been elided from what have come to be the dominant images and standard narratives of this period.

Thus, my readings here extend from canonical eighteenth-century works to those texts and elements of texts more usually ignored so that good taste, of a sort, may prevail. I argue, for example, that disgusting questions of incorporation, assimilation, and digestion are vital to the most refined and philosophical self-images of the Enlightenment. One way I pursue this argument is through unconventional pairings of writers and philosophers, such as Tobias Smollett and Immanuel Kant or D.A.F. de Sade and Georg Wilhelm Friedrich Hegel. These pairings enable me to take up some of the textual passages on which these writers' claims to canonicity are based and to analyze the part of the sentence that generally does not receive attention, the rest of the paragraph from which the sentence is excerpted, or the larger contexts out of which the passage is drawn. Through this strategy and others, I seek to draw attention to a figurative logic, a rhetoric of visceral embodiment and metamorphosis, that travels in and across the discourses of this era. One might say, then, that my argument does not concern an "underside" or "other side" of Enlightenment thought so much as it does the insides of this thought and of the wider culture in which it arose.

Given the title of this book, I should clarify from the outset that this is no more a work of philosophy than it is one of cannibalism. I do deal extensively with philosophical writings (in the broader sense that the term *philosophy* bore in the eighteenth century) as belonging to one form of discourse among others in this time. However, I do not treat them as having a special explanatory privilege in relation to these others. One of my contentions, in fact, is that our most familiar conceptions of the Enlightenment can prevent us from recognizing how the works and images of this age arose from visceral matters that we tend to exclude from our consideration precisely because we cling to an ahistorical conception of philosophy. Similarly, while cannibalism is a major issue in this book and the subject of its longest chapter, readers should be advised that for the most part this issue appears only in passing moments in the other chapters. At the same time, I would note that a reading of the book as a whole may suggest why such passing moments may yet be of great consequence for our understanding of culture, both in the eighteenth century and in our own day.

In the eighteenth century human flesh became a new thing, a flesh of sensibility, a surface of stimuli whence all knowing proceeds and against which it must be measured. As I explain in chapter 1, "In the Bowels of Enlightenment," this change gave new meaning to an old maxim, Nihil in intellectu quod non fuerit prius in sensu (Nothing is in the mind that was not first in the senses). Henceforth illumination would need come from the opening of the body: the new ideal of human autonomy would be forced to come to grips with human anatomy. Although it is too simplistic to state flatly that conjectural innate ideas were transformed into the palpable, dissectable, scrutable internal organs of the body, this statement captures a major aspect of Enlightenment thought, one that still continues to influence representations of this era and of the development of modern science with which it is identified.

As all concerned soon came to realize, however, one could not appeal to the senses without disrupting them or experiencing their disruptiveness. As they were brought under philosophical conceptions and made the basis for philosophical conclusions, the senses turned out to be torn by conflicts, including profoundly political conflicts. This was the case because in one form or another, the desire in any appeal to the senses was bound to find itself struggling for recognition in the historical conflicts of social life. Therefore, whether explicitly or implicitly, in appealing to the senses writers were compelled to articulate the cultural politics that they believed should determine how questions would be posed, answers formulated, and conclusions acted upon. As so many thinkers of this age were troubled to recognize, there could be no noncontroversial appeal to sense perception.

We can see attempts to work through this problem in the effort to imagine other possible orders of the senses, which became a topos of Enlightenment writing. In another contemporary response to this problem, writers often imagined metamorphoses in this world and in other possible worlds beyond the familiar reaches of sense experience. More generally, eighteenth-century natural philosophy frequently returned to an emphasis on metamorphosis because this was an image through which the assumption of a uniform nature could be correlated with the recognition of natural diversity. The problem of sense experience was especially exacerbated at this conjuncture of natural uniformity and diversity, for it was here that the fundamental relation between sameness and difference had to be articulated; and in this pre-Darwinian era, metamorphosis was the mechanism called upon to perform this articulation. The self-contradictory, self-abhorring, self-consuming figure of the cannibal, in which metamorphosis might find no proper beginning or end, then entered into this drama of knowledge to stand for all the uncertainties in the Enlightenment conception of the world. In the image of cannibalism, Western self-regard and its vision of otherness in nature, culture, and spirit came to a momentous crisis, which I analyze in the first chapter by focusing on writings by John Locke, William Blake, and James Joyce. The other writers who play a part here include Thomas Hobbes, Margaret Cavendish, Isaac Newton, Gottfried Wilhelm Leibniz, Benedict de Spinoza, Alexander Pope, Jonathan Swift, Laurence Sterne, Pierre Louis Moreau de Maupertuis, David Hume, and Voltaire.

The title of chapter 2, "Orifices Extended in Space," is designed to convey the eighteenth century's revision of the Cartesian definition of bodies. I reconsider the implications of Cartesian philosophy through the art of Jean-Siméon Chardin. In particular, I analyze Chardin's *The Ray* (1728) in the contexts of his other paintings, eighteenth-century aesthetics, and the reception of his work from his own time to the present day. My argument is that the totemic image displayed in this painting is designed to lead us to think through the status of art, systems of cultural classification, and the nature of human identity. By the way it calls forth and studiously deforms the image of geometry, which was closely associated in this time with Cartesian reasoning in particular and rationalist systems in general, this work may be seen as challenging contemporary conceptions about the differences of gender, the hierarchy of genres, the organization of society, and the revelation of divinity. It was, in fact, seen in precisely this way, as I explain through my discussion of contemporary critics such as Baillet de Saint Julien, the Abbé Raynal, and Denis Diderot, all of whom wrote about Chardin's work as an issue of a potentially unsettling visceral understanding. (I also take into account later critics, from the brothers Goncourt in the nineteenth century to twentieth-century writers such as Marcel Proust and Francis Ponge and scholars such as Ronald Paulson, René Demoris, and Michel and Fabrice Faré.)

Within my consideration of Descartes and of these critics, I also explain how Chardin's work may be usefully understood in the context of Enlightenment science as represented, for example, by the natural history of J. B. Robinet and the physiology of Albrecht von Haller (who was a great influence on Diderot, Chardin's critic and friend). I conclude that the wonder of Chardin's painterly line in *The Ray* stems from the way that it so suggestively anticipated a new philosophical climate of discourse. In this Enlightenment climate, the axiomatic foundations of human nature would wriggle out of their deductive confines and into a sensationist realm of experience in which categories such as *animal, man,* and *spirit* might seem to be consuming one another before one's very eyes. Similarly, in *The Ray*—in which the ray fish appears also as a human figure; as a paradigmatic object of display, utility, desire, and consumption; and even as the art of painting—Chardin stages the unsettling drama of vision seeing itself.

I then turn my attention to the androids made and exhibited by Jacques de Vaucanson in the middle of the eighteenth century: a flute-playing faun, a duck, and a Provençal musician. In chapter 3, "The Work of Art in the Age of Mechanical Digestion," I focus especially on Vaucanson's duck, which was famous for its apparent capacity to eat and digest grain. If we regard it from the perspectives offered by the scientific, philosophical, and social and cultural histories of its day, we can see that this duck was a work brilliantly designed to exhibit the meanings of bodies in the eighteenth century. I establish this point in relation to seventeenth- and eighteenth-century mechanistic theories and in terms of René Descartes's controversial conception of animals as machines. I also consider how Vaucanson's automatons were recognized by his contemporaries (such as Charles Bonnet, Voltaire, John Turberville Needham, the Marquis de Condorcet, and Diderot) as provocations to established conceptions of humanity.

This chapter is then concerned with issues of commodification, industrial manufacture, and technological form as they intersect with questions of aesthetic evaluation and philosophical meaning. For instance, I argue that in writings of and about the eighteenth century, the term *materialism* is a marker for a nexus of newly imaginable transformations, epitomized in Vaucanson's duck, which included the question of which cultural styles, social groups, and forms of life might "eat" others—even as Vaucanson's flute-playing automaton had symbolically incorporated its model, a statue by Antoine Coysevox (one of the favorite sculptors of Louis XIV). Most generally, I am concerned here to study the problem of delimiting sense perception in an age in which machines had taken the place of the senses not only through scientific practice, industrial process, and artistic design but in the very substance of the human body, insofar as it was imaginable. In addition to Descartes, the philosophers who enter into this argument include Leibniz, Julien Offroy de La Mettrie, Diderot, Hume, and Kant. I am also concerned to trace the aftereffects of the Enlightenment conception of the machine through certain Romantic representations (in the works of Jean Paul, Mary Shelley, and E.T.A. Hoffmann) and on into the art, philosophy, and literature of the twentieth century. Sigmund Freud and Walter Benjamin become important in this last regard, as do artists such as Jean Tinguely, Andy Warhol, and Karen Finley.

Whereas chapter 2 focuses on a painting and chapter 3 on a machine, chapter 4 focuses on a city. In "The Exchange of Fluids in the Beau Monde," I study the modern invention of Bath under Beau Nash, with special attention to the fluid exchanges among scientific, erotic, aesthetic, social, economic, and political matters in the practice of "taking the waters" at spas. At this time Bath came to be a byword for the heterogeneous orders of things, dissolutions of boundaries, and confoundings of bodies that were seen as typifying recent historical developments; and in the complex alliance of medicine, fashion, and commerce at Bath, I argue, we see an attempt to explore and symbolically manage these historical developments. For example, I consider attempts to deal with the perception that even as science was being constituted as a novel source of technological innovation and economic growth, its empiricist basis was bound also to suggest a phantasmic social equality and anthropological relativism. It even came to suggest an apologetic attitude toward cannibalism, such as we find in the writings of Robert Boyle (a pioneering analyst of mineral waters) as well as in those of Michel de Montaigne and Sade. Hence the way that cannibalism turns up as a central concern among those who are skeptical about modern medicine in Christopher Anstey's *New Bath Guide* (1766) and Smollett's *Humphry Clinker* (1771)—and as a concern that is as immediately social and political as it is physical.

In thinking through the implications of this situation, I study contemporary medical works about spas and mineral waters (such as those of William Oliver and Friedrich Hoffmann); popular guides to spas (such as those of James Schofield and Philip Thicknesse); relevant philosophical works by Boyle, Hume, and Kant, among others; and literary works by figures such as Daniel Defoe, Fanny Burney, Oliver Goldsmith, Jane Austen, and Sir Walter Scott. I then come to my conclusion about the cultural experiment that was the city of Bath through a comparison with Bishop Berkeley's *Siris* (1744), a highly influential tract that advocated "tar water" as an alternative to spa waters and, indeed, as a panacea for all human ills and a potential boon to the political economy of British industry and the slave trade.

In chapter 5, "Cannibalism, Trade, Whatnot," my concern with cannibalism as a topic and theme is brought to bear upon the "literal" figure of the cannibal in eighteenth-century European representations. My most central examples come from journals and narratives based on the voyages of Captain James Cook, but I analyze the figure of the cannibal from the time of early European encounters with the New World, as in the writings of Bartolomé de Las Casas and Montaigne, on into its theorization in twentieth-century psychoanalysis and anthropology. My argument, in brief, is that the figure of the cannibal ceased to be literal almost as soon as it appeared as such. Defined minimally as the consumption of human remains by other humans, cannibalism was obviously thinkable (human remains were even a regular part of the *materia medica* employed from the Renaissance through the eighteenth century). The real issue was how to deal with the tendency shown by the concept of cannibalism, once it was allowed to be thinkable in any case, immediately to overrun its own borderlines in all cases until nothing coherent, nothing literal, was left either of this behavior or of the flesh that was its nominal object.

Eighteenth-century writers were forced to confront this incoherence in the very notion of cannibalism, which depends upon an impossibly narrow conception of "eating" and an impossibly broad conception of one's "own kind." For instance, philosophers such as Voltaire and the Abbé Raynal came to see cannibalism as a displacement and disavowal of the European consumption of human flesh that was so grievously carried out in the slave trade but also in myriad forms of exploitation. We see a similar recognition worked out in Defoe's *Robinson Crusoe*, in which we may witness the transformation of cannibalism from a foreign category of behavior into a compelling and universal form of desire. Through this novel and the many voyages, narratives, and philosophical works that I use in the interpretation of Cook's encounters with the natives of New Zealand, I draw out the implications of the fact that during this era, in which the cannibal came to be merchandised as an object of consumption, the philosopher came to be seen as the cannibal's apologist. I conclude the chapter with a comparison of Sade and Hegel, who bring to a perverse conclusion the lines of thought about cannibalism that had been set down by Las Casas and Montaigne.

Having successively considered paintings, machines, spas, and cannibals as cultural forms, I bring this book to a close in chapter 6, "Kant Comes to His Senses," by focusing on a specific form of cultural behavior: the kiss. In particular, I analyze Thomas De Quincey's portrayal of the deathbed kisses of Immanuel Kant and Admiral Horatio Nelson ("Kiss me, Hardy!"). I argue that the kiss is, in effect, an attempt to articulate the body: to reassert and reenact its imaginary identification with the origins of transcendent cultural form. Consequently, an analysis of its representation in De Quincey's writings can bring us to see the fundamental assumptions bound up in this author's conception of culture. I bring out these assumptions about masculinity, nationality, race, and sexuality, among other things, by reading De Quincey's portrayal of deathbed kisses in relation to his sources and to other contemporary representations.

Because the aesthetic theory of the eighteenth and early nineteenth centuries is at issue in the beauty and sublimity attributed to these kisses, I also examine the aesthetics of De Quincey, Edmund Burke, and Kant, among others, in relation to contemporary physiological theory, which shared the term *sensibility* with aesthetics. (Jean-Baptiste van Helmont, George Ernst Stahl, Théophile Bordeu, Johann Friedrich Blumenbach, and Xavier Bichat are among the physicians and natural philosophers whose work I consider here.) Through my analysis of this relation I am able to explain, for instance, why Kant conceived of sex, if unsanctified by marriage, as being cannibalistic. We better understand Kant's thinking in this regard if we consider why his great admirer, De Quincey, made the kiss of the man-eating crocodile central to his *Confessions of an English Opium-Eater* (1821/1856). Finally, as with the arguments in the other chapters, my analysis here is also brought forward to cultural issues in our own time—most notably, in this case, through references to the work of Kiki Smith, the contemporary artist. Overall, the emphasis in this chapter on "coming to one's senses" then serves to sum up the visceral turn in understanding that I have identified from the outset as being definitive of the troubled epistemology of the Enlightenment.

ACKNOWLEDGMENTS

*F*OR THEIR GENEROSITY in responding to various parts of this book at various stages of its composition, I would like to thank Elizabeth Langland, Stephanie Smith, John Murchek, Caryl Flinn, Ellen Greene, Henry Golemba, Barbara di Genevieve, Eve Bannet, Michelle Lekas, Rick Barney, Ron Schleifer, and Brandy Kershner—invaluable comrades all. Encouragement I received from Nancy Armstrong and Rey Chow was especially timely and is hereby, very inadequately, noted, as is my good fortune in the form of my editor at the Johns Hopkins University Press, Maura Burnett. I am indebted as well to Carol Houlihan Flynn and Dennis Des Chene, for their careful critique of the entire manuscript, and probably above all to Leonard Tennenhouse, than whom I will not have a finer reader. I will not spurn the convention of noting that those I name are in no way to be held responsible for any infelicities that may remain.

I would also like to thank the editors and publishers of the journals *differences, Representations,* and *Novel,* in which abbreviated or otherwise different versions of chapters 2, 3, and 4 first appeared. Acknowledgment should also be given to the curators and librarians of the History of Science Collection at the University of Oklahoma, who made my research so much easier than it might otherwise have been; Sylvia Legare and Steve Wagner were especially helpful. Finally, for their help in obtaining the images reproduced in this book, I would also like to thank Erich Lessing and Simon Taylor of Art Resource, Jennie Rathbun and Roger E. Stoddard at the Houghton Library, Zoë Morley of the Anthony d'Offay Gallery, Jo Charlton of the Wallace Collection, Eileen Sullivan of the Metropolitan Museum of Art, and Kate Gillespie and Alma Pellicer of PaceWildenstein.

Cannibals
&
Philosophers

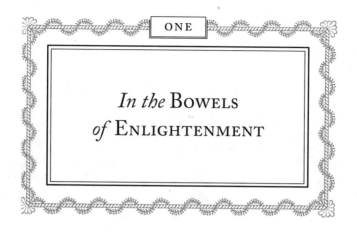

ONE

In the BOWELS
of ENLIGHTENMENT

All flesh is grass.
—Isaiah 40:6.

I N THE SEVENTEENTH and eighteenth centuries human flesh became a new thing, a flesh of sensibility, a surface of stimuli whence all knowing proceeds and against which it must be measured. According to early modern science, the establishment of knowledge depends on the organization of the human body and on our understanding of that organization. Voltaire helped to popularize this conception of knowledge in describing the era of the Enlightenment in terms of a desired progress from a condition bereft of certain possibilities of perception to one in which the human senses can function more fully, as they ought to do: "Before Kepler, all men were blind, Kepler had one eye, and Newton had two eyes."[1] Voltaire's suggestion that the conception of the human body had undergone a radical historical transformation reflected the new importance that this body had come to hold in the cultural imagination of his age. The transformation was certainly not as extreme as he suggested it to be, but his hyperbole does capture the importance accorded to the body in the establishment of knowledge in the early modern era. If one sought illumination, one would seek it henceforth from the revelation of the

[1]

flesh and so also, more profoundly, from what lay under the flesh. Consequently, the Enlightenment ideal of human autonomy would be forced to come to grips with human anatomy. No more would humankind imitate "the *Ancients*, whom a fond *Superstition* deterr'd from *Dissections*"; the *"Anatomy of humane Bodies"* should now be recognized, wrote Joseph Glanvill, as "this excellent *Art*, which is one of the most *useful* in a humane Life, and tends mightily to the *eviscerating* of Nature, and disclosure of the *Springs* of its *Motion*."[2]

As the epigraph to this chapter may serve to acknowledge, a concern with the nature of the flesh was not exclusively an issue of the Enlightenment. Nonetheless, a redefinition of the flesh is distinctive of this age and of its legacies unto the present day. For when Pierre Louis Moreau de Maupertuis opened his *Earthly Venus* (1744–46) with a sentence that might seem to paraphrase Isaiah—"We have received but a short while ago a life we are soon to lose"—he was yet saying something quite different about the nature of existence from what the prophet had traditionally been understood to mean. For a philosopher of nature like Maupertuis, writing "without the enlightenment of religion," the earth of flesh and grass was no longer a self-evident ground.[3] It had been transformed into a demanding new territory of pulsing organs and orifices, animals and instruments, vital processes and mechanisms and fibers shuddering with revolutionary hope. Flesh had become a new sort of substance, a flesh of worms and webs and machinery. The conception of human knowledge had taken a visceral turn, which I explore in this study by considering how certain eighteenth-century writers, artists, voyagers, and philosophers labored to come to terms with this corporeal transformation in the conception of human understanding.

If we investigate this visceral turn in the era of the Enlightenment, we discover unsettling experiences that are inseparable from what intellectuals now sometimes call "the project of the Enlightenment" and yet, in one way or another, unacceptable to it. In other words, we discover the driving contradictions of this age. These are contradictions that we fail to see when we too readily accept popularized images of this era such as the one I have just quoted from Voltaire or the one I am about to quote from Jean-François Lyotard. In the past as in the present, with disheartening predictability, the contradictions of social life tend to converge upon the sites of our greatest supposed certainty; and so as God was to Nicholas of Cusa and or as human rights appear to those who now live under the sway of democratic polities, so it was with viscera in this age of anatomical dissection and vivisection.[4] It is in the guts of this age that we can see into the puzzles of its reason. If we look into the body of this time, into this supposed basis for knowledge, we can learn something of how this knowledge was made out of contemporary uncertainties, anxieties, fantasies, hostilities, and desires. My argument, in fact, is that we must have recourse to the unsettling bowels of the Enlightenment, where distinctions were supposed to be made between what would be assimilated and what cast out in nature, culture, and spirit, if we wish to understand some crucial aspects of this era in European cultural history.

Lyotard's influential characterization of this age in terms of "grand narratives" of transformation in consciousness and society has helped to define, by way of contrast, the postmodern condition in which we are now said to live, bereft of the ancestral faith in universalizing narrative form.[5] The cues from which this postmodern characterization are taken, however, were already quite impressively articulated in the eighteenth century. They were communicated through an emphasis on visceral understanding that ate away at the seeming universality of narratives put forth in the name of reason. Like Voltaire's characterization, Lyotard's description of this age turns it into a polemical image that fails to capture the complexities of the cultural and social life of the time. In opposition to this sort of simplification, I am arguing (as Lyotard himself went on to argue elsewhere) that to miss what is visceral about the Enlightenment is in a sense to miss it all.[6]

In eras of dramatic social change such as the eighteenth century, in which events drive people to become more markedly self-conscious about their conditions of existence, reconceptualizations of the body are likely to follow.[7] As we can see today in popular images of the body as a computer, or as "wetware," one way people work to understand their lives so as better to satisfy their changing perceptions of the world is through such reconceptualizations. At the same time, in any representation of the body we end up binding ourselves to figurations whose implications we cannot entirely measure in advance of their historical development. This general consideration must be of particular importance to an era defined in large part, by its most influential spokespersons, through a privileging of corporeal knowledge. To recognize the unsettling visceral turn within this knowledge, we must attend to bodies not only in their most abstract formulations but also in the popularly reiterated images or tropes that traversed eighteenth-century philosophy, art, literature, anthropology, and medicine, among other fields of study, all of which were far from having attained the distinct disciplinary status that they suffer today. This is why the chapters that follow focus on the metamorphic relations among certain material forms—food, machinery, water, flesh, mucous —as they may be seen to incorporate newly demanding conceptions of filth and divinity, masculinity and femininity, race and reason, or manners and sexuality and national destiny, among other things. One of the results of this examination will be a questioning of certain categories central to discussions of this era, such as *science, aesthetics, morality,* and *materialism.* Another will be a reconsideration of some of the oppositions conventionally employed in analyzing the Enlightenment, including those between sensibility and reason, desire and disgust, and technology and spirit.

Of crucial importance in this era's visceral turn is the work of John Locke, which was perceived as giving a new significance to the old Scholastic maxim, popularly attributed to Aristotle, Nihil in intellectu quod non fuerit prius in sensu. When Denis Diderot cited this maxim, he did so in conjunction with a reference to Locke, whom he characterized as arguing that man "would have remained like a brute beast, an automaton, a machine in movement, if the use of his material senses had not set the faculties of his spirit to work."[8] "Locke has unfolded human reason to mankind," wrote Voltaire in 1734, "the way an excellent anatomist explains the inner works of the human body."[9] Yet at the same time as the senses were thus emphasized, in Locke's writings as in those of others, they were rendered terribly problematic. Before taking in the testimony of the senses, one had to figure out what these deponents actually were. Before evaluating their evidence, one had to come to grips with the consideration that the constitutive nature of the senses was not self-evident—quite the contrary.

One character who sought to trace the implications of the Lockean attitude was Laurence Sterne's Tristram Shandy. Tristram's droll and doleful excursus upon the threefold "cause of obscurity and confusion, in the mind of man"—specified as comprising "dull organs," "slight and transient impressions made by . . . objects," and "a memory like unto a sieve"—concluded in a summary identification of the senses with an obscure plug of "red seal wax" in the pocket of Dolly, his chambermaid.[10] This image marks a decided comedown even from the argument of Ralph Cudworth, the seventeenth-century philosopher, that nature "is but an image or imitation of wisdom, the last thing of the soul, which hath the lowest impress of reason shining upon it; as when a thick piece of wax is thoroughly impressed upon by a seal, that impress, which is clean and distinct in the superior superficies of it, will in the lower side be weak and obscure."[11] Yet while he certainly is an idiosyncratic character in other respects, Tristram was perfectly in tune with his age in thus suggesting that the organs of perception can be represented only through displacement and mockery. His complaint repeats a commonplace of empiricism with which Robert Hooke, for example, had prefaced his *Micrographia* (1665) and against which Cudworth had sought to maintain his reactionary neo-Platonic conception of nature.[12]

Tristram's account of the organs of perception is also comparable to that offered by Margaret Cavendish in her wonderfully zany fantasy, *Description of the New World, Called the Blazing World* (1666). In this work Cavendish emphasized the doubtfulness of sense evidence, the false testimony that might be had from telescopes and other optical devices, and the slipperiness in differentiations among various species of creatures. Similarly, Sterne recognized that once society turns to the senses for authority, it is bound to find no end of fantastic turns. "Well might Locke write a chapter upon the imperfections of words," Tristram says, employing the rhetorical turn, or trope, of litotes.[13]

In early modern science, a pressure toward universality was placed upon human anatomy and all its parts, up to and including "the brain, the most noble entrail of the human body," as it was called by Johann Friedrich Blumenbach.[14] Through this pressure, the fleshly envelope that was privileged as the originary site of knowledge was simultaneously abstracted from itself. It was not in vain that near the beginning of his *Principia Mathematica* (1687), Isaac Newton laid down the rule that "in philosophical disquisitions, we ought to abstract from our senses, and consider things in themselves distinct from what are only sensible measures of them."[15] The antinomy implied by this rule, which Immanuel Kant would seek to overcome in his distinction between phenomena and things in themselves, created a problem for philosophy that has endured to the present day. As Hilary Putnam has said, "Since the seventeenth century, philosophy has oscillated between equally unworkable realisms and idealisms."[16] This was also, however, an impasse with which people in every area of culture had to struggle, because the issues bound up in Kant's philosophical distinction between phenomena and noumena owed their compelling significance to ongoing movements in Western social history, science, medicine, exploration, trade, and colonization. These were areas of experience in which bodies had been asserting themselves in revolutionary ways, heedless of whether a philosophical justification for their demonstrations lay ready to hand.

Represented tendentiously by Voltaire in his *Elements in the Philosophy of Newton* (1738) and satirically by Diderot in the eighth chapter of his tale of garrulous vaginas, *The Indiscreet Jewels* (1748), the symbolic conflict between Cartesian tradition and the tradition of Newton has long been seen as marking a general advance from deductive to inductive reasoning or from metaphysical speculation to empiricist demonstration. As is commonly the case in such battles, however, there is no question but that this narrative of events is quite misleading as to the ins and outs of affairs at the time. For evidence of how misleading it can be, one need only think of René Descartes's concern with anatomical dissections or Newton's devotion to the doctrines of Christianity even unto their most speculative, apocalyptic modes. Self-declared spokesmen for the Enlightenment such as Claude-Adrien Helvétius might want to dismiss Newton's biblical exegeses as the sort of absurdity into which even geniuses can tumble, but Newton knew better.[17] When he felt it necessary to offer God as a foundation for human physiology, he did so because he recognized, more acutely than Helvétius would, that a security was needed for the testimony of the senses that they themselves, even when granted the frameworks of mathematics and science, were incapable of furnishing. "Every man, so far as he is a thing that has perception, is one and the same man during his whole life, in all and each of his organs of sense," he felt impelled to write near the end of the *Principia;* "God is the same God, always and everywhere."[18] Traditional authorities and beliefs could not be summarily eliminated from discussions that thenceforth might be devoted to a definitively objective analysis of physiology, natural history, sealing wax, chambermaids, and similar topics; matters were rather more complicated.[19]

Gottfried Wilhelm Leibniz, for example, did not want to have his understanding of that well-worn Scholastic maxim confused with the version that had been put forth by the notoriously irreligious Thomas Hobbes. Therefore, to Hobbes' "For there is no conception in a mans mind, which hath not at first, totally, or by parts, been begotten upon the organs of Sense," Leibniz would add the qualification *nisi ipse intellectu,* "save for the mind itself."[20] (A similar concern would lead Newton to speak ill of Locke and then to write him a letter of apology: "I took you for a Hobbist," he explained.)[21] We can see further evidence of how misleading the triumphalist narrative of empiricism may be in the fact that the nineteenth-century French translator of George Ernst Stahl's *Theoria Medica Vera* (1706) felt obliged to add a long footnote where Stahl cited this same adage. The anxious translator insisted that Stahl certainly should not be accused of materialism or sensationism; the eminent physician was referring only to the senses of fallen humanity, as distinct from the immortal soul.[22]

By this time, of course, other reinterpretations of the Enlightenment conception of the body had arisen, with William Blake railing against Newton and Locke and with Georg Wilhelm Friedrich Hegel emphatically declaring, "No prejudice is probably more false than the thesis that nothing exists in thought which has not existed in the senses."[23] Still, it is significant that this symbolic battle between Descartes and Newton did seem to be clearly delineated in the eighteenth century and so served to epitomize the growing conviction among learned persons that when it came to thinking about the nature of the world and of the humanity existing in it, it was necessary to turn away from conjectural innate ideas and toward the palpable, dissectable, scrutable organs of the body. From this conviction arose those images described by Anne C. Vila as being "typically associated with the figure of the Enlightenment philosophe: images of opening up, of uncovering what lies hidden in the human heart, mind, and body, and then of representing what one has seen with the feverish talent and enthusiasm of the natural genius."[24]

The Newtonian image of clockwork mechanisms did not simply and utterly displace metaphysical systems, not by any means. However, it did suggest a new understanding of what it might mean to say that there was nothing in the mind that was not first in the senses. Attention was turned toward the physical interiors of living things, as when Louis Bourguet defined the difference between minerals, on the one hand, and plants and animals, on the other, through the perception that the former grew by accretion from the outside whereas the latter grew from the interior: "The internal parts of plants and animals . . . are like the master wheels of the machine."[25] Similarly, while the Baron d'Holbach's *System of Nature* (1770) was generally seen as a terribly simplistic work, as well as an outrageous one, it but followed the dominant discourses of this time in attempting to trace historical events such as wars back to visceral causes such as "blood too inflamed in the heart" and "painful digestion in the stomach."[26] Although it would indeed be too simplistic to state flatly that in the eighteenth century innate ideas were transformed into internal organs, still this statement captures a major aspect of Enlightenment thought, one that continues to influence representations of this era and of the scientific developments with which it is identified. In the words of the distinguished contemporary philosopher W. V. Quine, "The most notable norm of naturalized epistemology actually coincides with that of traditional epistemology. It is simply the watchword of empiricism: Nihil in mente quod non prius in sensu. This is a prime specimen of naturalized epistemology, for it is a finding of natural science itself, however fallible, that our information about the world comes only through impacts on our sensory receptors."[27]

In the light of these considerations, we can see why it is important to examine how visceral understanding, in both the literal and the figurative senses of the term, became a locus for contradictions in the philosophy and everyday life of this era. The Marquis de Sade's Saint-Fond may have been an extreme case; but when he said that he favorably compared Nero to Vespasian on the basis of "the interior sensations that the one and the other must have received, as a result of the different inclinations with which the one and the other were endowed, the different vibrations by which they were moved," he was simply reproducing a language of sensibility increasingly shared by physiologists, philosophers, and novelists ever since the seventeenth century.[28] As a locus of difference, potential conflict, and outright contradiction, in other words, visceral understanding existed well within the supposed mainstream of Enlightenment thought. It is there to be read in the writings of figures such as Locke, Voltaire, and Kant. Yet it also was forced to exist outside the Enlightenment insofar as the thought of this era has been transformed into disembodied narratives such as the one that would sweep us forward from Descartes's subjective turn to Newton's physics, Kant's transcendental idealism, and contemporary philosophies of science such as Quine's. In contrast to the simplicity of bodies, or "sensory receptors," in such narratives, the antinomy of the body in the Enlightenment made it an anamorphic blot on the landscape of this era, at once showing too little and too much, exceeding the conceptual forms that had turned to it for their basic definitions, and so becoming a ground not only of definition but also of upsetting metamorphoses.

As they existed paradoxically both within and without the Enlightenment body, there at the interface of the body proper and of all that might be considered alien to it, the bowels proved especially well suited to represent this connection between definition and metamorphic transformation. It is with good reason that Friedrich Nietzsche saw fit to consider modernity through "the metaphor of nourishment and digestion."[29] As represented in this book through the still lifes of Jean-Siméon Chardin, the androids of Jacques de Vaucanson, the natives of New Zealand encountered by Captain James Cook, the city of Bath in the time of Beau Nash, and the act of kissing as Thomas de Quincey saw it memorialized in the dying moments of Kant and Admiral Horatio Nelson, the bowels of the Enlightenment were also bowers of imagination powerfully revelatory of the complexity of contemporary experience. To look at this matter from another direction, we might follow Julien Offroy de La Mettrie in noting that "the imagination plugs itself with the viscera" in this era.[30]

Obviously, this imaginative recourse to the bowels neither began nor ended with the Enlightenment. De Quincey was among those who would point out that the bowels possessed an ancient warrant as the site of the most profound and otherwise unimaginable experiences of humankind. In premodern societies it may have been the hiddenness of the viscera, their occult nature, that helped to qualify them for this role. In modernizing Western societies a more dramatic emphasis was placed on viscera in their connection with the primary physiological mechanisms of alimentation, digestion, and elimination. They were also associated with all the other processes internal to the body, such as the circulation of the blood established by William Harvey in his *De motu cordis* (1628) and then quickly made a metaphor for the revolutions empirical science was bringing to the basic understanding of nature and society. Moreover, to pay attention to the viscera, by the eighteenth century, was also to focus on orifices and thus on the body as a sexual, cultural, social, historical, and political entity existing in and through its exchanges with other bodies, human and otherwise. Accordingly, to have "entrails," in the jargon of the theater in France during this period, was to possess sensibility; to have *peu d'entrailles* was to be lacking in this distinguishing human virtue. In this context it made perfect sense for Diderot, in *The Dream of D'Alembert* (1769), to have Mlle. De l'Espinasse offer Doctor Bordeu the image of an arachnid's viscera as a figure for human sensibility. "Imagine a spider at the center of its web," says Mlle. De l'Espinasse. "Disturb a thread, and you will see the alert animal hasten forward. So then, what if the threads the insect draws from its intestines, and pulls back when it so desires, composed a sensible part of itself?" Bordeu promptly endorses this image and says that the threads of this metaphorical web run throughout the human body and thus communicate, through the impressions all things make upon one another, with the entirety of the universe.[31]

To some extent, the confusing impasses in the modern conceptualization of the body, as in this metamorphic identification of humanity with the guts of insects, represented a problem that had already been manifesting itself during the Renaissance. As David Hillman has explained, "The interior of the body . . . which (for Christianity) had always been the ontological site of belief, became, in the sixteenth century, *also* the epistemological site of rapidly growing medical and anatomical knowledge, and the two modes of understanding, incompatible in terms of the kind of access to the body's interior they deem possible, jostled against each other."[32] Even beyond these aspects of the situation, however, there were problems internal to the conception of the body in the new mechanical philosophy based on empirical analysis and demonstration. By association with traditional Christian beliefs but also in terms of any and all ideologies, Enlightenment bodies opened unto supernatural and perverse questions. It is for this reason that even in the writings of professed materialists such as La Mettrie, the new philosophy still resembled the old turn toward *haruspicina:* the practice of divination through the study of internal organs.

In the bowels of the Enlightenment, the same motivations that universalized the body also historicized it; the same developments that made the senses more fundamental to knowledge also rendered their perceptions more mysterious. (Insisting on this paradox in empiricism, Leibniz remarked that "sensible qualities" were in fact "occult qualities"[33]—in other words, dogmatically postulated entities of the sort for which scholastic reasoning had been discredited.) In suggesting knowledge, entrails also solicited belief—and vice versa. Questions that might lead to a transcendental conception of reason, as in the thought of Kant, led also to a fixation upon visceral understanding, such as we see in Kant's own writings. Characterizing human beings in terms of internal organs might displace and transform certain traditional questions, but this mode of figuration could not succeed in dismissing these queries, which were determined by matters of cultural politics that were not susceptible to resolution through any single image, logic, or methodology.

Cultural politics determine how questions will be posed, answers formulated, and conclusions acted upon. It would be insufficient to speak here of a cultural context to science or (in Quine's formula) of a "background language," because normalizing terms of this sort overlook the agon, the contestation and violence, without which there could be no determination of a controlling cultural authority. One cannot appeal to the senses without also disrupting them, or experiencing their disruptiveness, because in one form or another the desire in this appeal is bound to find itself struggling for recognition in the historical conflicts of social life.

Kant recognized this situation perfectly when he explained that his task in the *Critique of Pure Reason* (1781) was to provide "safe passage" for human reason between "fanaticism" (to which "Locke left the door wide open") and "skepticism" (to which David Hume "surrendered entirely"). In the imagery with which he describes his task, the desire to assign reason "determinate bounds, and yet keep open for it the entire realm of its appropriate activity," must involve a perilous passage between "two cliffs" that are figuratively identified both with "doors" and with the aforementioned "eminent men."[34] These are described as figures through which reason might break its bounds or, alternatively, through which one might recklessly throw reason entirely away. In rhetorical terms, Kant's images here combine to form a catachresis, a figure of speech considered improper because it is based on a strained or logically irreconcilable collocation of references. Yet this catachrestic image of cliff-door-men makes an apt figure for the senses as they were being reconceived in this time. Like the ludicrous red wax of which Sterne wrote, this figure makes evident how the senses that are supposed to ground representation are yet bound to disrupt their own representation and thus to drive reason into contradictions.

In regard to this problem it is crucial to remember that although Locke won tremendous fame for an anatomy of human understanding based upon sense perception, he was equally concerned to emphasize the shadowy status of this understanding relative to its presumed grounds. In the preface to the first edition of his *Critique of Pure Reason*, Kant proclaimed the failure of Locke's attempt to bring an end to metaphysical conflicts "through a certain physiology of the human understanding" (7), but Locke himself had fully recognized that any appeal to the ground of the senses opened as many philosophical problems as it closed. In this regard he was quite unlike Thomas

Sprat, in whose *History of the Royal Society* (1667) we are offered a utopian image of scientific culture. In this culture "the differences which should chance to happen, might soon be compos'd; because they could not be grounded on matters of speculation, or opinion, but onely of sence; which are never wont to administer so powerful occasions of disturbance, and contention, as the other." Contradictions to this image are certainly everywhere to be read in Sprat's *History*, as in his decision to characterize science, when he arrives at the topic of its relation to Christianity, in terms of an emphasis on the limits of the senses.[35] In Locke's work, however, the indecisiveness of any appeal to the senses is a most explicit and dramatically marked concern.

In fact, Locke considered ideas of spirit and body as being of a kind in this regard. "I think, we have as many, and as clear *Ideas* belonging to Spirit, as we have belonging to Body, the Substance of each being equally unknown to us," he wrote. "Constant Experience makes us sensible of both these, though our narrow Understandings can comprehend neither. For when the Mind would look beyond those original *Ideas* we have from Sensation or Reflection, and penetrate into their Causes, and manner of production, we find still it discovers nothing but its own shortsightedness."[36] He added that "whensoever we would proceed beyond these simple *Ideas,* we have from Sensation and Reflection, and dive farther into the Nature of Things, we fall presently into Darkness and Obscurity, Perplexedness and Difficulties; and can discover nothing farther, but our own Blindness and Ignorance" (314). In this respect he anticipated Alexander Pope's comment in his prefatory remarks to the *Essay on Man* (1733): "It is therefore in the Anatomy of the Mind as in that of the Body; more good will accrue to mankind by attending to the large, open, and perceptible parts, than by studying too much such finer nerves and vessels, the conformations and uses of which will for ever escape our observation."[37] Similarly, Hume would write, "The most perfect philosophy of the natural kind only staves off our ignorance a little longer: as perhaps the most perfect philosophy of the moral and metaphysical kind serves only to discover larger portions of it," concluding that "the observation of human blindness and weakness is the result of all philosophy, and meets us at every turn, in spite of our endeavours to elude or avoid it."[38] Indeed, though it may seem paradoxical to say so, Locke's emphasis on the limitations of the senses actually contributed to the tradition of antiempiricist rhetoric represented by works such as Thomas Shadwell's *The Virtuoso* (1676) and Jonathan Swift's *Tale of a Tub* (1710).

The most familiar quotation from *A Tale of a Tub*—"Last Week I saw a Woman *flay'd*, and you will hardly believe, how much it altered her Person for the Worse"—is generally cited without reference to its immediate context, which is an excursus against the modern scientific approach to natural philosophy, here characterized in terms of a focus on the internal organs of the human body. Swift writes,

> The two Senses, to which all Objects first address themselves, are the Sight and the Touch; These never examine farther than the Colour, the Shape, the Size, and whatever other Qualities dwell, or are drawn by Art upon the Outward of Bodies; and then comes Reason officiously, with Tools for cutting, and opening, and mangling, and piercing, offering to demonstrate, that they are not of the same consistence quite thro'. Now I take all of this to be the last Degree of perverting Nature. . . . I do here think fit to inform the Reader . . . that in most Corporeal Beings, which have fallen under my Cognizance, the *Outside* hath been infinitely preferable to the *In*.[39]

Following a similar logic, William Hogarth made the culminating image in *The Four Stages of Cruelty* (1751) (see fig. 1) a travesty of the anatomical theater of Vesalius and of the entire Renaissance tradition of the autopsy as "a quasi-religious event."[40] Also travestying the original meaning of *autopsy* as "seeing for one's self," Hogarth's horrific scene comes complete with a dog idly mouthing an internal organ, bones boiled in a pot to remove their flesh, a generally inattentive audience, and a knife stuck right through an eye of the corpse, which has its head mockingly elevated by means of a pulley attached to a drill stuck in its brain, that noble viscera. Voltaire labored to similar effect when he had his Leibnizian philosopher, Pangloss, come back to life as he was being dissected after having been hanged, ineptly, during the auto-da-fé following the Lisbon earthquake. Reworking the same tradition, William Wordsworth would famously damn the philosopher who "would peep and botanize / Upon his mother's grave," offering the epigrammatic warning, "We murder to dissect."[41] As this last example may indicate, what came to be called Romanticism was as much a continuation as a rejection of the En-

FIGURE I.
William Hogarth, *The Reward of Cruelty,* from *The Four Stages of Cruelty* (1751),
Giraudon/Art Resource, N. Y.

lightenment, especially as this preceding era may be characterized in terms of a troubling, sublime, or sadomasochistically tormenting insistence on the limits of the senses.

Although it may seem paradoxical enough that Locke's conception of the senses might foreshadow Swift's reactionary Christian satire of science, Hume's skeptical critique of the logic of empiricism, and the turn of Wordsworth's thought that has sometimes been characterized as pantheism, this is not the only convolution of intention to be found in Locke's work. Despite his insistence on the shadowy narrowness of the senses, for instance, he could not keep himself from indulging in an "extravagant conjecture," a "wild . . . Fancy," in which he imagined "that Spirits can assume to themselves Bodies of different Bulk, Figure, and Conformation of Parts" and "so frame, and shape to themselves Organs of Sensation or Perception, as to suit them to their present Design, and the Circumstances of the Object they would consider." For example, "What wonders would he discover, who could so fit his Eye to all sorts of Objects, as to see, when he pleased, the Figure and Motion of the minute Particles in the Blood, and other juices of Animals, as distinctly, as he does, at other times, the shape and motion of the Animals themselves" (*Essay*, 303–4). In proffering this conjecture Locke made reference to microscopes, which had done so much to lead thinkers of his age to reconceive the nature of sense perception, as in Bernard de Fontenelle's *Conversations on the Plurality of Worlds* (1686–87). Locke was remarkable, however, for the rigor with which he drew out his conclusion that the "extravagant" and "wild" implications of the microscope would prove disturbing to human reason no matter how apologetically—or, as would be the case in Swift's *Gulliver's Travels* (1726), disgustedly—these implications were advanced. His speculations about other conceivable orders of the senses became a staple of eighteenth-century physiological thought, as in Bourguet's *Philosophical Letters* (1729) and Claude-Nicolas Le Cat's *Treatise on the Sensations and the Passions in General, and on the Senses in Particular* (1739).[42]

Locke concluded his excursus on spirits by faithfully supposing that it is best that our senses should have been fashioned as they are, in accordance with God's wisdom. After all, as he had observed from the outset, "If our Sense of Hearing were but 1000 times quicker than it is, how would a perpetual noise distract us. And we should in the quietest Retirement, be less able to sleep or meditate, than in the middle of a Sea-fight" (302–3). This attitude, too, would be echoed by later writers such as Bourguet and Le Cat. In imagining various metamorphoses of the body in his *Essay on Man*, Pope placed himself among those who recapitulated this reasoning. "If nature thunder'd in his op'ning ears," he wrote of his titular character, "And stunn'd him with the music of the spheres, / How would he wish that Heav'n had left him still / The whisp'ring Zephyr, and the purling rill?"[43] Through the proclamation of his faith in the providentially ordered hierarchies of nature and in the reason that took human nature for its study, Pope sought to keep the body in general and its senses in particular within clear bounds:

> What if the foot, ordain'd the dust to tread,
> Or hand to toil, aspir'd to be the head? .
> What if the head, the eye, or ear repin'd
> To serve mere engines to the ruling Mind?
> Just as absurd for any part to claim
> To be another, in this gen'ral frame:
> Just as absurd, to mourn the tasks or pains
> The great directing MIND of ALL ordains. (1.46–47)[44]

Even in the absence of a traditional Christian faith, the influence of this line of reasoning would long continue to make itself felt, as in George Eliot's *Middlemarch* (1871–72). Like Locke's *Essay* and Pope's poem, this novel is also preoccupied with the imagery of microscopic and telescopic vision, and at one point its narrator declares, "If we had a keen vision and feeling of all ordinary human life, it would be like hearing the grass grow and the squirrel's heart beat, and we should die of that roar which lies on the other side of silence."[45]

Although Locke did not share Eliot's sense of irony, he did note various complications of reason that could not be put to rest even by the pious invocation of divinity. These revealed themselves especially in his analysis of the distinction between nominal and real essences as they might be exemplified by the human body. First of all, he noticed the problem evidenced by conflicting definitions of human nature, as in the ancient formulas of *animal rationale* and *animal implume bipes latis unguibus*. (In writing of "the old matter of featherless bipeds and rational animals," Quine, among others, has continued this line of critique into our own time.)[46] Locke noted as well the debatable ontological status of human fetuses, as evidenced in historical controversies over whether they might be baptized. He then considered the problem of deformities, both by quoting historical accounts—"When the Abbot of St. Martin . . . was born, he had so little of the Figure of a Man, that it bespake him rather a Monster"—and by extrapolating from the questions posed by monsters, fetuses, and inconsistent definitions to a world of virtually limitless metamorphoses:

> Who would undertake to resolve, what *Species* that Monster was of, which is mentioned by *Licetus* . . . with a Man's Head and Hog's Body? Or those other, which to the Bodies of Men, had the Heads of Beasts, as Dogs, Horses, *etc.* If any of these Creatures had lived, and could have spoke, it would have increased the difficulty. Had the upper part, to the middle, been of humane shape, and all below Swine; Had it been Murther to destroy it? . . . I imagine, none of the Definitions of the word *Man*, which we yet have, nor Descriptions of that sort of Animal, are so perfect and exact, as to satisfie a considerate inquisitive Person; much less to obtain a general Consent. (*Essay*, 454–55)

It was not for nothing that Locke had studied medicine under Thomas Willis, who wrote of man as "a manifold *Geryon*."[47]

Locke's nominalism in this regard is of a piece with his radically equivocal representation of the senses, which can find no security for their impressions, either within the body or without it, save by the postulation of divine ordinance. Within, the senses are bound to be disturbed by the theoretically illimitable contingencies of physiological form; without, they can find no ultimate stability but only further doubt through instruments such as microscopes that might seem expressly designed to establish a ground of knowledge. Thus, after describing certain experiments in microscopy of which he has heard, in which the "little Bodies that compose that Fluid, we call *Water*" have been magnified "to 10,000; nay, to much above 100,000 times," Locke concludes that any such magnifications must still leave the primary qualities of water, "when examined, to be as incomprehensible, as any thing belonging to our Minds, and *a solid extended Substance, as hard to be conceived, as a thinking immaterial one*, whatever difficulties some would raise against it" (310).

It only makes sense, then, that in Locke's writing the mind is assimilated to the senses in all their metamorphic contingency. Although Benedict de Spinoza had scorned the adage that "there are as many differences of brain as of palates" (by the same logic that made him contemptuous of the adage, Nihil in intellectu quod non fuerit prius in sensu), Locke embraced it almost as fully as would Pierre-Jean-Georges Cabanis a century later.[48] "Men may and should correct their palates," wrote Locke, "and give a relish to what either has, or they suppose has none. The relish of the mind is as various as that of the Body, and like that too may be alter'd" (280). This metamorphic quality of the mind means that it is, on the one hand, manipulable but, on the other, so analogous to differentiations within and among species as not to be consistently swayed or defined. "We have our Understandings no less different than our Palates; and he that thinks the same Truth shall be equally relished by every one in the same dress, may as well hope to feast every one with the same sort of Cookery" (8). As Locke envisioned it, the problem is not simply one of addressing different minds appropriately so as to arrive at the same "truth"; rather, it lies in the need to recognize that there may be no ultimate convergence except in the tropological terms of simile or analogy. "Men may chuse different things," he wrote, "and yet all chuse right, supposing them only like a Company of poor Insects, whereof some are Bees, delighted with Flowers, and their sweetness; others, Beetles, delighted with other kinds of Viands" (270).

As played out in his conceptions of language, monsters, the senses, and bodies in general, the semiotic permutations in Locke's reasoning might even be taken to suggest that La Mettrie was following in Locke's tradition when he found it perfectly imaginable that a monkey might be transformed into a man—despite the fact that the materialist, atheistic, and libertine premises that La Mettrie claimed for his work would not otherwise seem to bear reference to the God to whom Locke paid obeisance. Similarly, Locke's reasoning helped to prepare the way for philosophers in the second half of the eighteenth century to be popularly identified as apologists for the palates of cannibals. The possibility of such transformations was prefigured not only in Locke's own words but also in those of other pious propagandists of Enlightenment, such as Pope, for whom man was yet a creature characteristically "in doubt" (2.7), a "being darkly wise, and rudely great" (2.4) and hence a "Chaos of Thought and Passion, all confus'd; / Still by himself abus'd, or disabus'd" (2.13–14).

Following Locke, Pope invoked boundaries beyond which "no eye can see, / No glass can reach" (1.239–40) while still maintaining that man's senses were appropriate to his condition. At some points he even laid claim to a certainty that was more blunt and, perhaps, more anxious than Locke's. "Man is not a Fly," he insisted (1.194), and presumably not a monkey or a bee, either. Not for him the conclusion to which John Turberville Needham would come in his *Observations upon the Generation, Composition, and Decomposition of Animal and Vegetable Substances* (1749), that all living things "return by a slow Descent to one common Principle, the Source of all, a kind of universal *Semen*"; not for him the conclusion to which the Academy of Projectors in Lagado arrived, that the best way to judge of thoughts was by examination of excrements.[49] Nevertheless, Pope did insist on doubt even in the midst of faith and delighted in vividly imagining metamorphoses of the human body, as of a sense of smell that would cause one to "die of a rose in aromatic pain" (1.100). Such passages in his writings may serve to indicate how the corporeal perversities of Joris-Karl Huysmans's *Against Nature* (1884), say, should be said to represent a further blossoming of the Enlightenment, not a turn away from it.

In fact, just as imagining other possible orders of the senses became a topos of Enlightenment writing, so did imagining metamorphoses in the perception of this world and in others beyond the senses. So Robert Hooke suggested, "'Tis not unlikely, but that there may be yet invented several other helps for the eye, as much exceeding those already found, as those do the bare eye, such as by which we may perhaps be able to discover *living Creatures* in the moon, or other Planets." (He also went on to imagine "*many* Mechanical Inventions" that would improve the other senses in the same way that optical devices had altered the sense of sight.)[50] Newton helped further to establish this emphasis on metamorphosis when he considered that God—"an uniform Being, void of Organs"—might so exceed the properties of "our little Sensoriums" as "to vary the Laws of Nature, and make Worlds of several sorts in several Parts of the Universe." Even looking out at the natural world as it was presently available to the human senses, he saw metamorphoses throughout:

> The changing of Bodies into Light, and Light into Bodies, is very conformable to the Course of Nature, which seems delighted with Transmutations. Water, which is a very fluid tasteless Salt, she changes by Heat into Vapour, which is a sort of Air, and by Cold into Ice, which is a hard, pellucid, brittle, fusible Stone. . . . Mercury appears sometimes in the form of a fluid Metal, sometimes in the form of a hard brittle

Metal . . . or in that of a red opake volatile Earth, call'd Cinnaber. . . . Eggs grow from insensible Magnitudes, and change into Animals; Tadpoles into Frogs; and Worms into Flies. All Birds, Beasts and Fishes, Insects, Trees, and other Vegetables, with their several Parts, grow out of Water and watry Tinctures and Salts, and by Putrefaction return again into watry Substances. . . . And among such various and strange Transmutations, why may not Nature change Bodies into Light, and Light into Bodies?[51]

This passage bears more than a passing resemblance to Cavendish's earlier *Blazing World,* in which "nature is eternal and infinite, and her particulars are subject to infinite changes and transmutations by virtue of their own corporeal, figurative self-motions" and in which we meet with creatures such as "some fly-men, some ant-men, some geese-men, some spider-men, some lice-men, some fox-men, some ape-men . . . and many more."[52] The resemblance does not bespeak a direct influence but instead is testimony to the way that the new mechanical philosophy naturally, as it were, turned the imagination toward vivid thoughts of metamorphoses of bodies, species, and customs, including customary perceptions. Locke and Newton were certainly more systematic thinkers than Cavendish, and so was Robert Boyle, who criticized "the vulgar doctrine of forms" by instancing the "paradoxes" of bodies, including parasites and grafts, which "seem to have a title to more than one form."[53] In the hybrid species of *The Blazing World,* however, as among Locke's monsters, Newton's tadpoles, and Boyle's example of an overwhelming mistletoe on a small hazel tree, we see just how fantastic the order of nature claimed by empiricism could turn out to be. Furthermore, given the traditional connections between the representation of nature and of the body politic, this recognition of a fantastic natural order would tend to suggest that the nature of fantasy was also implicated in the cultural politics of specific social, historical, and political orders. In a dialogue that prefaces *The New Heloise* (1761), Jean-Jacques Rousseau identified the radical conception of his work with this unsettling situation by allowing his interlocutor to complain that his novel's characters belonged to "another world" and that any attempt to justify them would also permit the conception of nature to include "unheard of monsters, giants, pygmies, chimeras of every type" until "everything would be disfigured."[54]

Eighteenth-century natural philosophy so frequently returned to an emphasis on metamorphosis because this was the figure through which the assumption of a uniform or minimally differentiated nature—whether this be imaged as semen or excrement, conceived of as corpuscular or void of organs—came into a critical conjuncture with the assumption of a diverse natural order exemplified in a continuous hierarchy of fixed species. This was precisely the conjuncture that Cudworth, through the conception of "plastic nature" in his *True Intellectual System of the Universe* (1678), had sought to protect against atheistic speculation. Even as they were being transformed, his concerns persisted into the next century. Those who then resisted the image of metamorphosis in nature, such as David-Renaud Bouillier in his *Philosophical Essay on the Soul of Beasts* (1728) and Kant in his *Critique of Pure Reason*, did so because, like Cudworth, they feared for the stability of nature, the foundations of language, and the dignity of humanity.[55] Those who promoted the image of metamorphosis did not necessarily differ from these others in respect to this fear. They might simply consider, with Georges-Louis Leclerc Buffon, that too great an emphasis on the distinctness of species would lead one to mistake human categories for divine reality. So Jean-Baptiste-René Robinet argued, in his *Philosophical Considerations on the Natural Gradation of the Forms of Existence* (1768), that even seemingly monstrous forms of life "are metamorphoses of the prototype as natural as any other"; that "far from troubling it," such forms "contribute to the order of things"; and that there might be other worlds populated by creatures "among which we would be the monsters."[56]

Of course, writers such as Diderot did press the point to a more unorthodox effect. "Every animal is a man, more or less; every mineral a plant, more or less; every plant an animal, more or less," he had D'Alembert say in *The Dream of D'Alembert*. In the same work Théophile Bordeu is made to declare, "If man is not resolvable into an infinity of men, he is at least resolvable into an infinity of animalcules whose future and former metamorphoses and organization it is impossible to envision."[57] Similarly, Maupertuis advised his readers to remain calm even if he should tell them that they had undergone metamorphoses—"if I tell you that you have been a worm or an egg, or a kind of slime." He then went on to imagine natural events that might bring forth "new unions of elements, new animals, new plants, or rather totally new things."[58] After such predecessors, the stage was set for the Marquis de Sade to make his appearance and to carry this sort of perspective about as far as it could go.

Whatever the attitude toward it might be, however, metamorphosis was the issue around which nature was conceived in this era. Fontenelle would try to regard metamorphosis as a sign of outmoded, prescientific thought—"All metamorphoses are the physics of the early ages of the world"[59]—but this image was not so easily to be patronized or controlled. There at the critical juncture of sameness and difference, the image of metamorphosis was called forth to speak to the questions of first causes and final ends—and thus to the politics of culture. (Accordingly, even as he rejected the notion of unstable species, Bouillier did not find it contradictory to write that "the carnal man, the man enslaved by his body and his sensual habits . . . undergoes a metamorphosis into a beast.")[60] Neither a static tableau nor a dynamically evolving organic whole, the nature of this pre-Darwinian era was articulated in and through the troubled figure of metamorphosis. The conjunction of the ground of universality with the diversity of bodies, species, and customs simply could not be stabilized even if one invoked, in the manner of Newton, an unquestionable divinity. The problem was that such an invocation was so out of keeping with Newton's other precepts, as of not feigning hypotheses, that it was bound to be disturbingly transformed in its very utterance. In this respect, Newton's biblical exegeses positively invited Helvétius's condescending interpretation.

Bodies in their singularity posed the question of metamorphosis especially through the internal process of digestion and in their plurality especially through the external process of incorporating relations to other lands, behaviors, and beliefs. The inside and the outside of the human body might then become as one in the image of the cannibal, the figure in which metamorphosis can find no beginning or end in nature, culture, or spirit. For in the cannibal the distinction between the same and the different threatens either to disappear entirely or to appear entirely arbitrary. Either cannibalism destroys the identity of the human species, reducing it to an undifferentiated bestial ground, or it makes the pretension to humanity seem adventitious— a matter of taste, as it were. It is because he feared such a confounding of self and other that Pierre Bayle, in his *Historical and Critical Dictionary* (1696), unfavorably contrasted the metamorphoses suggested by Spinoza's philosophy to those given to civilization by Ovid. It makes sense to us, he argued, that men may hate and kill one another, and even that "the victors sometimes eat the vanquished," because "we suppose that they are distinct from one another and that the 'mine' and the 'thine' produce contrary passions in them." If there is no distinction between God and matter, however, as he understood Spinoza to maintain, then these other distinctions must also prove unfounded. If different men should be nothing but a "modification of the same being," cannibalism could not be seen as an extreme or perverse act. We would be in a miserable world such as that which Bayle judged Epicurus to have described very aptly, given his pagan viewpoint: one in which the Creator would find that his creatures, including "the most perfect of these animals," would "do nothing but eat one another, incapable as they are of continuing to live if the flesh of some does not serve as the food of others." Moreover, we would find that this devouring approach to life would extend to humans becoming "Anthropophagi" as a matter of course.[61]

Finding a similar image of things in Ovid, and reflecting upon a traditional motto of alchemical philosophy—Generatio unius est corruptio alterius (The generation of one thing is the corruption of another)—Bayle expressed wonder that "a cleft as small as the human mouth" could turn out to be "a gulf and an abyss."[62] Like Sterne's sealing wax, Kant's cliff-door-men, and Locke's monsters, this image of the abysmal mouth marks the catachrestic end toward which the representation of the senses was driven by the visceral turn in eighteenth-century culture. The catachresis makes manifest the paradoxical necessity and unacceptability of the image of metamorphosis in this age. It might even be seen as foreshadowing one of Nietzsche's more striking formulations almost two centuries later, wherein he sought to sum up the nature of the world: "It lives on itself: its excrements are its food."[63]

Bayle both acknowledged and sought to disavow the image of metamorphosis at the conjuncture of natural diversity and universality. In the eighteenth century, which saw many editions and republications of his work, his troubled position would be reoccupied by many others, whether or not they had actually read what he had to say on this topic. Gnawing at the heart of the age of Enlightenment was the self-contradicting, self-abhorring, self-consuming figure of the cannibal: the unavoidable figure of radical metamorphosis. In the image of cannibalism, Western self-regard and its vision of otherness in nature, culture, and spirit came to a momentous crisis. We see one aspect of this crisis in the fish-man of Chardin's masterpiece, *The Ray* (ca. 1728), which shuttles its viewers among transformations in species, rank, gender, and aesthetic form so as to anticipate the provocations of La Mettrie's monkey-man, machine-man, and plant-man. We see another in Vaucanson's androids, which were recognized virtually from their first appearance as casting into question established standards for representing humanity. In the city of Bath, a resort designed to encourage encounters among all sorts of people, this crisis was played out as an issue of pollution in bodies no less than in manners. It showed itself as well in the voyages of Captain Cook, through which students of the incipient cultural relativism of this age, and of the correlative metamorphoses imagined in other possible worlds, came face to face with the cannibal: the figure in which such metamorphoses threaten never to resolve themselves into a formal, social, or theological order. The cannibal might then turn out to be all but indistinguishable even from the philosopher, that leading figure of the Enlightenment. In De Quincey's meditations on Kant, as in his thoughts on another type of cultural hero, Admiral Nelson, this last metamorphosis is imaged through one of the most intimate of civilized acts: the pressing together of lips.

What Locke's nominalism, Charles Bonnet's gradualism, La Mettrie's materialism, Diderot's transformationism, and Sade's eroticism had in common was a recognition that the determination of species was the compelling cultural problem of this age in which empiricism was being established as the basis of knowledge. In order to settle anything else, one had to establish how to delineate and comprehend the nature of identity in the terms of sense perception. Far from being resolved, the drama of identity in Descartes's *Meditations on First Philosophy* (1641) was then heightened even more under the influence of figures such as Newton and Locke. In order to base knowledge on sense perception, it seemed, one first had to come to one's senses and bring others to theirs. Certain boundaries to what would count as perception had to be established even though the nature of these boundaries would ultimately be imaginary and could not be maintained without violence.

For those who professed the cause of enlightenment, even—and especially—if their senses were secured by the authority of the Christian God, the senses still had to define themselves within the politics of culture. In the sixteenth century, Bartolomé de Las Casas had recognized this problem in the European demand that the natives of the New World come to their senses; Kant sought to place himself between Locke and Hume in his attempt to resolve it; De Quincey would struggle with it in his meditation on those moments when Kant may or may not have been in possession of his senses while he lay dying in Königsberg. What exactly might it mean, then, in the context of the Enlightenment, to come to one's senses?

If we seek to answer this question, Blake is one of the immediate heirs to the Enlightenment from whom we still have much to learn. The poetic mythologies he invented often prove so excruciatingly difficult to follow for good reason: because they are designed to lead us into and through the catachrestic passages that compose sensory experience. It was precisely because he shared so many of the premises of Locke and Newton, in fact, that Blake was driven so viscerally to repudiate their names.[64] Blake may have gone Locke one better when he memorably imaged "the Optick Nerve" as being "like the black pebble on the enraged beach,"[65] but in itself this characterization was not in contradiction with the argument of Locke's *Essay*. (It may even recall to us Newton's characterization of himself as a boy playing with pebbles on the seashore "while the great ocean of truth lay all undiscovered" before him.)[66] Locke, after all, was no less concerned with the corporeal dubiety of human understanding than with its apparent nature. "For how much the Being and Operation of particular Substances in this our Globe, depend on Causes utterly beyond our view," Locke had written, "is impossible for us to determine." He went on to comment,

> We see and perceive some of the Motions and grosser Operations of things here about us; but whence the Streams come that keep all these curious Machines in motion and repair, how conveyed and modified, is beyond our notice and apprehension: and the great Parts and Wheels, as I may so say, of this stupendous Structure of the Universe, may, for ought we know, have such a connexion and dependence in their Influences and Operations one upon another, that, perhaps, Things in this our Mansion, would put on quite another face, and cease to be what they are, if some one of the Stars, or great Bodies incomprehensibly remote from us, should cease to be, or move as it does. This is certain, Things, however absolute and entire they seem in themselves, are but Retainers to other parts of Nature, for that which they are most taken notice of by us. Their observable Qualities, Actions, and Powers, are

owing to something without them . . . and we must not confine our thoughts within the surface of any body, but look a great deal further, to comprehend perfectly those Qualities that are in it.

If this be so, it is not to be wondred, that *we have very imperfect* Ideas *of Substances;* and that the real Essences, on which depend their Properties and Operations, are unknown to us. We cannot discover so much as that *size, figure,* and *texture* of their minute and active Parts, which is really in them; much less the different Motions and Impulses made in and upon them by Bodies from without. (587–88)

Concession granted, Blake might have said, as he then opened up Locke's premises to reveal this philosopher's epistemological constructions as prisons to human understanding. To the extent that they were based on the avowed limitations of human senses, and so also on a disavowal of any imaginative knowledge of their conceivable metamorphoses, Locke's constructions were understood by Blake to be nothing but "a delusion of Ulro." They represented a capitulation of the body to the abysmal measures of its own privation. So he wrote,

> As to that false appearance which appears to the reasoner,
> As of a Globe rolling thro Voidness, it is a delusion of Ulro
> The Microscope knows not of this nor the Telescope. They alter
> The ratio of the Spectators Organs but leave Objects untouchd
> For every Space larger than a red Globule of Mans blood. opens
> Into Eternity of which this vegetable Earth is but a shadow:
> The red Globule is the unwearied Sun by Los created
> To measure Time and Space to mortal Men. (*Milton* 1.29.15–24)

Like Newton, Locke is seen by Blake as a devilishly cunning apologist for the very limits of the senses beyond which he proudly claims to locate divine reality:

> I turn my eyes to the Schools & Universities of Europe
> And there behold the Loom of Locke whose Woof rages dire
> Washed by the Water-wheels of Newton. Black the cloth
> In heavy wreathes folds over every Nation; cruel Works
> Of many Wheels I view, wheel without wheel, with cogs tyrannic
> Moving by compulsion each other: not as those in Eden in which
> Wheel within Wheel in freedom revolve in harmony & peace.[67]

Nominally worshipping the same savior to whom Newton and Locke had professed their faith, Blake came to radically different conclusions about the nature of bodies because he willed a past, present, and future different from theirs.

To observe this difference in the cultural politics in their writings is by no means to dismiss the other mechanisms through which these differences might find an accounting, including that which has proven to be the most historically powerful of such mechanisms: the modern distinction between scientific knowledge, on the one hand, and imaginative or mythological representation, on the other. I do not wish to suggest here that Blake's desperate effort to prevent the eternal forging of this distinction was in some way an anticipation of the recognition that the philosophy of science has sometimes allowed, from the time of Kant and Hegel on to the work of Quine, to the historically constructed nature of scientific representations and thus to some form of "ontological relativity." To make Blake a precursor to a lineage of theoretical self-consciousness in the history of science would be to do his work a double injustice. In the first place, one would then be utterly trivializing all that is most distinctive in his work not only in terms of its poetics, narrowly defined, but also in its demand that poetics be expansively defined to incorporate actions toward liberating transformation in every aspect of social life. The second and equally important consideration is that to see Blake as being preoccupied with the epistemological margins of science would mean turning our vision away from all the evidence of how Blake's visceral response to Locke and other icons of the Enlightenment was called forth by metamorphic figures such as those that were central to Locke's own conception of human understanding. Like the cult of sensibility, the fad for the Gothic, and all that has come to be called Romanticism, Blake's poetry certainly may need to be distinguished from sweeping generalizations about the age of Enlightenment, but then so does this age deserve to be rescued from the Urizen-like abstractions into which it has sometimes been frozen. After all, the Blake who had his Eternal Ones amusingly refer to human organs "Contracting into Worms, or Expanding into Gods" (*Jerusalem* 3.55.37) was not simply opposing claims such as those made by Sprat: "*Experimental Philosophy* . . . will cure our minds of *Romantic swelling*, by shewing all things familiarly to them, just as large as they are."[68] He was also summarizing his own themes in terms of the wager on sense experience that gave the Enlightenment its very name.

Similarly, in conceiving that digestion, along with all the other processes of the human body, was animated by spirits,[69] Blake was quite faithful to the Enlightenment concern to investigate what entrails entail with respect to the ultimate reaches of human understanding. It was in following the Enlightenment turn from innate ideas to bodily organs that Blake identified the bowels of humanity with Ulro, which is a world of death because it is a state of natural generation that knows nothing of spiritual regeneration. Moreover, in describing "the Stomach & Intestines terrible, deadly, unutterable" (*Milton* 2.34.16), he found the image of Ulro in that recent discovery of natural science, the polyp, which plays a role in Blake's prophetic books akin to that played by monsters in Locke's *Essay*.

A follower of Hermann Boerhaave and other heroes of natural philosophy, Abraham Trembley reported in 1744 that if one cut up the polyp, or freshwater hydra, each of its pieces would regenerate into a distinct creature, even if one sliced the polyp entirely through its gut. From his observation that it could be turned inside out and continue to eat and thrive in that reversed form, Trembley concluded that the polyp "consists of but a single skin," which, moreover, has no proper head and mouth.[70] When the creature was turned inside out or cut into pieces, mouths sprouted on different areas of its skin.) Sexually undifferentiated and seeming to exist on the border of the animal and vegetable kingdoms, this thing then became famous among intellectuals because its heedlessness toward the distinctions of sex, species, and corporeal organization threatened to confound conventional assumptions about spirituality as well. It might even be seen as bringing before one's eyes precisely the phenomenon of "thinking matter" that Cudworth had singled out as the reductio ad absurdum of atheistical materialism; and at the very least, as Bonnet wrote, "The polyps then teach us to use induction soberly."[71] La Mettrie made polyps serve his purposes in his *Machine Man* (1748); Diderot used them in *The Dream of D'Alembert;* Maupertuis did likewise in his *System of Nature;* and so did many others, thus preparing the way for Blake.

Relating it to Beulah, a world or state of dreamy imagination, and to Los, the figure of tormented desire in whose labors we find the hope for humankind's eventual transformation into the divine state of Jerusalem, Blake described the abysmal world of Ulro as

> . . . a vast Polypus
> of living fibres down into the Sea of Time & Space growing
> A self-devouring monstrous Human Death Twenty-seven fold
> Within it sit Five Females & the nameless Shadowy Mother
> Spinning it from their bowels with songs of amorous delight
> And melting cadences that lure the Sleeper of Beulah down
> The River Storge (which is Arnon) into the Dead Sea:
> Around this Polypus Los continual builds the Mundane Shell.
> (*Milton* 2.34.24–31)

The autocannibalistic deathliness that characterizes Ulro is also, for Blake, the character of science when it is treated as the basis for "natural religion." He sees this form of religion as epitomizing Enlightenment thought: "How is this thing? This Newtonian Phantasm / This Voltaire & Rousseau: this Hume & Gibbon & Bolingbroke / This Natural Religion! This impossible absurdity" (*Milton* 2.40.11–13). Thus it is that in *The Four Zoas* (ca. 1796–1807) the Eternal Man speaks to Urizen—the figure associated by turns with the deathliness of the Old Testament Jehovah, the deceptiveness of Satan, and the spectral mathematical abstractions of empirical demonstration—about Urizen's "self-destroying beast formd Science" (*Milton* 9.120.40). This description is comparable to the one Los offers of Satan as "Newtons Pantocrator weaving the Woof of Locke / To Mortals thy Mills seem every thing" (*Milton* 1.4.11–12).

In contrast to what he sees as the "crucifying cruelties" of science, when it becomes natural religion and so represses the metamorphic possibilities of the senses (*Jerusalem* 1.24.55), Blake demands in all his works that the senses be conceived of within narratives that dramatize their implication in history and in the imaginative will of historical agents. That is why, in describing the sons of Urizen in *The Book of Urizen* (1794), he rewrites the biblical story of creation as the fall of the senses into the net of natural religion. Whereas Enlightenment philosophers such as Etienne Bonnot de Condillac and Charles Bonnet had sought to imagine the growth of the senses in terms of a process of empirical discovery, Blake sought to imagine their degeneration into the world of sensationist philosophy embodied in such thinkers:

> The Senses inward rush'd shrinking,
> Beneath the dark net of infection.

Till the shrunken eyes clouded over
Discernd not the woven hipocrisy
But the streaky slime in their heavens
Brought together by narrowing perceptions
Appeard transparent air; for their eyes
Grew small like the eyes of a man. . . .

Six days they shrunk up from existence
And on the seventh day they rested
And they bless'd the seventh day, in sick hope:
And forgot their eternal life.[72]

When Blake proclaimed "the intire abrogation of Experimental Theory,"[73] he was not so much rejecting science pure and simple as rejecting its idealized simplicity and purity. In its place he sought to put a historical conception of human nature, one that would never be capable of justifying tyranny, for example, in the name of natural hierarchy, or cruelty and suffering in the name of Providence, or a child's fear of a "Blackmoor" (an example in one of Locke's analyses) with this child's supposedly natural disgust toward "*Wormseed* or *Mustard*" and its supposedly natural taste for "*Apple* or *Sugar*" (Locke, *Essay*, 62). In other words, in waging mental war against experimental theory, Blake drew out the implications of a visceral understanding that was no less definitive of the Enlightenment than was this theory itself. He could turn Enlightenment philosophy against itself because he had intuited that it had in fact been turned against itself, twisted in its bowels, right from the start. Even in its most central and orthodox conceptions it had been turned against itself because of the passages to multiple worlds of metamorphic possibilities that it had been compelled to open, and yet also to deny, there at the conjuncture of theoretical universality and natural diversity.

Among those who have since recognized how fully Blake belonged to the age whose dominant narrative he nonetheless labored so fiercely to revise, I would single out James Joyce as perhaps his most brilliant exegete; and it is with Joyce's attention to metamorphoses that I wish to bring this chapter to a conclusion. Blake is repeatedly invoked in *Ulysses* (1922), in which another heir to the Enlightenment, Leopold Bloom, is characterized from the outset in visceral terms. "Still he knows a lot of mixed up things especially about the body and the insides" his wife reflects on Bloom, whom the novel characterizes as a "physicist," "philosopher," and "physiologist" and who is mentioned in the company of two eminent eighteenth-century natural philosophers, Blumenbach and Lazzaro Spallanzani.[74] (In a related moment Bloom assumes the semblance of Jean-Jacques Rousseau and Robinson Crusoe, among other historical figures [495].) Indeed, Bloom is consistently associated with science and with a visceral emphasis on the body, and often with the two together, as when his scientific temperament is illustrated through the mention of hypothetical inventions "of which he had cogitated when reclining in a state of supine repletion to aid digestion" (683). This comment is related to a passage much earlier in the novel wherein Bloom is meditating on the nature of digestion after lunching at Davy Byrne's and successively contemplates "Röntgen rays," closestools, the "insides entrails" associated with the latter furnishings, and how said entrails are illuminated by Röntgen rays in the name of "Science" (179–80). We may recall that Bloom is first characterized in terms of a relish for "the inner organs of beasts and fowls" (55) and through the ritualistic easing of his own bowels in an outhouse.

Bloom is also attentive to viscera, of course, through his sympathy for Mina Purefoy, whose difficult labor preoccupies him throughout *Ulysses*. In fact, in *Ulysses*, as in Blake's prophetic books and in Enlightenment culture in general, the specifically female capacity to give birth gets generalized into the creation and reproduction of identity through the viscera.[75] Like the acts of eating and of sex, stomach and womb get conflated through the philosophical turn that drives matters of the body toward the demand of universality or, in other words, toward a theory of organized bodies in general. (Hence Blake's horror at the parthenogenesis in the polyp, which imaged for him the elimination of sexual difference in the drive toward abstraction definitive of Enlightenment science.) Here the anatomical confusion between anus and vagina that Sigmund Freud saw as representing infantile confusion proves instead to be a laborious product of civilized reason, just as it is in the writings of Sade. In this respect as in others, Freud's identification with a grand narrative of the Enlightenment—the one popularly termed *science*—led him to underestimate the material differences between the perdurable clichés of childhood experience and the metamorphic complexities of cultural formations.

Bloom himself identifies with the Enlightenment ideal of progress: "He desired to amend many social conditions, the product of inequality and avarice and international animosity." Again like Freud, however, he cannot believe "that human life [is] infinitely perfectible." His optimism is restrained by his attention to "the generic conditions imposed by natural, as distinct from human law," which include the killing of prey, "agonies of birth and death," menstruation, accidents, disease, cataclysms, and "the fact of vital growth, through convulsions of metamorphosis from infancy through maturity to decay" (696–97). This comment illustrates the Enlightenment conflation of the female body with a generalized physiology that in turn is made to embody a philosophical understanding comprehending "the human whole" and the universe in general. On the other hand, Bloom's Enlightenment differs most from that of his renowned contemporary, Freud, in his conviction that the reproduction of identity is more profoundly a cannibalistic than a sexual process. In this respect Joyce's protagonist evinces a visceral understanding of Enlightenment culture more historically telling than the version deployed in Freud's efforts to demystify religion, social conventions, and cultural ideals.

Thinking of Mina Purefoy with her "swollen belly on a bed groaning to have a child tugged out of her," Bloom is led to dwell upon the monotonous, mechanical repetitiousness of life in the modern metropolis: "trains in, out." Death and life are but as the trains—"Cityful passing away, other cityful coming"—and by the same token the notions of property and identity are conjoined and dismissed: "This owner, that." The experience of exploitation appears hopelessly banal: "Slaves. Chinese wall. Babylon." Arriving at the stultifying idea that "no one is anything," Bloom concludes, "This is the very worst hour of the day. . . . Feel as if I had been eaten and spewed" (164). In other words, moving on from his hopeful thoughts about those attending upon Mrs. Purefoy—"Humane doctors, most of them" (161)—he experiences a passage through the bowels of Enlightenment, in the course of which he must undergo a metamorphosis into everything from trains and corpses and "the blood of the lamb" to houses and cities and the dusty remains of civilization.

In this passage he is figuratively consumed and eliminated by his own body and by every imaginable form of culture. Shortly thereafter he stops in at Davy Byrne's for a restorative gorgonzola sandwich and glass of Burgundy, but there, too, cannibalism remains—albeit in a lighter tone—the defining obsession of modern civilization. The sight of some tins of Plumtree's potted meats must naturally, as it were, lead Bloom to think of the funeral for Paddy Dignam that he had attended that morning—"Dignam's potted meat"—and then, just as naturally, of eating the dearly departed. "Cannibals would with lemon and rice," he muses. "White missionary too salty. Like pickled pork. Expect the chief consumes the parts of honour. Ought to be tough from exercise. His wives in a row to watch the effect. *There was a right royal old nigger. Who ate or something the somethings of the reverend Mr MacTrigger*" (171).

In this passage Dignam's body, Bloom's sense of taste, and the vaguely remembered racist limerick are all swallowed within Bloom's perception of the body of Plumtree's "stupid ad," which begins, "What is home without Plumtree's potted meat? Incomplete," and which concludes, immediately after the consumption of the martially surnamed MacTrigger, "with it an abode of bliss" (171). The effect is to suggest, among other things, that there is no getting outside the maw of cultural clichés about cannibalistic relationships. This lesson naggingly repeats the more subdued thoughts that had come to Bloom during a mass at All Hallows: "Shut your eyes and open your mouth. What? *Corpus*. Body. Corpse. Good idea the Latin. Stupefies them first. Hospice for the dying. They don't seem to chew it; only swallow it down. Rum idea: eating bits of a corpse why the cannibals cotton to it" (80). Although he goes on fleetingly to recall kosher dietary laws—"No meat and milk together" (171)—Bloom cannot sustain such orthodoxy, either literally or metaphorically. His reflections on the Haggadah at the newspaper office offer no relief: "Justice it means but it's everybody eating everyone else. That's what life is after all" (122). His scientific speculations on "cells or whatever" at Paddy Dignam's funeral had come to the same conclusion: "Nothing to feed on feed on themselves" (109).

Bloom does, of course, go on to enjoy his meal at Davy Byrne's: "Mr Bloom ate his strips of sandwich, fresh clean bread, with relish of disgust, pungent mustard, the feety savour of green cheese" (173); and Mrs. Purefoy is, in the end, safely delivered of her child. The paradoxical "relish of disgust" in this meal, however, like the hint of cannibalism in the cheese's "feety savour," still indicates the bowels within which Bloom is fated to live in the universe of this novel. Accordingly, Bloom and the other characters in *Ulysses* are represented as metamorphic figures. Through these figures we see the defining relationship between insides and outsides generally, as of the internal organs of bodies and the external organs of culture more particularly, endlessly defining and redefining itself. This relationship between interiority and exteriority suffers continual transformations in the intermediary flesh, which also appears here as the substance of any imaginable religion, philosophy, or literature.

"Without Contraries is no progression," Blake wrote in *The Marriage of Heaven and Hell* (3.6);[76] and in this matter of the flesh the brilliance of Joyce consists in having so effectively dramatized the Blakean Contrary to the epigraph of this chapter. What *Ulysses* suggests is that we do not know, we cannot possibly know, that our flesh is grass, because we would have to become something other than ourselves in the very moment in which we would claim such knowledge. I might add that despite all subsequent efforts to turn it into a matter of knowledge, our flesh must still remain an open question today.

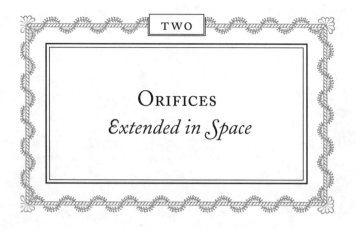

TWO

ORIFICES
Extended in Space

$\mathcal{A}$T THE CENTER of the painting, or at once everywhere and nowhere, geometry is mortified. Hanging ever so slightly off-kilter, its right wing curling toward the viewer, the diamond of the ray fish has been slashed open (see fig. 2). In place of its smooth, pale, bilaterally symmetrical ventral surface, we are shown gaping hollows and ungainly, blood-tinged internal structures. It is as if a curtain has been yanked aside in the theater of this creature, which greets us as a tragicomic mask. Its surface conflates genres just as the entire painting, a still life, presents itself also as a caricatural portrait and as a mock-historical treatment of martyrdom. No less compellingly than Pablo Picasso's *Demoiselles d'Avignon* (1907), the canvas in question here embraces seemingly incompossible moments, forms, and teleologies of representation.

Directly below the ray, two open-mouthed fish repeat the dumb grimace of its mouth, above which we see its tragic "eyes," which would in fact be its gills. In the lower right quadrant of the picture we see a knife, which conceivably is the very one that gutted this lozenge, this fish, this face, this body—this thing of generic ambiguities. The handle of the knife is offered to the viewer, its blade half covered (but only half covered) by a fold of a napkin. The length of this knife is crossed from above by the handle of a pan, over the side of which another fold of the napkin is draped as if to obscure—and thus ironically to emphasize—all the imaginable connections among the activities of cutting and cooking and painting, on the one hand, and viewing

FIGURE 2.
Jean-Siméon Chardin, *La Raie* (ca. 1728), Erich Lessing/Art Resource, N. Y.

and eating and understanding, on the other. In fact, the right side of the canvas shows three handles—of skimmer, pan, and knife—poking out at different angles, contributing to the sharp diagonals of the composition, which are
accentuated by the light coming from the upper left. Through these lines a
pressing assemblage of human intentions frames the martyred form in the
center, which the pot at the right seems poised to swallow. The weight of all
these lines is balanced, even as it is jostled, by the cat entering at the left and
stepping into one of the opened oysters scattered on the counter between the
fish and the scallions. A trick of its coloring, a dark slash under its nose, draws
attention to the mouth of this animal, which is borrowed for this work from
its familiar role at laden tables in Dutch and Flemish still lifes.

With the diamond and diagonals set against the rough-hewn rectangles of the stone wall and accompanied by the oval, circular, and spherical figures of the plate, mortar and pestle, pepperpot, oysters, and vessels, the rectangle of this canvas appears to be grounded on the lines, planes, and forms of geometry. It might have been expressly designed to prepare us for Paul Cézanne's most famous remark: that the artist should get a handle on nature "by means of the cylinder, the sphere, the cone, everything brought into proper perspective."[1] Cézanne, as it happens, was an admirer of Jean-Siméon Chardin; and in this dictum he would seem to have been reiterating an artistic practice founded upon the mathematized space of Renaissance art, among whose inheritors Chardin must be numbered. Yet just as this dictum may seem inconsistent with all that is most striking in Cézanne's own practice, so does this painting, cut out of a household interior, direct our attention beyond the balanced surfaces and volumes of geometry toward disturbing openings in these forms. It does so not only through the mouths of the ray, the fish, and the cat but also through the vessels standing at the right: one corked, one half-covered, and one fully open, with the systematic logic of a textbook diagram. Most notably, and centrally, the maw carved in the belly of the ray draws our attention to orifices. The composition is further structured, left to right, by a progress from vegetable to animal nature and from animality to an absent but implied, by its instruments, humanity—but what sort of humanity?

Certainly its creator showed a flair for the dramatic in this performance, which Michael Baxandall has referred to as that "outrageously flash piece of paintwork, the superb and savage *The Ray*."[2] This chef d'oeuvre was accepted as a presentation piece along with another work, a *Buffet*, when Chardin was welcomed into the Royal Academy of Painting and Sculpture in 1728.[3] So theatrical is the central subject, in fact, that I cannot help but think that Pierre Rosenberg was troubled by this quality, as well as by the style of the painting as a whole, when he commented on the composition of Chardin's presentation pieces. "Our admiration of the two works which gained the young man admittance into the Academy is tempered with a certain reluctance," he wrote, "for he seems to have used them primarily as showpieces for his precocious technical skill and to have put too little of himself into them. An artist of Chardin's calibre soon outgrows this kind of exhibitionism."[4] In any case, it may be difficult to dispute the taste, or the lingering distaste, with which

Rosenberg advanced his judgment and suggested its universality. After all, those who commented on Chardin's work in the eighteenth century, including those who most highly praised it, even then generally saw it as skirting the boundaries of distastefulness, of the *dégoutant*.

The alleged exhibitionism of this painting might also be argued to be historically demonstrable from another perspective, which is indicated by the immediate impression it made on Chardin's contemporaries and by its continuing acceptance up to the present day.[5] (If not necessarily repulsive, such popularity might be said to be presumptively so, and particularly for those who are concerned with modernist conceptions of aesthetic mastery.) Furthermore, it cannot be denied that Chardin never did return to anything like the drama that he placed at the center of this painting. In this drama the ray fish appears also as a human figure; as a paradigmatic object of display, utility, desire, and consumption; and as painting itself, inasmuch as the inexact parallelogram of the fish is made to represent, synecdochically, the surface of the canvas on which it appears.[6] There is nothing like this dramatic figuration in Chardin's later works, although in saying so I mean only to suggest that they are markedly different, not lesser.

It is as if Chardin had summed up to his own satisfaction, at the very outset of his career, all that might lie on the far side of painting's space of representation—all that might lead, for instance, to Cézanne, cubism, and abstract expressionism. In fact, just as the history of critical response to *The Ray* provides evidence that it may tease viewers into all sorts of metaphysical contortions by way of religious, class, political, psychological, and anthropological considerations, this work seems virtually to offer itself to the invention of traditions. (Another would lead through Gustave Courbet's notorious *Origin of the World* [1866] to the *poupées* that Hans Bellmer made in the 1930s, the slit paintings in Lucio Fontana's *Concetto spaziale* series of the 1960s, and Cindy Sherman's photographs of grotesque anatomical models in her work of the 1990s; and yet another through Philippe Rousseau's nineteenth-century *natures mortes* and Marcel Duchamp's early-twentieth-century ready-mades to Andy Warhol's pop artifacts.) Exhibitionism, then, there certainly may be—but perhaps of a kind undreamed of in Rosenberg's aesthetics.

It is also of a kind that may lead us beyond Ronald Paulson's splendid formal analysis of this painting, which alludes as well to other still lifes and genre scenes by Chardin:

The essential may be the opened skate, which denies the shape's solidity as it does its smile, mediating between the full bodies of the cat and fish on the left and the hollow, empty pitchers and pans on the right. Some kind of an inner area is always implicit in Chardin's definition of outside area. The pots and pans are only the final reduction that proceeded from the revealed inside of a skate or dead animal to the space created by a house of cards or by a bubble, by an urn or an egg. The pots and pans are the most distinctively Chardinesque of the subjects because they express at its simplest the relationship between solid and hollow.[7]

No sign of distaste shows up here, but Paulson's analysis of what is "most distinctively Chardinesque" is still in keeping with Rosenberg's. What Rosenberg achieves by characterizing *The Ray* as an immature work, Paulson accomplishes by turning our attention away from the livid viscera imaged at the center of the painting and toward an abstract "relationship between solid and hollow." Even though Chardin himself emphasized this painting's singularity (for instance, by the very different handling of the central figure in his *Ray-Fish and Basket of Onions* [1731]), both critics deemphasize its distinctiveness so as to assimilate it to a comprehensive sense of Chardin's biography—in Rosenberg's idiom, what Chardin's self was when he really put himself into his work. What remains to be considered is whether the very conception of the self in the eighteenth century, and even in our own time, might not face a challenge in *The Ray*.

Without wishing to underestimate the writings of scholars such as Rosenberg and Paulson, to which my work is deeply indebted, I would suggest an approach that does not presume a congruence between aesthetic forms and biographical contents. This may allow us to focus on all the matters that we are apt to miss not only in our eviscerating formalisms but even in more fleshly schools of criticism, those which seem to pay more attention to the body, such as psychoanalysis.[8] Beyond what such approaches can teach us, there is an abstraction to be found in *The Ray* that is not of the thing or the species but of biomorphism itself, in its very grounds. Biomorphism is here carried beyond the noncontradictory space of Renaissance art into a historical dimension in which it is impossible even to draw a line between vitality and death. (To see this dimension, imagine the detail of the ray's interior as an image complete in itself, enlarged to cover the surface of the entire canvas: this is the invitation we are given by Chardin's handling of things.) Ostensibly presenting the materials of a meal, this painting offers its viewers the slippery substance of self-perception. *The Ray* cuts into the eye no less dramatically than does the famous scene of Luis Buñuel's *Un chien Andalou* (1929). In doing so, it dramatically suggests that the eye has a gender, although this is not a simple categorical distinction; a body, although this cannot be defined in terms of geometrical extension; and a history, although this will not suffer itself to be framed in the conventional terms of biography.

In Claude Lévi-Strauss's memorable phrase, natural species are chosen as totems "not because they are 'good to eat' but because they are 'good to think'";[9] and the totemic image here is designed to think through the status of art, cultural classification, and human identity. At the literal and figurative center of *The Ray* we encounter a heterogeneous form that is simultaneously reified (as a parallelogram), anthropomorphized (as a face caught in the tragic rictus of a grin), objectified (as food), aestheticized (as an image of its own artistic ground), and allegorized (as the messy cutting, emptying, and ritualistic display of form in all these aspects). In contrast to the characterization that Jonathan Crary has offered for Chardin's still lifes—"a last great presentation of the classical object in all its plenitude, before it is sundered irrevocably into exchangeable and ungrounded signifiers or into the painterly traces of an autonomous vision"[10]—*The Ray* presents the perversion of this supposed object. Accordingly, although the semiotic structuring of mineral, vegetable, animal, and human natures in this painting might seem to exemplify the tables of taxonomic classification through which Michel Foucault, on whose work Crary relies, epitomized the "Classical episteme," this tableau is also deformed through the commitment of this painting to the topology of the orifice.[11] Foucault's notion of the "Classical episteme" can no more hold its ground here than it can in the "taxonomic fissures" that Paul Ilie has traced in Francisco Goya's *Caprichos* (1799).[12] It is not going too far to suggest that in addition to anticipating future traditions of realism and surrealism, of modernism and postmodernism, *The Ray* still has something about it that subsequent practices of art and criticism have yet to comprehend.

Consider first the issue of geometry. In the seventeenth century, in his *Discourse on the Method* (1637) and other works, René Descartes had drawn a connection between the foundations of geometry and the existence of God. Divinity was conceived of as a figure necessarily presupposed by all philosophy and, moreover, as the guarantee that humanity could not be reduced to animality and that our sense experience would not lead us into endless confusion. ("The proofs I employ here," Descartes wrote in the dedicatory letter to the Sorbonne prefacing his *Meditations on First Philosophy* [1641], "are in my view as certain and evident as the proofs of geometry, if not more so.")[13] In pursuing this line of thought, Descartes was continuing a tradition that goes back to Platonic metaphysics and that would live on long after him. In the eighteenth century, however, in which it came to be considered emblematic of rationalist systems, geometry was symbolically identified with Cartesian metaphysics as distinct from, and opposed by, Newtonian physics in particular and an empiricist orientation in general.[14] That is why Albrecht von Haller, in the beginning pages of his immensely influential *Elementa physiologiæ corporis humani* (1747), was careful to delimit the scope of geometrical reasoning in relation to his study. He thus distinguished himself from earlier physiologists such as Giovanni Borelli, who had based his iatromechanical principles on the image of God as a geometer. It was in part as a result of this same association between the image of geometry and speculative reasoning that Immanuel Kant took care to insist, in his *Critique of Pure Reason* (1781), that "geometry and philosophy are two quite different things—although in natural science they offer their hands to each other and . . . therefore the procedure of the one can never be imitated by the other."[15]

In this context, the emphasis on geometry in *The Ray* was bound to be fraught with metaphysical significance, and at first glance we might see a treatment of geometry in this painting fully in accord with Cartesian precepts. Within this unsettling composition, the definitive line traditionally drawn between reality and dreams is treated as an unmeaning distinction—just as it was for Cartesian geometry. ("For whether I am awake or asleep," wrote Descartes, "a square has no more than four sides.")[16] As they shuttle us among heterogeneous orders of being—inanimate/animate, natural/cultural, mineral/vegetable/animal/human—the geometrical lines of Chardin's composition are oblivious to the oneiric transfigurations in the body of the ray fish, which virtually insists on being perceived also as a mock-human face and tortured body. (Here the contrast with Chardin's *singeries* is instructive, in that these works use an entirely conventional, satirical association of humanity and animality; the contrast with the fish and game portrayed in Chardin's other still lifes is also noteworthy, in that these creatures are in no way designed to emphasize a human semblance.) Yet this very similarity to the Cartesian conception of geometry has the effect of driving Descartes's assumptions into various forms of nonidentity, with consequences that still may prove impossible for us to face head-on.

Descartes spent years dissecting animals and attributed much of his knowledge to this practice.[17] In the circumstances of this painting, however, the gaping line of the cut in the ray's belly is anything but a revealing opening. The generic ambiguities figured through the ray ensure that we cannot clearly grasp what it is an opening *on* or *to*—or even that it is finally an opening at all, as opposed to just another passage of sensuous brushwork. An anatomical diagram of a ray's physiology cannot help us here, for any literal naming of the parts portrayed by Chardin would be no more satisfying, for our understanding of this painting, than the pedantic identification of the ray's "eyes" as its "gills." It may be significant in this respect that according to Charles-Nicolas Cochin, who described his friend as having "an extreme sensibility," Chardin himself had warned against an overly literal conception of the materials of art. Interrupting an artist who was annoying him with his talk about the use of color, Chardin is reported to have said, "But who told you that one paints with colors?" and then to have added, "One makes use of colors . . . but one paints with feeling."[18]

The Ray would be an entirely different sort of work if the heterogeneous identifications its central figure is designed to elicit could be resolved into an optical pun. Then the painting would be a simple amusement or novelty, like an outline of a vase that appears also (when the eye switches foreground and background) as the silhouette of two faces. *The Ray* proves compelling, however, because it is neither opposed to nor congruent with conventional pictorial representation. The design of this painting invites us to see the ragged line drawn through the ray's body as of a kind with all the others in its composition: the edges of the fish, the angles of the handles, the rays of sunlight, and so on, all the way down to and including the very brush strokes composing these lines. Just as the ray's dehiscence is a caricature in miniature of the painting as a whole, or a brush stroke writ large, this central line is a caricatural magnification of the ideal line of geometry, or a microcosm of metaphysics. No less than George Berkeley's *New Theory of Vision* (1709), it leads us to scorn "the humour of making one see by geometry."[19] Furthermore, this slash in the ray fish is like the strokes of distinct colors for which Chardin

was famous, which would not make sense or look like anything when regarded too closely. This incision then deforms the metaphysical line of figuration in which the interior of a thing is made to signify its essence or truth.[20]
Instead of revelation, the decisive movement that would show us the ground
of things, we meet with perversion, the repetitious movement that multiplies
phantasmic forms ateleologically. The deliberate perversity in Marcel Proust's
characterization of the ray's interior as "the polychromatic nave of a cathedral" brilliantly captures the frustrated desire for revelation that Chardin
worked into the hallucinatory forms in the center of this painting.[21]

The napkin draped so as to form a kind of ectoplasmic double to the
lozenge of the ray, a spotless "soul" leaving its bloody "body," makes this
mockery of the desire for revelation even more emphatic. Once noted, the
dark passage at the center of this napkin is startling, even hilarious. If the napkin is an emblem of divine spirit—or simply of the manners supposed to be
definitive of civilization—it is an emblem that must lose its coherence in the
dark necessity of this orifice. Guiding the eye from background to foreground
and from left to right, from the rectangular stones of the wall to the ray and
thence to the drooping napkin, this painting tells the story of a parallelogram's descent out of a fixed geometrical regularity and into a soft and sinu-
ous material whose form disappears into itself. In the paintings in which he
reworked Chardin's image in 1924, it was this identification of formative lines,
brush strokes, and gaping orifices to which Chaim Soutine would draw attention.

Through the theatrics of the line in *The Ray*, the design of colors, spaces,
and figures that Chardin plays off against the central image of geometrical
form is also identified with that form, supposed exteriors with interiors and
with the brush strokes differentiating the two, so that we are led to think of
the nature of the ideal line as luscious, violent, visceral. This line rippling
through the geometrical figure of the ray bodies forth geometry as a science
productive of no metaphysical pride whatsoever. In effect, this painting proposes that the ideal line of geometry, the axiomatic shortest distance between
two points, is more accurately to be seen as a grotesque, groundless, unaccountable passage through the swirling substance of the world. Writ large in
the grain of recognizable forms, the geometrical line appears as the stuff of
deformation; writ small, in brush strokes on a painted surface, as an enchanting, baffling mechanism of deception. Each aspect of representation

mocks the other: image and technique, figure and ground, literal and figurative reference. According to this painting, the forms of geometry are not distinct from the real world of history, as the traditions of metaphysical idealism would have it. Instead, geometrical form is made out to be a sensuous bodily affair, viscerally compelling and profoundly self-deceiving. Like the categorical forms of generic hierarchies and orders of being, geometrical forms are suggested to be historical through and through—which is to say, painted with the substance of feeling.

Here again the resemblance to Haller's understanding of physiology is notable. In his argument about the elemental basis of anatomy, Haller displaced mathematical with visceral form: "The fiber is to physiology what the line is to geometry."[22] In a work on physiology that he adapted from the writings of Haller, among others, Denis Diderot expanded upon this notion. The fiber, he wrote, "is soft, elastic, pulpy, drawn out almost without breadth or of a breadth with scarcely any extension." As such, it is "like an animal, a worm" that serves as "the principle of the entire [human] machine."[23] Accordingly, in *The Dream of D'Alembert* (1769) we are given a moment in which D'Alembert asks whether he was talking of geometry in his sleep and is told no, his talk was a "gallimaufry of vibrating cords and sensible fibers." Similarly, Doctor Bordeu tells Mlle. De l'Espinasse that if she wishes an image of her original form, she must "return to a moment in which [she was] nothing but a soft, filamentous, formless, vermicular substance, more analogous to the bulb and root of a plant than to an animal."[24]

Like Haller, Diderot certainly did not scorn the value of mathematical science. Elsewhere he was capable of referring approvingly to the notion that the supreme being "*geometrizes* perpetually in the universe."[25] His adoption of Haller's fibrillary theory of anatomy was in accord with his aesthetics, however, which asserted that "the artist will shun parallel lines, squares, and all that comes close to geometrical figures, because out of a thousand cases in which chance arranges objects, there is but one in which he encounters these figures."[26] Therefore, in his praise of the "harmony" in Chardin's *Attributes of the Arts* (1766), this pioneering critic of art and friend of Chardin would adopt the image of the serpentine line of beauty popularized by William Hogarth. "It snakes [*elle serpente*] imperceptibly in his composition, completely underlying each part of the expanse of his canvas," wrote Diderot. "It is as the spirit of which theologians speak, perceptible in the whole and hidden in each point."[27]

Diderot's little joke in this passage, in his identification of snake and spirit, appears less trifling when one considers the cultural implications of this displacement of divine geometry by the visceral fiber. For instance, this displacement made it possible for Julien Offroy de La Mettrie to mock Haller's piety by devoutly adopting and enthusiastically developing his physiological theory. When Diderot criticized geometry on the grounds that experience would forever destroy its dreamlike lines, the potential implications of his argument were no less scandalous.[28] The wonder of Chardin's painterly line in *The Ray* is that it so suggestively anticipated this philosophical line of discourse in which the axiomatic foundations of human life were wriggling out of their deductive confines and into a realm of experience in which categories such as animal, man, machine, and spirit might seem to be consuming one another before one's very eyes. No less than Jonathan Swift, in his satire of the Laputians' fondness for geometry, Chardin brought this science down to earth, earthiness, and orifice. He went beyond even Swift, however, in that his imagination did not seek abstraction from the body.

Considering how the ray serves as a face can help further to clarify this point. As a preliminary context to this consideration, it is useful to note that the human figures Chardin would go on to paint in his portraits and genre scenes are remarkably composed and self-contained images, their expressions calm and abstracted, their lips sealed.[29] (The lips of the girl in *The Game of Knucklebones* [ca. 1734] are slightly parted, but this work is really no exception to the rule.) Whether viewed from this context or from within the frame of this specific painting, the opening of the ray is bound to stand out as a gesture, a dramatically staged event, directed to the image of humanity. It is at once a line, a cut, a wound, a mouth, and a sexually suggestive orifice. Especially when one takes into account the marked absence of the human figure from the genre of the still life, an absence here literally maintained and yet figuratively violated, this eventration is remarkable. The geometry of the ray makes this creature an apt figure for the "face" of the entire painting and, indeed, for the face of objects in general. At the same time, the caricatural features of the image imply a human face and body. Therefore, the distinctions among animate, inanimate, and representational things appear to be slashed through, disgorged of their contents, right there in the center of the painting.

In their provocative meditation on *The Ray* in a collaborative essay published in *Critique,* Yve-Alain Bois and colleagues characterized the central image as, among other things, "a parody, a personage miming the human, whose mask unmasks latent animality."[30] This analysis describes one line of implication traced out in Chardin's painting (and retraced, for instance, in the role played by the cat). Yet there is still more to be seen in this line. In the midst of a wonderfully cranky, bombastic analysis of still lifes, in which Chardin is used to beat up on Cézanne, Camille Mauclair provided a valuable formulation in this regard:

> Do you remember those childhood images in which one sees eyes or mouths sketched on houses, on trees, or on vases, through the use of windows, knots of wood, or handles, in an amusing deformation? This is a rough image of what Chardin knows how to suggest through his divination of the thoughts of objects. . . .
>
> Chardin's objects are psychological documents that express the entirety of an epoch. But they are also visages, and whoever contemplates them discovers strange velleities, menacing or peaceful. Many great masters have placed still lifes that are magnificent bits of painting within their pictures, but these are ornaments, decorative elements. No one or almost no one has dared, has suspected, the very singular psychology of intimacy that Chardin has attempted, and through which he directly recalls certain propositions of Edgar Allan Poe.[31]

Mauclair was referring to Chardin's still lifes in general, but the effect thus described is already figured, summed up, in *The Ray*. It is not that the human face is displaced but that the face is defined *as* displacement. It is made a matter of openings repeatedly figured in and through heterogeneous surfaces, and so it is made to open onto a potentially endless series of metamorphoses. *The Ray* shows us that one may regard this situation with either childish amusement or sardonic inhumanity—or with a recognition of the interdependence of such apparently contradictory attitudes. The ray looks like a clownish mask; the ray looks like a nightmarishly disfigured human body, quite beyond anything imaginable even in the Marquis de Sade's tableaux or, more recently, in Francis Bacon's tortured perspectives on the human form. Finally, then, the geometrical elements in *The Ray* seem to metamorphose into an elemental non-Euclidean geometry of visceral transformations.

Traditionally, to approach the human body through still life is to approach it as light, color, texture, design, and association. Despite its literal absence, the human body makes its presence felt in still lifes by serving as the implicit context for the visual designs we do see. By proposing that this ground is also the surface, this interior the exterior, this informing soul the matter of scattered individual brush strokes and lines, *The Ray* stages the drama of vision seeing itself.

After all, it is through our viscera (through "a feeling in our guts") that we typically provide ourselves with an image of the ultimate ground of perception. This is the habit that Descartes literalized when he placed the principal seat of the soul in the conarium, or pineal gland. By the way he imaged the eviscerated fish at the center of *The Ray*, Chardin mocked this supposed ground of revelation. Figuring the senses in their fundamental obliquity, the center of this painting opens onto a visceral understanding that is not revelatory but is, on the contrary, thoroughly upsetting of the desire for revelation. Rather than exhibiting the soul of humanity, the face appears as a thing at once animate, inanimate, and representational. This is a face gaping with displacements, unaccountable to metaphysics, its orifices exposing an irreducible heterogeneity of form in which beauty must be seen to touch upon nausea.

No wonder Edmond and Jules de Goncourt, for all their praise of Chardin, complained about his painting of human flesh. ("He does not sufficiently differentiate it from fabrics and accessories. He does not grant it its lightness or its transparency.")[32] For in his portraits and genre scenes Chardin would go on quite calmly to do to the human face explicitly what he did to it implicitly through the geometry of *The Ray:* flay it of its metaphysics. An eighteenth-century critic, Louis-Guillaume Baillet de Saint Julien, recognized perfectly well this line of implication in Chardin's work, which does more than bring out the latent animality of humanity. As this critic argued, in Chardin's work we see an artist playing with the metaphysical conventions of the human visage, heedless of a science of truth based on the law of noncontradiction. "There is no one who does not consider himself a physiognomist," he wrote, "and there can be no science in the world more false than physiognomy. But that chimera is by no means useless for painting. We are accustomed, in all that regards the productions of this art, to judge things by their form and external figure. Consequently, a painter can act freely, and we will not contradict him."[33]

In other words, in *The Ray* the Cartesian *res extensa*, the generalized body, appears instead as a matter of passages from one form into another. Geometric lines are made to appear as passages among various categories, forms, orders of being, and conditions of existence. Furthermore, in these passages these sorts of distinctions must at a certain point lose their pertinence as they turn into orifices, those decidedly un-Cartesian vortices. Whether animate or inanimate, whether human or animal, however it is generically classified, the body moves among forms. This movement emphasizes that the consumer may become prey and vice versa, and it also stresses the centrality to the body of digestive processes, within whose boundaries one can never be quite sure of what is or is not the stuff of one's own self.[34]

This design of Chardin's painting is in keeping with the tendencies of seventeenth- and eighteenth-century natural philosophy. We may compare it, for example, to Robert Boyle's definition of a body as a "convention of essential accidents." Boyle explained, "I would not say, that any thing can immediately be made of every thing. . . . Yet since bodies, having but one common matter, can be differenced but by accidents . . . I see not, why it should be absurd to think, that (at least among inanimate bodies) by the intervention of some very small addition or subtraction of matter . . . and of an orderly series of alterations, disposing by degrees the matter to be transmuted, almost of any thing, may at length be made any thing."[35]

In his qualifications here, as in his insistence elsewhere on the immutability of the human species, Boyle was careful to place limits upon the metamorphoses that he saw within any seemingly static tableau of nature. Similarly, in writing of the "metamorphoses that take place before our eyes," in which "all things serve mutually as nourishment for one another," Jean-Baptiste-René Robinet would still seek to maintain a conception of nature as an uninterrupted continuity and plenitude of which humanity was the cynosure. His adherence to the doctrine of preformationism was meant to assure all this. Nonetheless, in Robinet's natural philosophy, as in Boyle's, we see how nature was coming to be viewed through an image of metamorphosis within which the figure of the cannibal would appear as the most extreme term of philosophical comprehension.

Robinet's philosophy relied on the writings of naturalists such as Carolus Linnaeus and Georges-Louis Leclerc Buffon as well as on ancient histories, the works of physiologists, and travelers' tales. Robinet was able to draw upon these sorts of materials so as to account for curiosities such as anthropomorphic fish (fig. 3) or stones shaped like human genitalia (fig. 4). He concluded that these puzzling phenomena were signs and tokens of the fact that all elements of creation "have relations, more or less close, with all the others, and the extremes still communicate."[36] Yet this argument, like Boyle's theories of corpuscles and cannibals, could not help but suggest that there were passages among species, or orifices within creatures, that rendered suspect their seemingly distinct identities.

One such passage was noted and momentarily resolved through a racist trope that lay ready to hand, in Robinet's consideration of the Hottentot. "It has been said that the orangutan is an animal," he wrote. "Under a human mask. One could say that the Hottentot is a man disguised under the features, the voice, and the manners of an animal." In this instance as elsewhere, Robinet still sought to maintain his assurance: "All these metamorphoses change nothing in its essence and remove nothing that is inherent to any organism."[37] Yet his defensiveness on this score amply reveals his anxiety. It is as if he were gazing upon Chardin's *Ray* and seeing in it a shocking reproduction of some of his very own words, one that distorts their proper meaning or at least what he had imagined their meaning to be when he composed the following passage:

> The houses we inhabit, with all the materials of which they are built— metal, sand, cement, etc . . . ; the furniture with which we decorate these houses, as much for luxury as for utility; the utensils we use; the clothes we wear: all of this comes from organic matter. . . . It is for this that towns are devoured and reduced to cinders in the vast bowels of the earth. There all these works of art dissolve and return, little by little, to their natural state. The earth nourishes itself with their debris. It forms a juice that serves as nourishment for minerals and vegetables. Thus matter successively becomes metal, stone, plant, animal.[38]

The Ray focuses on the body in its materiality, which is us but not ours. It is less ours, anyway, than the objects with which we consider ourselves to be familiar—less ours even than a fish fit for our pot. For it is indeed a body of metamorphoses, as another eighteenth-century naturalist, Charles Bonnet, labored to explain: "The machines of animals have been constructed with such a marvelous art that they convert alimentary matter into their own substance. The preparations, the combinations, and the separations that these

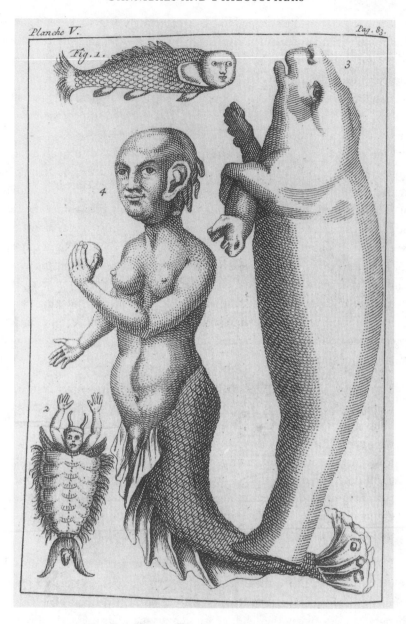

FIGURE 3.
Jean-Baptiste-René Robinet, "Anthropomorphic Fish," from *Considerations philosophiques de la gradation naturelles des formes de l'être* (1768), History of Science Collections, University of Oklahoma Libraries

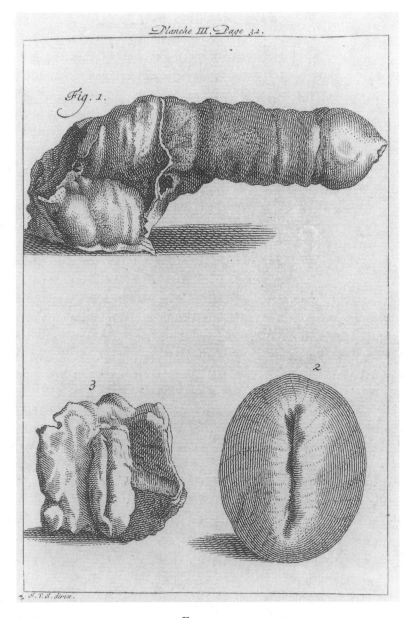

FIGURE 4.
Jean-Baptiste-René Robinet, "Rocks that Represent the Sexual Parts of Man and Woman," from *Considerations philosophiques de la gradation naturelles des formes de l'être* (1768), History of Science Collections, University of Oklahoma Libraries

matters undergo insensibly change them into chyle, blood, lymph, flesh, bone, etc. Thus, as soon as circulation has begun in the embryo, as soon as it has become a living animal, the same metamorphoses take place in its interior." Like Robinet, Bonnet sought to stabilize this vision of metamorphosis through an insistence on a continuity and hierarchy of nature, which he articulated in Leibnizian terms. ("There is no true metamorphosis in nature," he noted, because "the elements are invariable.") The marvelousness of Trembley's experiments with polyps might put pressure on his philosophy, taking possession of one's spirit "to such a point that there is no more room for simple and natural explications," but even in this case Bonnet could reassert the role of divine providence. Where his picture of creation really faltered—and so where it proves assimilable to Chardin's *Ray*—is in his observation, "We lack a *Logic* that would be infinitely useful not only in the physical sciences, but also in the moral sciences; I mean a *Treatise on the Use and Abuse of Analogy*."[39]

The study of nature necessitated that one employ analogies in differentiating and organizing the categories of things. Therefore, one could not hope to recognize a particular species—or even a particular organism—without the use of analogy. This is the problem posed, on the one hand, by the metamorphic combinations and arrangements of natural elements and, on the other, by liminal cases such as those presented by polyps, orangutans, Hottentots, monsters, grafts, wars, and cannibals. In this context, the lack of a treatise on analogy must mean that despite all protestations to the contrary, one cannot be sure where metamorphoses begin or end. Identities, species, and systems of classification must then be seen as subject to just such an overdetermined play of analogies as we can see in the alimentary and digestive matters that come alive in Chardin's *nature morte*.

In *The Ray* the body turns us away from life and death alike. It dissolves this distinction, turning us instead toward our perverse communications with objects. These communications are appropriately termed perverse because in these objects, which are supposed to be radically differentiated from the human subject, we see ourselves or parts of ourselves as we might see mouths in houses or eyes in vases; and we treat these things accordingly, narcissistically, without batting an eye. As no genre of art illustrates more clearly than the still life, our relations with objects share the same structures of identification and feeling as our relationships with other people.

Recognizing this perversity, Chardin's painting teases out an ambiguity in Descartes's writings, which might be argued to be viscerally, if not literally, central. For the philosopher who in his *Meditations* conventionally associated paintings with delusory perceptions nonetheless compared his work, as a philosopher, with that of a painter. In his *Discourse on the Method* he proposed to "represent [his] life . . . as if in a picture."[40] Recalling an earlier treatise he had begun to write but then suppressed after Galileo was condemned by the Inquisition in 1633, he offered this troubled image of himself:

> Now a painter cannot represent all the different sides of a solid body equally well on his flat canvas, and so he chooses one of the principal ones, sets it facing the light, and shades the others so as to make them stand out only when viewed from the perspective of the chosen side. In just the same way, fearing that I could not put everything I had in mind into my discourse, I undertook merely to expound quite fully what I understood about light. Then, as the occasion arose, I added something about the sun and fixed stars . . . about terrestrial bodies . . . and finally about man, because he observes these bodies. (132, 134)

This use—or abuse—of an analogy holds telling implications for the self-presentation of this philosopher, for the problem of representation from an illusionistic point of view, and for the metaphysics of identity in general.[41] The vacillation of perspectives within it is precisely comparable to the problem that Chardin organized for his viewers by bringing heterogeneous forms into communication with one another at the center of his canvas. The force of this comparison becomes all the more pressing when Descartes—still very conventionally, to be sure—presents himself also as an authority on physiology and invites anyone "unversed in anatomy" to observe the dissection of an animal before reading any further. Things do not get any simpler when he presents his work "only as a history or . . . a fable" shortly before he proceeds to point out the dangers of deception in both genres.[42] This is the Descartes—the philosopher seeing himself as like and yet unlike a painter, anatomist, historian, and fabulist, dividing himself among their perspectives onto different things, writing in self-confessed fear of the Inquisition, believing he had located the primary dwelling place of the soul in a gland of the body—who met his match in Chardin, who made himself a philosopher through his visceral handling of paint.

No doubt the foregoing may seem a great deal too much to claim for *The Ray*, which was made by a man who we have no reason to believe ever read a word of Descartes. Certainly it may seem strange that I have compared the metaphysician of the seventeenth century, tutor to members of the royal houses of Bohemia and Sweden, with an eighteenth-century painter who regretted that his background, as the son of an artisan who made billiard tables, had not afforded him a humanistic education. However, the pertinence of this comparison was established long before Baxandall illustrated his analysis of Chardin with a diagram of the eye reproduced from Descartes's *Discourse on the Method*.[43] It antedates as well André Gide's more impressionistic analogy between the effect of Chardin's still lifes and "the rapt profundity of one of Descartes' meditations."[44] The metaphysical significance of Chardin's still lifes has been argued by admirers as various as Diderot, the artisan's son and philosophe who helped to inaugurate modern art criticism in the eighteenth century; the Goncourts, who rediscovered Chardin's work on behalf of nationalist, realist, bourgeois ideologies in the nineteenth century; and Francis Ponge, who viewed this work as inimical to all ideologies, both in the past and in his own twentieth-century present.

Apostrophizing Chardin in his *Salon of 1765*, Diderot wrote as follows: "If it is true, as the philosophers say, that our sensations are the only reality; that perhaps neither the emptiness of space nor even the solidity of bodies has anything in it of what we experience; then can these philosophers, at a distance of four feet from your paintings, teach me what difference there is for them between the Creator and you?"[45] Here Diderot was obviously alluding to philosophers more closely resembling John Locke and David Hume than Descartes, but this is just the point: Chardin's art was seen to pose a sensational challenge to the intuitive grounds of geometry, of extended things in space, and to all that was implicated therein. To be sure, Diderot himself was being more than a touch exhibitionistic in this passage. Even so, he was simply trying out the logical implications of the dominant contemporary characterization of Chardin's work, which he had already summarized in writing of it in his *Salon of 1763*: "It is nature itself."[46] Similarly, Baillet de Saint Julien had earlier represented an encounter with Chardin's paintings as a drama in which their "enchanting mechanism" compelled viewers to surrender their identities, to dissolve, in the repetitious, ateleological pleasure of the artist's hand: "Through concentration and repeated investigations, the eye fooled by so much delicacy, and by the apparent facility that reigns there, desires in vain to learn the secret; it is engulfed, it loses itself in your touch; and wearying of its efforts, without ever being surfeited with its pleasure, it distances itself, approaches again, and never finally leaves without vowing to return."[47]

Diderot presented Chardin as an artist whose works so thoroughly epitomized sensationism, the epistemology through which the Enlightenment searched for its grounds, that they ended up mocking it. In doing so, he made it clear that the premises of this art might threaten to be distasteful or at the extreme—as in Descartes's figurations—demonic, upsetting man, philosopher, and God all at once; and his was by no means an exorbitant commentary, either in contemporary terms or from the retrospective viewpoints afforded us by our own time.

To begin with, simply to concentrate on still lifes and genre pictures, as Chardin did, was markedly to turn away from the history painting that was most esteemed in the contemporary hierarchy of genres. It was as a painter "of animals and fruits" that Chardin was originally accepted into the Academy;[48] and even an extremely sympathetic critic such as the Abbé Raynal, writing in the November 1753 *Mercure de France,* would automatically frame his appreciation by noting that the artist's works "make no pretension to the heroic style."[49] If Chardin was commonly praised for making humble things sublime, this praise was always accompanied, implicitly or explicitly, by a sense of defensiveness over the possibility that this way of handling things could prove to be a form of aggression. The aesthetic violence that André Malraux was to see in his work, by a retrospective glance through the fractured lens of cubism—"Chardin's seeming humility involved not so much subservience to the model as its destruction in the interests of his picture"[50]— was already noted in the eighteenth century, and to an effect far more consequential than Malraux's formalist concerns would let on.

Even within the boundaries of the painting of still lifes and, beginning in the 1730s, of domestic scenes and portraits, Chardin's attention was markedly turned away from the more elevated subjects within these categories. He did not focus on lavish arrangements of food and luxurious tableware such as those found in some Dutch and Flemish still lifes, displays of game within tableaux designed to idealize the royal and aristocratic diversion of the hunt, or representations of prosperous male figures. As has often been noted, such human figures as his pictures include are almost without exception women, children, and servants. In the words of Marianne Roland Michel, "Chardin takes pains to evoke domestic scenes in such a way that the presence of the painter does not disturb the arrangement of the scene. He flows through the feminine space, without straining or forcing his way; it is as if there is an osmosis between the work of the painter and that of the house that surrounds him."[51]

Not only are adult male figures generally absent from his paintings, but the kitchen interior in which Chardin typically set his still lifes was a specifically feminine space. This consideration marks another aspect in which his works transfigured Cartesian geometry.[52] Made feminine by cultural associations and common social practices, the kitchen interior is also a figure, by metonymy and analogy, for the guts of the body. Here we may recall the Renaissance commonplace that identified the stomach as "a little cook, a little kitchen, or a little oven."[53] In this respect, too, the visceral exposure of the central figure in *The Ray* is a synecdoche for the entire pictorial space and, moreover, a suggestion of the female sex. It is only an oblique suggestion, to be sure, and yet arguably a more telling one than a supposedly frank representation such as that in Courbet's *Origin of the World*. For here the visceral opening, gendered as feminine by association with this space and with the vessels in this space, as well as by contrast with the phallic knife and handles, is made to suggest the impossibility of objectively representing sexual difference. This suggestion is reinforced if we recall that oysters, such as those made a prominent element in this work, were popularly seen as reproducing "without the combination of the two sexes," as Voltaire put it, and were often used in the eighteenth century to represent the lowest scale of animal creation.[54] Accordingly, in the place of sexual difference—canvas, kitchen, viscera, wound—we are presented with an event in which we can distinguish elements of beauty, violence, disgust, lusciousness, and confusion, but this is an event in which we are prevented from focusing on any one privileged line. Instead, straight lines are shown to hesitate, yield, drift: to see themselves in a dreamy geometry that is feminine and yet, contrary to the developing eighteenth-century bourgeois ideal popularized by writers such as Samuel Richardson and Jean-Jacques Rousseau, not at all proper.

The drama is yet more complex, for the setting of *The Ray* also figures, by metonymy and analogy, as an image of the genre of still life itself. Because it was traditionally regarded as a relatively minor, secondary art, and in this regard paralleled the status of the kitchen in relation to the public rooms of the house as well as the status of women in relation to men, the still life as such must be seen as being ceremonially elevated when geometry is mortified in *The Ray*. (One remembers, of course, how still lifes were long considered the most proper subject for women artists.) The comestibles in this still life, too, suggest the general image of the interior, of the visceral passage, and of sex (oysters having been associated with venery since antiquity). In this regard it is important to recall that although the contemporary hierarchy of genres did have considerable power—enough, by contemporary accounts, to make Chardin feel lifelong regrets that he had not had the humanistic education and the formal training that would have qualified him to be a history painter—this power was never absolute and was always being renegotiated, as nothing demonstrates better than Chardin's successful career.

To use the rhetoric with which Chardin's work was contemporaneously received, when "simple," "naïve," "truthful" matters of "private life" can gain a public standing, arousing a public appetite, it is clear that certain cultural classifications may be redrawn, broadened, crossed, or otherwise messed with. Although engravings made from his genre scenes were widely sold to a bourgeois public, Chardin's paintings were purchased primarily by aristocratic patrons and cognoscenti, and he was very much a central part of the artistic establishment in Paris from the time of his induction into the Academy to the day of his death. However qualified by the inevitable mark of condescension—as in Baillet de Saint Julien's backhanded compliment that among painters whose talents were "contained within a particular genre," he was the one whose work came closest to history painting—Chardin's success was considerable. (It was sufficient, for instance, to lead Baillet de Saint Julien to go on to urge that Chardin ought not "to abandon . . . the painting of fruits and animals" even though he had proved himself so talented at rendering scenes of "private life.")[55] Under these circumstances, any painting of a still life, much less one designed to be a masterpiece, was bound to be an allegorical elevation of genre as well as of the painter of artisanal heritage. Genre, rank, and gender were all perforce implicated in one another, together with theological and philosophical concerns, when the abstract universe of Cartesian metaphysics was rendered as a definitively visceral space.

Still, it is vital to remember that Chardin's success was always questionable. It could not escape anyone in his time that Chardin provokingly chose as his subjects utterly commonplace interiors and objects or "familiar subjects," as the contemporary idiom would have it. Although such a choice was not without precedent, those who were accustomed to the standard of "la belle nature" in art could find it positively disgusting.[56] Precisely by their emphatic insistence on the differences between Chardin's images and distasteful subjects, even the most sympathetic critics, such as Raynal, could not help but emphasize their provocative similarity: "But the appropriateness of the choice and charm of the images offers a strong criticism of the Flemish painters in general. The fact of the matter is that smokers' kits, fist fights, the needs of the body—in short, Nature captured at her most abject—are the subjects most frequently treated by the Brauwers, the Ostades, the Ténières [sic], etc. M. Chardin has always avoided these images humiliating for humanity."[57] More concisely, Mathon de la Cour, writing in 1763, said that Chardin had found "the art of pleasing the eyes, even when he presents them with distasteful objects."[58]

Diderot faced this provocation directly in writing about The Ray. Remarking that he would recommend this piece for his son to study, were the boy to desire an artistic vocation, Diderot argued as follows: "The object is distasteful, but it is the very flesh of the fish. It is its skin. It is its blood. The very appearance of the thing would have no effect otherwise. Monsieur Pierre [Jean-Baptiste-Marie Pierre, a contemporary history painter], look well at this piece when you go to the Academy; and learn, if you can, the secret of redeeming, through one's talent, the distaste in certain temperaments."[59] In thus characterizing Chardin's work, Diderot was making a point about the "nature itself" that Chardin was widely praised for representing (praise that Diderot made as literal as possible: "O Chardin, it is not the white, the red, the black that you mix on your palette; it is the very substance of objects, it is the air and the light that you take on the tip of your brush and fix on the canvas.")[60] As opposed to Raynal, who insisted that Chardin's work repulsed all abject things, Diderot insisted that the potential for disgust in the subject of The Ray not only was true to the nature of nature but also was necessary to the aesthetic impression of this work.

In the present context we need not worry about passing judgment in favor of Raynal or Diderot. The important point is that the understanding of Chardin's work was fixated in his era, through various perspectives, on the visceral issue of disgust, which was prominently symbolized in the central image of The Ray. This issue was to show its continuing importance when the brothers Goncourt rediscovered Chardin for their own time in *The Art of the Eighteenth Century* (1873).

The Goncourts did not neglect to touch upon the viscera while upbraiding the nation that had given birth to Chardin but then neglected the works he created. "What!" they exclaimed, " . . . this is France, the France so protective of her other glories, which has neglected these, though they be the living issue of her temperament, her character, her entrails, made in the image of all her features!" Chardin himself was characterized in similar terms: "What is Chardin, indeed? The bourgeois painter of the bourgeoisie. It is to the petite bourgeoisie that he turns for his subjects; it is among the petite bourgeoisie that he finds his inspirations. He confines his painting in that humble world from which he comes and where his habits, his thoughts, his affections, his entrails remain." Finally, with a certain inevitability, not only this painter and the nation for which he stood but his art itself was characterized by the Goncourts in visceral terms: "Nothing humiliates his brushes. He reaches into the larder of the people. He paints the old cauldron, the pepper pot, the wooden mortar with its pestle, the most humble furniture. There is nothing in nature that he disdains. In an hour of study he will tackle a rack of mutton cutlets; and the blood, the fat, the bones, the lustrous sinews, the meat—his brush will express it all and make it exude from his impasto like the juice of that flesh."[61]

Needless to say, the Goncourts' vision of Chardin, their effort to recover his work and the heritage it represented, was a kind of invention. Chardin's art was not confined to the petite bourgeoisie so much as it was imprisoned within it by these nineteenth-century champions who portrayed themselves as liberating him from the darkness of cultural amnesia. Because no historical object, no effort at recovery of the past, and for that matter no form of representation of any sort can entirely avoid such effects of projection—cultural, ideological, libidinal, and so on—I do not mean to belabor this very general point. The specific terms in which the past is framed are more interesting, as in the difference of emphasis between the Goncourts' lexicon of nation and class and the eighteenth-century categories of nature and genre. Contemporary critics certainly had noticed the relation of Chardin's work to the Third Estate, as the Goncourts for their part had taken note of a certain conception of nature within it; but the emphases and crucial idioms had changed. In this respect, what is most notable in the Goncourts' representation of Chardin is that the artist himself was made out to be a martyred figure central to the image of France.

As the Goncourts portrayed him, Chardin was a humble man of the people. He was one who had not feared to touch any bloody, oozing, disgusting thing and one whom fashion had then cast into a revolting oblivion from which he would have to be redeemed if the French were to find any hope for the present and future of their nation. ("Before this prodigious example of neglect, before the excess of ingratitude and the insolence of disdain of its immediate posterity for the great century of art of Louis XV, one is brought to doubt the justice of France.")[62] In this respect, Diderot's literal equation of pigment with natural substance was not merely equaled but was gone one better by the Goncourts' emphasis on the artist's entrails in the reproduction of national identity. In the eighteenth century the transfigured geometry of the canvas marked by the central figure in *The Ray* had brought Diderot to image a godlike artist who displaced the traditional architecture of the universe by dissolving all the structures of the perceived world into tantalizing sensations; in the nineteenth century it moved the Goncourts to image a Christlike artist whose own flesh, along with the flesh of his canvases, was the sacred nourishment necessary to save France from dissolving into vacuous frivolity.

This focus on Chardin's work as an issue of visceral understanding would continue in the twentieth century, from a variety of perspectives. Ponge, for instance, in writing of Chardin, compared the arrangements of everyday objects that one finds in still lifes to "the disposition of the entrails of sacred chickens."[63] Proust opened his essay on Chardin by imagining himself introducing a discontented youth to the artist's work, including *The Ray*, which he characterized as a spectacle bound to "repulse" the young man.[64] Michel and Fabrice Faré have gone so far as to call the choice of subject in *The Ray* "a declaration of principles." In their words, Chardin,

> concerned with a new aesthetic and with the practice of an original vision, was not afraid to turn to so repugnant a model: the ray exhibits bloody insides; red reflections and touches of blood are spread everywhere like so many attacks brought against the integrity of the form. The knife rests below the ignoble wound, beside the skimmer. The green jug and the scallions indicate culinary servitudes with an indifference to which the oysters add the note of a derisory refinement within a climate of violence underlined by the savage cat, its fur still bristling.[65]

In apparent reference to the Farés, as well as to the *Critique* collaborators (Bois and colleagues) and René Demoris, another critic who has written extensively on Chardin, Marianne Michel has adopted a more restrained interpretation of *The Ray:* "One hesitates to follow those who see in this painting the horror of an ignoble wound or a sexual content—or even a representation of the crucifixion—and it is hardly likely that Chardin wanted to put in it all that one may recognize there today, even if he wished to make this painting a demonstration of his talents." However, even she calls it a "horrible" as well as "magnificent" painting and sees in it "a choice, a refusal of concessions to all purely decorative representation."[66]

Again, the interesting task here is not to decide among these opinions but rather to note their common ground. Writers of this century have attributed various characters to Chardin, in accordance with the critical perspectives they have brought to bear on his work even when they disclaim any such intervention, as in Michel's hallucinatory insistence on what Chardin "wanted to put in."[67] Consistent within this inconsistency, however, is a toning down of the visceral question of the *dégoutant* that preoccupied critics in Chardin's own time and that continued to obsess the Goncourts. Despite the challenging views offered especially by the *Critique* authors, by some of the work of Demoris, and most recently by Mieke Bal, the general tendency has been to suggest that although there may be some cause for disquietude, especially in *The Ray,* it is not of a kind in which one need fear being personally implicated.[68] Whereas Diderot's Chardin proved repulsive to shallow metaphysicians and the Goncourts' to frivolous modes of fashion, the Chardin of the twentieth century seems ultimately to repulse only childishly naïve viewers. This Chardin is a pussycat—and not one bristling with tension while invading a different being's table and stepping into the juice and flesh of yet another displaced creature of marked and yet markedly indeterminate sexuality. In effect, the disturbed and disturbing center of *The Ray* has been contained, if not in a hierarchy of genres, then in a historical framing of Chardin's art and, through his art, of his self. Neither God nor son of God, Chardin now has been deemed a human being like unto ourselves; and so it might seem that the totem of *The Ray* is now so easily consumed that it is no longer "good to think."

If this is not to be the case—if we may yet be perverse enough to wish to confront all over again the implications of the viscera of which *The Ray* makes such an exhibition—then we must begin by reconsidering the history of Chardin's art, as I have sought to do here. We may then recognize that historical understanding is precisely what is at issue in *The Ray*. Geometry is mortified in this work so that history may make itself apparent, though not the sort of history that can hang Chardin's paintings in museums and gut them of their power to threaten us with disgust. It is rather a question of such history as exists in the inexpressiveness of fact even within its supposed yielding to forms of taste, utility, or humanity. In focusing our attention on viscera, in directing us to the body in its materiality, *The Ray* exhibits a thing that we can strive to regulate and to which we can give organized form but which ultimately remains beyond our control. Therefore, this visceral body seems naturally to figure as the self's other, as the animal, and as the inanimation of death both within and without us. Through this overdetermination it suggests a non-Euclidean geometry through which perception endlessly opens onto the ever frustrated desire of cultural organization. As far as this mortified geometry is concerned, becoming historical, being recognized as historical, means yielding to a stubbornness of fact that cannot be consumed by aesthetics, morality, or reason.

Metamorphic in a way that incorporates and digests biomorphism instead of privileging and being contained by it, this is the geometry, and the materiality and history, of orifices. To look at it closely is to confront a formlessness that is not behind, before, or under but is rather *of* geometry and all that it is conventionally taken to signify, whether that be divinity, nature, beauty, rationality, or the creative self. Through a series of symbolic equivalences (canvas-fish-face-food-form-object-ground), *The Ray* proposes that the basis of representation, the foundation of all our knowing of things, is not a surface but an orifice. In other words, it proposes that the basis of representation is a disorienting line that opens onto heterogeneous surfaces of potential identification. In the central figure of *The Ray*, ripped from the justifications of theodicy and aesthetics and all other cultural mechanisms for organizing perspectives, the line appears as an evisceration of the human will to see itself affirmed in all things; as the oneiric law of classification in nature and culture; as the boundary in which beings like ourselves give themselves away by showing that they understand all too well the ideal of disgust.

With a similar concern for "everything that happens at the edge of the orifices (or orality, but also of the ear, the eye—and all the 'senses' in general),"

Jacques Derrida has offered an appropriate comment: "The question is no longer one of knowing if it is 'good' to eat the other or if the other is 'good' to eat, nor of knowing which other. One eats him regardless and lets oneself be eaten by him. The so-called nonanthropophagic cultures practice symbolic anthropology and even construct their most elevated socius, indeed the sublimity of their morality, their politics, and their right, on their anthropophagy."[69] As is emphasized by the exposed insides of the oyster shells, those primitive habitations, the trench in Chardin's ray fish is also a crude mockery of a dwelling place, a *mise-en-abîme* of the environing kitchen, which is itself the belly of the house, that microcosm of the *socius*. The world in general is thus imaged as a space of digestive and reproductive processes. This is a world of uneasy and partial transformations, not of formal bodies and fixed orders of being. It is akin to the world of cannibalism described by Sir Thomas Browne in his *Religio Medici* (1642):

> *All flesh is grasse,* is not onely metaphorically, but literally true, for all those creatures we behold, are but the hearbs of the field, digested into flesh in them, or more remotely carnified in our selves. Nay further, we are what we all abhorre, *Anthropophagi* and Cannibals, devourers not onely of men, but of our selves; and that not in an allegory, but a positive truth; for all this masse of flesh which wee behold, came in at our mouths: this frame wee looke upon, hath beene upon our trenchers; In briefe, we have devoured our selves.[70]

As the ray's opening suggests multiple orifices (mouth, eyes, anus, vagina), it offers an image of the body that is most emphatically not self-enclosed and not a substance extended in space. This body is rather a heterogeneous concatenation of figurations in which no line is completely direct and no form unequivocal, independent, or self-evident. This, we are informed, is what it means to be a human thing: to be forever transfigured by disgust, whether through denial, transcendence, avoidance, reification, rationalization, or some other mechanism of culture—or, if you prefer, this is what it is to think: to imagine that one may draw lines without a knife.

To think: to entertain the hallucination of an art that does not wound, that does not bleed. It would take a sentimentalist of a later day to proclaim that we murder to dissect, as if works of imagination were not also, always, works of evisceration of one's own supposed self as well as of putative others. *The*

Ray offers us a vision of a totem as different from the Wordsworthian self as it is from the Cartesian cogito: not the thing of sublime imagination, not the thinking thing, but the visceral thing, in which vision sees itself and in its own sight is forced to turn away.

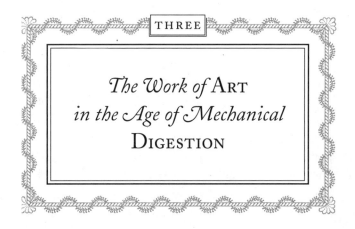

THREE

The Work of ART in the *Age of Mechanical* DIGESTION

*T*HE DUCK BORE no resemblance at all, he insisted, to the famous "cock of the clock" in the great mechanical masterpieces of Lyons and Strasbourg. No, the movements of its wings were anatomically accurate, in keeping with the extraordinary nature of its overall conception. In addition, because Jacques de Vaucanson did not wish simply to exhibit *(montrer)* but also to demonstrate *(démontrer)* his creation, he proclaimed that its mechanism would be open to public view. "Perhaps some ladies, or gentlemen who like only the exterior of animals, would have preferred to see it completely closed; but except where that request has been made, I am well pleased that one should not be misled and that one should see all the interior works."[1]

So Vaucanson wrote in his "Letter from M. Vaucanson to the Abbé d[e] F[ontaine]," which was published along with the memoir of his inventions submitted to the Royal Academy of Sciences in 1738. He had already gained considerable renown by the time the general public got a chance to peek into the innards of his duck, for he had previously given exhibitions of an amazing automaton that played a flute. In his account of Vaucanson's life, Marie-Jean Caritat, the Marquis de Condorcet, would later mock the skepticism of those contemporary spectators who "saw nothing in the flute-player but a serinette and regarded the movements of its fingers, which imitated those of man, as charlatanism."[2] For this life-size figure of a seated shepherd, modeled after the *Faun Playing the Flute* (1709) by Antoine Coysevox, did actually perform on its instrument, moving its fingers and blowing across the embouchure, as opposed to miming these actions while the music box of a "bird organ," or serinette, played in a concealed interior.

Nothing quite like this figure had ever before been seen. Automatons of various kinds had been known to the world since antiquity, including some works of considerable sophistication, such as the *jaquemarts* that struck the hours on cathedral towers or the rooster of the "great clock" that Tristram Shandy hoped to see at Lyons.[3] This flute-playing android, however, had outdone them all. For good reason, the entry on "android" in the *Encyclopédie* (1751–65) was almost entirely taken from the description of this invention given in Vaucanson's memoir.[4] It was only after his faun had been put on display in a number of French cities that Vaucanson launched a new series of exhibitions in which it appeared alongside his duck and a third figure, a Provençal shepherd who performed on a drum while also playing the three-holed pipe known as the *galoubet*. Not long thereafter, in 1742, Vaucanson's memoir was translated into English when his creations were put on display at the King's Theatre in London. They went on to tour Germany in 1747 and 1748, and they were also seen in Russia before a series of sales and misadventures resulted in their disappearance from the historical record in the course of the next century.[5]

All three figures were greatly admired, but it was the duck that came to be most closely associated with Vaucanson, symbolizing the remarkable achievement that made his name a byword for mechanical genius.[6] Its emblematic status in the history of technology has lived on to the present day, in both scientific and popular literature.[7] The history of this duck can then contribute to our understanding of the Enlightenment, and it can do more. It offers us a way to think through a constitutive problem in the formation of modern and postmodern Western art: the task of distinguishing the desired products of culture from the unmeaning refuse of human life. In other words, this mechanical duck can help us better to comprehend the vexed aesthetic continuities between Immanuel Kant's *Critique of Judgement* (1790) and Andy Warhol's Factory.

An engraving by Hubert-François Gravelot (fig. 5) served as the frontispiece for Vaucanson's memoir presented to the Royal Academy of Sciences (to which he would be admitted in 1746). In this engraving the duck stands in profile on its modest pedestal between the two androids, which are ele-

H. Gravelot delin.   Vivares Sculp.

FIGURE 5.
Hubert-François Gravelot, frontispiece to *Le mécanisme du fluteur automate,*
by Jacques de Vaucanson (1738), by permission of the Houghton Library,
Harvard University

vated and frontally posed. Perched glumly between these pastoral types, the duck certainly must look sufficiently absurd to the twentieth-century eye. Nonetheless, it fully deserves its central position, for in addition to being a great technical accomplishment, this duck was a semiotic marvel. Whether viewed in the context of the mechanical musicians pictured on either side of it or from the perspectives offered by the scientific, philosophical, and social and cultural histories of its day, Vaucanson's duck was a work brilliantly designed to exhibit the meanings of bodies in the eighteenth century. Its power in playing this role was recognized at the time, as when Charles Bonnet remarked in his *Reflections on Organized Bodies* (1762), "If VAUCANSON has known how to construct an artificial duck that moves its beak to seize the food presented to it, could not the CREATOR of VAUCANSON have constructed an automaton that would imitate the actions of man?"[8] To others as well, it seemed that this machine might prove central to the way all of creation would be imagined; and so, as absurd as it may appear, the duck in that engraving is standing right where it belongs.

In putting forward this argument I am assuming that for their part, the musicians do not look particularly outlandish to our eyes. Indeed, it is difficult to imagine the setting that could prove disconcerting to their idealized composure. In any event, they seem at home on their pedestals, and they also make perfect sense as elements in Vaucanson's career. Just as it is logical that the novelist Richard Powers, in *Galatea 2.2,* should have revised the legend of Pygmalion in the terms of computer circuitry, it is obvious why Vaucanson chose to animate pastoral figures. For all their differences, what makes these representations comparable is that the machine appears in them as an easily recognizable compound of contemporary cultural ideals and anxieties. (In Powers' novel, this means that the frightfully ideal impersonality of digital code is made to give birth to a decidedly imperfect—and so adorable—personality.) The case is similar with Rabbi Loew's legendary Golem, a clay figure animated by a written formula as if demonically to parody the inspiration of scripture; Auguste de Villiers de l'Isle-Adam's late-nineteenth-century "future Eve," which is invented by Thomas Edison so as to mock both spiritualist and empiricist epistemologies by exhibiting their erotic identity; Fritz Lang's *Metropolis* (1926), in which the figure of woman is split into violently industrial and pathetically sentimental enemy twins; and Ridley Scott's *Blade Runner* (1982), whose viewers are given the dismaying news that in the postpunk stylings of twenty-first-century culture, desire will still be channeled through the codes of *film noir*. Without meaning to suggest that there is nothing more to say about the images of machines in these instances, I would note that they all obey a similar logic of ambivalence—quite unsurprisingly, of course, given the massively overdetermined traditions through which human nature has been articulated in opposition to a presumably spiritless technology.

In all these instances we are witness to a representational logic that knows how to explore the borderlines of a generalized humanity without crossing the powers that be of a given society. In the case of Vaucanson's musicians, this logic entailed that aesthetic ideals from the age of Louis XIV would be formally carried over to the age of Louis XV, but with a crucial and definitively modern change, which therefore had to convey a certain aggressiveness as well. This change was especially marked in the case of the first automaton, the flute player whose image Vaucanson appropriated from Coysevox. Like the contemporaneous still lifes of Jean-Siméon Chardin, which made a success of this painter even though the humble objects represented within them were often viewed as skirting the boundaries of the *dégoutant,* Vaucanson's faun challenged the standard of *la belle nature* in a fashion that managed to appear both highly sophisticated and decidedly bourgeois. Whereas Louis XIV had symbolically inserted the workings of his court inside the mythological figures of Latin and Greek antiquity, even as Coysevox had inserted himself into tradition through his rivalrous refashionings of antique masterpieces, Vaucanson had introduced his modern self into the courtly icon.[9] In taking a sculpture that decorated the gardens of the Tuileries to serve as a mere shell for his machinery, Vaucanson effectively outmarveled Coysevox's pastoral while simultaneously transforming a fixed and restricted aesthetics of royal display into a mobile and commercial public spectacle. While not neglecting to note that their inventor had been awarded a pension from the king, a prospectus for one of the exhibitions of the automatons specified the conditions for four levels of admission, from thirty-one to eight sous a head, and added, "We hope that everyone in town will be pleased to profit from the chance to see them and will note their difference from the various bagatelles that are shown in public every day."[10]

As Barbara Maria Stafford has noted, "Vaucanson's virtuosity, ostentatiously displayed in expensive artifacts, provided a counterimage to virtuous rural labor. His clever handling epitomized those provocative and fashionable goods beguiling big-city dwellers."[11] Accordingly, rather than being shaped by the artist's hand, the parts of the flute player were constructed by a number of artisans entrusted with Vaucanson's designs. Moreover, in place of the classical materials of sculpture, Vaucanson made use of steel, brass, leather, and other manufactured materials, including a paint that gave his faun's exterior the simulated appearance of marble. A traditional symbol of nature's harmony and an innovative work of human art, his faun was also a product implicitly representing the potential for commodified industrial reproduction that would be explicitly represented in the business of silk manufacturing that was to provide Vaucanson with his occupation later in life. This business would then prove to be philosophically evocative in its own right, as when John Turberville Needham, in seeking to counter mechanistic conceptions of life with a vitalist theory, used Vaucanson's silk-weaving machines to image the divine fabrication of living beings.[12]

Coysevox, the celebrated sculptor of the seventeenth and early eighteenth centuries, a favorite of the Sun King, thus was reincarnated as the engineer of the Enlightenment, who would choose to decline Frederick the Great's invitation to join his showpiece court in Prussia. Like Chardin, who became a member and officer of the Royal Academy of Painting and Sculpture, Coysevox and Vaucanson were sons of artisans who worked their way up to prominent positions in their social worlds. As distinct from the celebrated sculptor who earlier had risen through his art to become a director of the Academy, however, Vaucanson became an innovator in technology, an inspector of manufactures for the silk industry, and an active proponent of industrial reorganization, in which role he was said to have had stones flung at him by artisans from Lyons who were infuriated by his plan "to simplify the crafts."[13] If only in frustration, his career even touched upon the colonial economy. One of his projects, an automaton meant to illustrate the circulation of the blood in the human body, was put aside because of the difficulty in arranging for rubber to be sent from Guiana (that land of reputed cannibals) to serve as the raw material for its vascular system.

For those who had eyes to see, the unsettling social changes for which these paralleled careers might be an allegory were already visible in that first android whose skin Vaucanson had appropriated from the stone sculpted by Coysevox. When Voltaire, in his versified "Discourse on Man" (1738), and

Julien Offroy de La Mettrie, in his *Machine Man* (1748), both identified Vaucanson with Prometheus, even readers with only the most superficial knowledge of the classics would have recognized this as somewhat worrisome praise for any man who valued his liver.[14] Nonetheless, as with the other images of machines I have mentioned, the gods might still look benignly on this one; for in Vaucanson's faun aggressive innovation was meticulously cloaked in the figuration of the ideal. In this regard it is notable that while its panpipes were left to rest at its feet, this figure played the transverse or "German" flute—the modern concert instrument of relatively recent devising—whereas the Provençal shepherd, "like the successors of our ancient Troubadours" ("Éloge," 211), was provided with comparatively rude traditional instruments. So the duck in Gravelot's engraving is framed by two versions of pastoral, modernized and archaized, markedly urbane and decidedly provincial, cosmopolitan and native, which are balanced as well in their complementary postures, seated and standing. Nothing could be more civilized; and it may be noted that when he was still at the Jesuit school he attended in his youth, Vaucanson was said to have decorated its chapel with "little angels that moved their wings" and with "priest-automatons that imitated several ecclesiastical functions" ("Éloge," 204–5).

Questions of technological complexity aside, the duck is finally a more provocative object than these docile androids, and for reasons that have everything to do with the development of challenges to the very notion of humanity in this age. To look into this provocation, one needs first to recall that René Descartes was as important a context for the duck, and for Vaucanson's automatons in general, as Coysevox was for the faun in particular. Notoriously, and with effects that his own declared intentions were quite unable to control, Descartes had pronounced animals to be machines. It followed that the human body, qua body, was just such an animal. In his *Discourse on the Method* (1637), while referring to the fact that his earlier *Treatise on Man* (1629–33) had sought to explain how parts of the body can move without being guided by the will, Descartes had elaborated on his contention:

This will not seem at all strange to those who know how many kinds of automatons, or moving machines, the skill of man can construct with the use of very few parts, in comparison with the great multitude of bones, muscles, nerves, arteries, veins and all the other parts that are in the body of any animal. For they will regard this body as a machine which, having been made by God, is incomparably better ordered than any machine that can be devised by man, and contains in itself movements more wonderful than those in any such machine.[15]

In fact, in his *Treatise on Man* Descartes had compared the body not only to automatons and to the artifact that would become the inevitable post-Newtonian reference point for philosophical speculation—the clock—but also to the machinery of the royal gardens. To clarify the movements of the animal spirits in the body, he had offered this analogy: "Similarly, you may have observed in the grottos and fountains in the royal gardens that the mere force with which the water is driven as it emerges from its source is sufficient to move various machines, and even to make them play certain instruments or utter certain words depending on the various arrangements of the pipes through which the water is conducted."[16] (He had also pioneered another comparison that would enjoy a notable popularity in the following century, in which a parallel is drawn between human physiology and the mechanisms of harpsichords or organs.) This line of thinking became the basis for the physiological theory of iatromechanism, which was associated especially with Hermann Boerhaave, the famous Dutch physician; the influence of Descartes, as combined with the examples of Isaac Newton, Robert Boyle, Pierre Gassendi, and Gottfried Wilhelm Leibniz, among others, also was cited in various other mechanistic theories.

Henry Fielding's Tom Jones was very much irked by those who adopted such a strenuous reading of Descartes's argument as to insist that animals could not properly be said to suffer: "for he was by no means agreed with the Opinion of those who consider Animals are mere Machines, and when they bury their Spurs in the Belly of their Horse, imagine the Spur and the Horse to have an equal Capacity of feeling pain."[17] In general, however, this image of animals as machines did not in itself prove especially remarkable to those who came after the seventeenth-century philosopher. Of greater import was the evident failure in Descartes's attempt to forbid the image of the machine, once it was identified with animals and the workings of bodies, from trespassing into the image of human nature proper.

This is a tendency that continues to look for its *terminus ad quem* in our own time. We see this search equally in the philosophical rigors of artificial intelligence and in the popular form of the Borg ("You will be assimilated") on the television and movie series *Star Trek: The Next Generation*. From today's perspective, we can see that the deceptiveness of the machine in *Blade Runner,* which challenges our perception and thus our conception of the human, mirrors the candor of the machine in the Enlightenment, which offered the same challenge but with very different effects, in accordance with the difference in the reigning conceptions of humanity at the time. Environed by the organs of cathedrals, the water organs of the Château de Saint-Germain, and the bird organs of the bourgeois parlor, the organs of the body of this time obliged the metaphysician to attend upon the physician, aesthetics upon physics, and nature upon its own self-consuming art. "Thus physics is in a way the mother of metaphysics," wrote Bonnet, "and the art of observation is the art of the metaphysician as it is that of the physician." In a more frolicsome mood, Denis Diderot brought Mlle. De l'Espinasse to voice a similar conclusion: "Now I can assure the whole world that there is no difference between a doctor who is awake and a philosopher who is dreaming."[18]

Inevitably, to evaluate the animal as a mere machine seemed to suggest that the same consideration might be given to humankind. As Théophile Bordeu stated in his *Researches in the History of Medicine* (1768), "One must admit that this was never the intention of this great man, but his system could offer room for falling into that error."[19] With one look at the *machina* from the inside out, not only might the deus ex machina come to seem supererogatory, but so too might all putatively higher values, such as those of art. *Machine* was an idiom in eighteenth-century French for indicating, among other things, the manipulation of light in a painting—"One says, 'There is a beautiful *machine;* this painter understands the *machine* very well'"[20]—but this term of approbation, which no doubt owed something to the conception of painting as an artisanal craft, easily could and eventually would be turned against itself to suggest aesthetic failure on the grounds of lifeless artificiality. As with the illumination of painting, so with enlightened reason. Leibniz had noted in his *Elementa physicæ* (ca. 1682–84), among other works, that the mechanistic philosophy of his time could not help but carry a suggestion of profanation or even of atheism. From his very different philosophical perspective, John Locke had also found cause to worry that "*Morality*" and "*Mechanism*" were "not very easy to be reconciled, or made consistent."[21] Like all other philosophers in this time, they had to confront not only the shades of Epicurus and Lucretius but also the bogey of Thomas Hobbes' *Leviathan* (1651), which opened with an identification of the human body and the state as "*Automata.*"[22]

The theological consequences of the Cartesian "room for error" were spelled out in the Abbé Yvon's entry on the "Soul of Animals" in the *Encyclopédie*. Taking his words from David-Renaud Bouillier's *Philosophical Essay on the Soul of Animals* (1728), and agreeing with Bouillier and La Mettrie in identifying Descartes as the first philosopher to treat animals as pure machines, Yvon demanded, "Let us admit it from the start: if God can make a machine that, solely by the disposition of its forces, performs all the surprising actions that we admire in a dog or a monkey, he can form other machines that imitate perfectly all the actions of men."[23] Implicitly, this statement spoke to Descartes's evident anxiety over the potentially disturbing implications of his *Treatise on Man*, which he had chosen to abandon after he heard of Galileo's condemnation by the Inquisition. Explicitly, it replied to the distinction between animality and humanity that Descartes had sought to maintain. As he had put it in his *Discourse on the Method*,

> I made special efforts to show [in the suppressed *Treatise on Man*] that if any such machines had the organs and outward shape of a monkey or of some other animal that lacks reason, we should have no means of knowing that they did not possess entirely the same nature as these animals; whereas if any such machines bore a resemblance to our bodies and imitated our actions as closely as possible for all practical purposes, we should still have two very certain means of recognizing that they were not real men. The first is that they could never use words, or put together other signs. . . . Secondly, even though such machines might do some things as well as we do them, or perhaps even better, they would inevitably fail in others. (*Discourse on the Method*, 139–40)

Despite Descartes's insistence on this point, it seemed to others that if machines were allowed to form identifications beyond themselves, as with animals and the physical bodies of humans, nothing could prevent them from taking over human nature in its entirety. This likelihood might then be met with the argument (here Yvon diverged from the cheery La Mettrie) that such a progression was an impious threat demanding the most vigorous refutation. In the *Encyclopédie* and other writings, such as Charles-Georges

Leroy's *Philosophical Letters on the Intelligence and Perfectibility of Animals* (1781), the riposte was made that Cartesian reasoning must logically lead to a self-evidently absurd conclusion, which was that God is a deceiver.[24]

Of course, one could oppose Descartes without adopting this particular reductio ad absurdum, which rather flagrantly failed to engage with the premises of the philosopher's thought. Insignificant as an example of rigorous reasoning, this argument remains important as a sign that the machine had entered so unobtrusively into the traditional styles of eighteenth-century thought that by the time it was evaluated as something more than a mere amusement or tool, it had already rendered those styles antique, superficial, and innocuous. It was all very well for Fanny Burney's Evelina to enjoy, in all innocence, the singing mechanical birds at Cox's Museum, which was famed for such automatons; but when the pious Joseph Berington turned his attention to Cox, he fantasized darkly about how this showman might collaborate with the heterodox Joseph Priestley. He imagined them constructing "two or three *men machines* . . . that might really operate in a *human* manner, might gradually advance to the summit of knowledge in all the arts and sciences, and perhaps present the public with their several discoveries in religion, philosophy, and politics."[25] In other words, he thought of a fearsome machine of the soul that by its very conceivability would destroy the governing conceptions of humanity and divinity in this age. Similarly, in the last sentence of "What Is Enlightenment?" (1784), Kant would answer his own question in terms of a human being "who is now more than a machine"—thus calling his readers' attention to the metaphor that somehow had sneaked up and all but engulfed them.[26]

Early in the eighteenth century, the noted chemist and physician at Halle, George Ernst Stahl, in his *Disquisitio de mechanismi et organismi diversitate* (1706), had articulated what would prove to be an influential argument for a vitalist conception of the human body, "which the common herd of modern philosophers consider as an *automaton*."[27] He was far from alone in challenging the iatromechanists. By midcentury, in fact, the *Encyclopédie* could refer to the contemporary "ridicule of the system of automatons" ("Ame des bêtes," 1:344). Despite Stahl, Robert Whytt, and others who sought to oppose or revise mechanical models, however, they were not so easily dismissed.

For his part, as if anticipating Franz Kafka's "Report to an Academy" (1919), La Mettrie did not even balk at the idea that a monkey might learn to speak, thereby leaping over the crucial Cartesian distinction between men and beasts. "Then this would no longer be either a savage or a failed man," he wrote, adding that "it would be a perfect man, a little man about town, with as much material or muscles as ourselves for thinking and profiting from his education."[28] Here it might be objected that La Mettrie is an unusual case, despite the fact that his conclusion on this point was substantially in accord with that of Pierre Bayle, whose famous *Dictionary* (1696) went through numerous reprintings.[29] Yet La Mettrie's example may serve to point out that the "ridicule of the system of automatons" must be considered to have been rather more wish than reality, unless we are to construe this phrase quite narrowly, as referring only to Descartes's attempt to construct a systematic theory of the physical universe.

Even within these bounds, such mockery of the system of automatons was bound to ring rather hollow. The problem was that this criticism could not help but call to mind the most powerful force currently discrediting Cartesianism, which was the theory of the Newtonians popularly represented, for instance, in Voltaire's *Elements in the Philosophy of Newton* (1738). While specifically Cartesian automatons might be put out of play in this new theory, the figure of the automaton in general was to enjoy, if anything, even more room to wander and incorporate other things.[30] Voltaire's objections to the idea that animals were machines did not prevent him from describing the soul of man as a clock. Others, such as Diderot in his *Elements of Physiology* (ca. 1765–84), put the matter more strongly still. "The peasant who sees a watch move and, not being able to understand the mechanism, infers a spirit in the hands," wrote Diderot, "is no more or less stupid than our spiritualists."[31] By the mid-eighteenth century the word *machine* had become an idiom synonymous with *body* in both French and English, as if faithfully trailing after the philosophical usage summarized by the famous friend of Voltaire and La Mettrie, the Marquise Du Chatelet, in the primer on contemporary physics that she based on the work of Leibniz and Newton. "Thus, all bodies, all parts of matter are machines," she noted, firmly and formally, as she proceeded to build up her description of "this great automaton of the universe." Similarly, David Hume would move easily from a description of the "vast variety of springs and principles" in nature, philosophically regarded, to the "mighty complicated machine" that was the human body.[32]

It is entirely natural, in a sense, that the idioms of the machine and the automaton should have gained such power. After all, even Abbé Yvon had felt compelled to admit that the effects of modern technology might seem to give the mechanistic theory an overwhelming impression of truth:

> Another consideration in favor of Cartesianism, which would seem to have something dazzling about it, is taken from the productions of art. We know how far the industry of man has gone in certain machines: their effects are inconceivable, and to the minds of those who are not well versed in machinery, they appear to be miraculous. Reassemble here all the marvels of this type of which you have ever heard—statues that walk, artificial flies that soar and buzz, spiders of the same manufacture that spin their web, birds that sing, a head of gold that speaks, a Pan that plays the flute—one would never have done with the list. . . . The celebrated three-footed works of Vulcan, which paraded on their own into the assembly of the gods—those slaves of gold, which seemed to have learned the art of their master and which labored next to him— are a type of marvel that does not at all go beyond verisimilitude; and the gods who admired them so strongly were less enlightened, apparently, than the mechanicians of our days. ("Ame des bêtes," *Encyclopédie*, 1:345)

There is a problem indeed when even a writer who wishes to defend God against the image of the machine has to admit that the machine must appear to have divinity on its side, though it be of a pagan, Vulcanian, or potentially rebellious Promethean sort. This is, then, all the more a problem for anyone who would look into the political works acting in the interior of this image. When machines figure as "slaves" that might appear miraculous to those who are "not well versed in machinery," then they are liable to be identified with workers in general. Through this identification, workers might come to see themselves as being capable of learning the art of the master, of laboring next to him, and even of displacing him.

In mentioning the happy chance that brought the youthful Vaucanson to pause in the manufacturing center of Lyons before he went on to his fame and fortune in Paris, Condorcet touched upon just this issue. Writing after Vaucanson's death in 1782, he addressed it in a way that seemed to evince certain democratic sympathies. "The great manufactures present a multitude of mechanical inventions that we would admire," he commented, "if habit had not familiarized us with them and if their use, or the conditions of those who operate or employ them, did not seem to degrade them in the eyes of the prejudiced; but they are a fertile source of instructions for a man born with a true talent who takes in everything, and for whom almost everything is still novel" ("Éloge," 205–6). Condorcet even went so far as to anticipate, so that he could demolish, the objection that "a mechanician [is] like an artist who owes his talents or his success [only] to practice" (213), as opposed to abstract reasoning or innovative genius. Still, as might have been expected, the good marquis showed some ambivalence on this point. Having separated himself from those who sniffed at Vaucanson as a commoner or charlatan, he yet used the last words of his account to draw a distinction between Vaucanson's fame among the vulgar on account of his automatons, "the ingenious productions that were the amusement of his youth," and among the enlightened, for "the useful labors that were his life's work" (232). He thus carefully placed Vaucanson on a pedestal between riotous workers, on the one hand, and disdainful fops, on the other. In this way Condorcet allowed him to be identified with enlightenment only so long as his machines remained docile and productive things, as distinct from the "dazzling" images adverted to in the *Encyclopédie,* which might lead helots to think themselves the familiars of gods. Just as Bouillier had been concerned that "the pure mechanism of the organs" of animals could create "deceptive appearances" that might lead the human species to raise animals out of their properly "subaltern" position, Condorcet was concerned that machines should know their place.[33]

Of course, even those who saw the image of the machine as having the potential to proliferate endlessly, aggressively forming identifications everywhere and rendering innocuous all models beyond itself, did not necessarily fear this situation. One did not have to conclude that the result must be a mechanical universe such as La Mettrie's, much less a world of despair such as that which Jean Paul was to limn in his "Personal Matters of the Servant and the Machine Man" (ca. 1796–98). In this odd little fable, Vaucanson's flute player and duck are made to be prominent symbols of the eighteenth century, which is identified as the grotesque age of the "Machine King." With its culmination in the following century's "nihilistic omnipotence,"[34] Jean Paul's world of machines governed by yet other machines, and so on unto infinity, was designed to appear both ludicrous and nightmarish; but mechanism could just as easily be configured religiously and optimistically. It was seen in

precisely this way by numerous thinkers of this era, including Ralph Cudworth, in *The True Intellectual System of the Universe* (1678); Boyle, in *The
Christian Virtuoso* (1690); George Cheyne, in his best-selling medical work
The English Malady (1733); Claude-Nicolas Le Cat, in his *Treatise on the Sensations and the Passions in General, and on the Senses in Particular* (1739); and
the character of Cleanthes in Hume's *Dialogues Concerning Natural Religion*
(1779).[35]

In fact, Leibniz had directly responded to Descartes on the matter of his
notorious room for error. He had written, "Those who point out to the Carte-
sians that their way of proving that beasts are only automatons tends at length
to support the view that it is possible, metaphysically speaking, for all other
men except themselves also to be simple automatons, have said exactly and
precisely what I need in order to prove the half of my hypothesis which concerns the body." This half of his hypothesis, as eventually developed in his
Monadology (1714), was that "each organic body belonging to a living being is
a kind of divine machine or natural automaton infinitely surpassing all artificial automata"—indeed, that living bodies "are still machines in their small-
est parts, into infinity."[36] The other half of his hypothesis, which was meant
to cloak and contain the first, was that these machines were organized in all
their workings according to divine ordinance and providence.

In the present context, the differences between Leibniz's machines and
their caricature in the work of Jean Paul, like the differences between Condorcet's account of Vaucanson and Yvon's allusion to him in the *Encyclopédie,*
are less important than the common ground they share in their preoccupation with the proliferating image of machinery. This same consideration
holds for the differences between the philosophy of Leibniz and the gleefully
materialist writings of La Mettrie, who referred to himself as "Monsieur Machine" and who, unlike Vaucanson, did accept an invitation to join Frederick
II at his court. Their conflicts are less significant here than the imperative to
which both men testify: the need to assign the provocative machine a determinate cultural role. As in Diderot's *The Indiscreet Jewels* (1748) and Nicolas
Réstif de la Bretonne's *The Perverted Peasant Girl* (1787), the automaton might
be invoked as a figure for the dull, animalic, clockwork routine of ordinary
people disdained by a libertine elite, or it could figure as the modern identity
eagerly embraced by the libertine, as it does in the works of the Marquis de
Sade.[37] Whether the viewpoint upon it was fervently optimistic or satiri-

cally despairing, religious or anticlerical, and so on through the many variations on such themes, the machine was obviously felt so fully to compel one's attention as to define the very substance of all contemporary thought. "The Philosopher," an essay that was adapted for an entry in the *Encyclopédie*, offered a succinct summary of this situation: "The philosopher is a human machine like any other man; but this is a machine that, by its mechanical constitution, reflects on its movements."[38]

Vaucanson appeared Promethean in this context because his creations did not simply record this compelling issue of the cultural role of machines. They addressed it in a theatrical form that displayed the play of identities in which machines had come to do their potentially upsetting work. Vaucanson's duck, perched there between the two androids, is not simply an animal in contrast to the figures that bear the familiar signs of human semblance. To adopt Vaucanson's language, only those who prefer to look at nothing but the exterior of animals could think so; or to adopt the bucolic perspective that gave rise to the faun, only those who know nothing of mythology could so imagine humanity. On the other hand, this duck was not the same sort of thing as the speaking heads fashioned by the Abbé Mical, presented to the Royal Academy of Sciences in 1783, and subsequently exhibited to the public, which were designed to say, "The King brings peace to Europe," "Peace crowns the King with glory," "Peace makes the people happy," and "O adorable King, father of your people, their happiness shows Europe the glory of your throne."[39] Communicating something else entirely, this duck was more modern, more human than human. Le Cat, the celebrated physician, sensed as much when he fantasized about an automaton that would possess human organs and mimic bodily functions, such as respiration, digestion, "and, God forgive us, all that follows." As if carried away from himself by his own imaginings, he wrote that such an automaton "would resemble a man too much."[40]

What made the duck so interesting as it posed with its companions was the fact that it was not obviously a different species of thing from these others. The dramatic question posed by Vaucanson's exhibition was whether the mechanical duck was not, in fact, the spitting image of the man—or the faun, or the monkey—about town. Furthermore, as the duck could body forth the worker, either rebellious or docile, it also suggested the racial alien, whether savage or noble, through which questions about the human species were pursued in theological, anthropological, physiological, and historical discourse in the eighteenth century. In the duck's contemporary setting it was not at all clear but that the faces of the androids, designed as they were to satisfy the codes of pastoral, were actually less recognizable in their representation of humanity than was the face of the duck, though it was a beaked and artificially feathered thing.

To say this is not to compare this duck to conventional zoomorphic representations of humanity, as in the *singeries* of eighteenth-century painting. In regard to this question, it is important to recall precisely what it was that made Vaucanson's duck so distinctive, for the history of automatons had long included many examples of avian artifacts. Indeed, these had been one of the most popular subjects for such manufactures, and their popularity would only increase later in the eighteenth century, as in the form of the serinette.[41] This duck was something else again because in addition to moving its wings, extending its neck, raising its body, playing in water, and quacking, it was able to eat, digest, and excrete its food. In Vaucanson's words,

> It extends its neck to take grain from the hand, swallows it, digests it, and voids it, completely digested, by the usual passages. All the gestures of a duck that eats hastily, and that redoubles this quickness in the movement of its throat in order to make its meal pass into the stomach, are copied after nature. The food is digested there as it is in real animals, by being dissolved, and not by trituration as some physicians claim; but this I wait to discuss and show when the occasion permits. The digested matter in the stomach is conducted by pipes, as by the bowels of the animal, to the anus, where there is a sphincter that allows it to exit.[42]

In the seventeenth century, the Count de Gennes was said to have constructed a peacock that ate and digested its food;[43] but whatever this invention's merits may have been, it neither attained the celebrity nor represented the physiological ambition attendant upon Vaucanson's duck. At least one twentieth-century commentator, who was interested in Vaucanson's machines as harbingers of cybernetic technology, has suggested that this matter of digestion "was but a flourish of Vaucanson's" in comparison with his more central concern with "artificial man";[44] but he could not have been more wrong, and precisely in drawing this distinction.

Vaucanson's emphasis on the mechanism of digestion, in the case of the duck, paralleled his emphasis on the playing of music, in the case of his androids. Both activities represent the iatromechanical and iatrochemical principles that he appears to have learned from his youthful studies in anatomy. (We see these studies reflected in his 1731 description of one of his first mechanical creations: "a physical machine in which there are several automatons and in which the natural functions of several animals are imitated by the movement of fire, air, and water.")[45] In this regard, we may recall that Vaucanson at one point worked on a project for an automaton that would demonstrate William Harvey's discovery of the circulation of the blood; and it is noteworthy as well that when Bouillier listed examples of cases in which "men are so many automatons," musicians in the act of playing their instruments led the list (which also included somnambulists, dancers, and orators). The trained musicians' movements were said to be comparable to "the internal movements" of the body, "those of the heart, the diaphragm, the intestines, the arteries, the blood, and the [animal] spirits."[46] Furthermore, the duck's digestion paralleled the musicians' playing in that both actions, in following the same mechanical and in imitating the same physiological principles, dramatized the problem of defining human nature in a time when it seemed that the traditional conception of art might be turning to waste matter—and not only among artists such as David Teniers, Chardin, and others of their species, who appeared to some refined eyes to have given over their discipline to the abject refuse of society.

To see that this last point is not an anachronistic view from the era of late-twentieth-century postmodernism, or from the smoky aftermath of the self-destroying machine that was Jean Tinguely's "Homage to New York" (1960), or even from the era of Jean Paul's edgy satire and of the dire "Sexual Machine" in William Blake's Ulro,[47] one need only turn to that pioneering critic of art and assiduous student of physiology, Denis Diderot. In *The Dream of D'Alembert* (1769)—a dialogue that takes place by a sickbed, where the physician attending D'Alembert is the aforementioned Théophile Bordeu, the better to focus attention on the metaphysics of bodily matters—Vaucanson is referred to as a type of genius (177). A reference to the example of a chicken's egg in the prefatory "Continuation of a Conversation between M. D'Alembert and M. Diderot" helps to explain why the designer of the famous bird, which artfully made wastes just as other machines made music, was so lauded here. Referring to the egg in terms of its course of development, Diderot wrote, "It is with this that one can overthrow all the schools of theology and all the temples of the earth" (103–4). As a matter of course, he anticipated that one might seek to counter this assertion by raising the example of Descartes, and he responded accordingly. "Would you claim, with Descartes, that [the grown chicken] is a pure imitative machine? Little children would mock you, and philosophers would reply that if this is a machine, you are another" (104). Thence comes his conclusion: "There is but one substance in the universe, in man, in the animal. The serinette is made of wood, the man of flesh" (107).

Even the fact that the duck was left unsexed is significant in the light of eighteenth-century physiology, within which (in the words Diderot gives to Mlle. De l'Espinasse, at whose salons contributors to the *Encyclopédie* used to gather), "Perhaps man is but the monster of woman, or woman the monster of man" (152). As Thomas Laqueur has explained, this sort of statement derives from a conception of sexual anatomy that goes back to antiquity, within which male sexual organs are envisioned as being the inside-out homologues of female sexual organs, and vice versa.[48] Perched between the two male androids, the duck of indeterminate sex must then again be a brilliantly apt figure for the body of this era, in which the sexual difference insisted upon in certain respects, as in theories of sensibility, would be swallowed up in others, in which universality was sought in the principles of anatomical organization.

In this regard it may be worth remembering that the figure Vaucanson took for his first automaton, the faun, originally had been grouped with a hamadryad and a Flora, also by Coysevox, so that they could be seen by a contemporary observer as ideal types of masculinity, femininity, and beneficent deity.[49] Certainly it is appropriate to remember that the descendents of Vaucanson's automatons would include, in addition to things made by other mechanicians, the body made by Mary Shelley's "new Prometheus" in *Frankenstein* (1818). As Vaucanson had refashioned Coysevox's faun, her creation put new works inside the skin of Milton's man while also reworking the imaginary "first man" in the third volume of Georges-Louis Leclerc Buffon's *Natural History* (1749), the heuristic "statues" in Etienne Bonnot de Condillac's *Treatise on Sensation* (1754) and Bonnet's *Analytic Essay on Faculties of the Soul* (1760), and the infantile "automaton" in the first (Favre manuscript) version of Jean-Jacques Rousseau's *Emile* (1762). In doing so, Shelley's creature reflected back on the reciprocal monstrosity described by Mlle. De l'Espinasse so as to reveal the patriarchal and misogynist guts that were cloaked within the seemingly undifferentiated, egalitarian substance of Enlightenment man.[50] To be sure, when she composed her novel, she probably did not have writings on natural philosophy, such as the following quotation from Boyle, literally placed before her eyes: "I consider the frame of the world . . . as a great, and, if I may so speak, pregnant automaton, that, like a woman with twins in her womb, or a ship furnished with pumps, ordnance, &c. is such an engine, as comprises, or consists of several lesser engines."[51] Nonetheless, her vision encompassed the catechrestic violence and confused desire revealed within such writings.

Although it is commonplace to refer to the eighteenth century as a mechanistic age, in presumed contrast to the organicism said to characterize the Romantic sensibility that followed upon it, it is rather less noted that this was a visceral age. On this point insufficient attention has been paid not only to Mary Shelley's most famous narrative but also to that most notorious work by David Hume, his *Dialogues Concerning Natural Religion*. In this work Hume has Philo slyly observe that the theological argument from design, based on an image of a mechanical universe, might just as easily follow from an animal universe, such as one spun from a spider's bowels: a universe then "from the belly" instead of "from the brain."[52] It is less noted still that this visceral identification is what the popular Romantic and Victorian criticisms of the Machine Age, as in the fulminations of Thomas Carlyle, were obsessed with expelling from art. Machines, after all, were never simply machines. That is why La Mettrie was able to write *Plant Man* (1748) as well as *Machine Man* and why philosophers as diverse as Locke, George Berkeley, and the Marquis de Sade also spoke of animals, plants, and machines in the same breath.[53]

They did so because these had long been seen as complementary, not contradictory, images. For instance, in his *Philosophical Letters on the Formation of Salts and Crystals* (1729), Louis Bourguet used the term "organic materialism" to sum up his corpuscular, vitalist, preformationist, neo-Leibnizian refutation of soulless materialism. In much the same fashion, Nehemiah Grew, in the late seventeenth century, had accepted mechanistic theory to explain the "Bowels" of plants while also arguing that "a *Plant* is, as it were, an *Animal* in Quires, as an *Animal* is a *Plant*, or rather several *Plants* bound up into one Volume." Similarly, in *An Account of Some New Microscopical Discoveries* (1745), Needham argued that the supposed "Animalcules in the Semen" were really "minute Machines" and as such were to be thought of through an "Analogy between the Animal and Vegetable World."[54] The ease with which these writers turned between the alternate metaphors, which Romantic and Victorian aesthetics would often see as utterly opposed, may be taken as a sign of the misprision at work in any history that would delineate a passage from mechanical reason to natural supernaturalism or, for that matter, from an era of supernaturalism to an age of mechanical reproduction. The identification of man with machine might displace from the former to the latter term the pressing question of teleology—which is also the question of cultural and political demands—but it could yield no automatic conclusion, attitude, or response in this regard.[55]

Here we may also see the problem of overreliance on the term *materialism* in writing of this era. This formal token in the definition of philosophical systems can obscure, in this case, the extent to which the representation of machines in the seventeenth and eighteenth centuries was no less a matter of soulful bodily organs than of artificial tools and works.[56] The furious imagery in which Jonathan Swift had attacked the conflation of scatology and eschatology, in his "Discourse Concerning the Mechanical Operation of the Spirit" (1704), had been meant to reincorporate and lay waste to this emerging identification; Kant would later use much the same joke.[57] Nonetheless, this identification would continue to make itself felt through the examples of Vaucanson's duck and Shelley's monster, not to mention innumerable works of the twentieth century.

In writings in and about the eighteenth century, *materialism* is a marker for a nexus of newly imaginable social and cultural transformations, brilliantly represented in Vaucanson's duck, which included the question of which cultural styles, social groups, and forms of life might "eat" others, as Vaucanson's machinery had incorporated Coysevox's statue while maintaining the pious pretense of paying homage to it. Similarly, La Mettrie had incorporated the physiological theories of Albrecht von Haller and duly dedicated his *Machine Man* to him—with a satirical intent that had enraged Haller, whose piety was well known—and he had played a similar trick in appropriating material from a lecture by Jerome Gaub, a professor of medicine and chemistry at the University of Leiden. (Gaub complained that as a result of La Mettrie's borrowings, in which material on cannibalism figured prominently, the good food of his 1747 lecture had been "corrupted into bile by a disturbed stomach.")[58] Even as it was caught up in the complex ideological dramas of this age, the artificial machine was an organic image, a visceral image, of the inner sensibilities and transformative paroxysms at the very core of any imaginable human nature. One did not need to await the dada and surrealist movements of the early twentieth century to witness this identification of the organic and the mechanical, in which we can see a carefully measured appreciation of history in its breathtaking carelessness—in the automatism of its signification on the pulse, through the eye, in the slippery guts of our every machine.[59] Hence the questions raised by Diderot in his reworking of the image of the human body: "Does one think when one is vigorously tickled? Does one think amidst the pleasure of the union of the sexes? Does one think when one is strongly affected by poetry, by music, or by painting? Does one think when seeing an infant in danger? Does one think in the midst of combat? In how many circumstances would you respond, if you were asked why you had not done this or said that, 'It is because I wasn't all there.'"[60]

I would not wish to leave the impression that Mary Shelley was the only writer of the Romantic era who recalled Swift's lesson about the visceral identity at stake in modern proliferations of the mechanical image. For instance, we have an 1816 tale by E.T.A. Hoffmann, "The Jesuit Church in G.," in which music boxes are incidentally, or not so incidentally, associated with the Promethean animation of matter. In this tale we meet the character of Professor Aloysius Walther, whose views the artist-protagonist, Berthold, summarizes in the following words: "In the end the Professor was right: animals and we ourselves are well-regulated machines."[61] By this point in the story the implications of this idea have been clearly established to be a matter of visceral understanding. As the narrator puts it,

> This icy coldness of the Professor in regard to Berthold was already annoying me; but the talk that he pursued with the colleagues who took their place at our meal convinced me that despite all his learning and worldliness, his sense for higher things was entirely closed, and he was the crassest materialist there could be. As Berthold quoted his words, he had completely adopted a system based on consuming and being consumed. He attributed all spiritual strivings, discoveries, and works to a certain state of affairs in the viscera and the stomach, and in this

regard he brought forth many examples of foolish, abnormal fancies. For instance, he maintained very earnestly that every human thought was produced by the mating of two fibers in the brain. I understood how the Professor, with this kind of craziness, tortured and stuck knives in the still bleeding wounds of Berthold, whose despairing irony clouded all promising impressions of higher things.[62]

In his most famous tale, published in the same year as "The Jesuit Church in G.," Hoffmann developed even further this identification of engineering with entrails. It is significant in this regard that when Spalanzani, the father of Olympia in "The Sandman," is first introduced, this "famous professor of physics" is associated with the "famous naturalist" of the eighteenth century, Lazzaro Spallanzani (24, 27)—who, incidentally, was the first to fertilize eggs artificially.[63] The mechanistic context is further established by the way the story associates Coppelius, the nightmarish lawyer and alchemist, with Coppolla, "a most respectable machinist and optician" (35), whose products include eyeglasses and telescopes. It is through one of Coppolla's telescopes that Nathanael looks at Olympia, the women he does not yet know to be an automaton, and falls in love with her. In the narrator's words, "It seemed as if her eyesight was only now being illuminated; her gaze burned with ever more life" (36). Makers of optical instruments were not historically associated with automatons as were those pioneers in mechanical engineering, clockmakers —many inventors of automatons actually began their careers as clockmakers—but Hoffmann's design here draws upon the equally telling relationship between optical devices and the discoveries of modern science. These discoveries were exemplified not only by Galileo's telescope but also by experimenters such as Anton van Leeuwenhoek and Robert Hooke who had exposed the limits of ordinary vision, with its attendant metaphysics, by using microscopes.

In Hoffmann's tale, this issue of vision is also raised by Nathanael's first encounter with "the sandman," when he views the experiments of his father and Coppelius: "It was as if human faces were visible all around me, but without eyes—with horrible deep black holes instead" (17). It is notable that when Sigmund Freud addressed this tale, he completely overlooked its scientific allusions and, in effect, remained blind to his own identification with scientism.[64] From the perspective of eighteenth-century physiological speculation, the interpretation that Freud gave to this aspect of the text, in the theme of castration, is not so much wrong as beside the point, in that it presumes a belief in the normative integrity and teleological comprehensibility of the human body that was far from being the case in this era. Cross-referenced as it had come to be with invisible organs, diverse machines, and the generalized workings of the universe, the body of this era could be regarded quite calmly, without horror, as a fantastic construction of separate parts, each of them an individual animal. "The eye is the dog that leads us," wrote Diderot, adding, "Man can then be regarded as an assemblage of animals in which each one assumes its particular function and cooperates either naturally or by habit with the others."[65]

This is not to say that the body of this era was a stable entity—quite the contrary. The same forces that had brought eighteenth-century theorists to concentrate upon the evidence of the senses also brought them to see these senses as black holes within which one's entire intellectual focus was put into question. In the last analysis, any authority derived from the testimony of the senses could be established only outside the body, through mechanical instruments, or inside the body, in imperceptible visceral processes that were the counterpart to those foreign instruments (see figs. 6 and 7). As Aileen Douglas says, "If the body, newly privileged as the instrument of sensation, cannot be isolated satisfactorily from a multiplicity of animate and inanimate forms, if it is lost within a confused heap of shapes both quick and mechanical, then it cannot be used to assuage societal crises: its 'sheer material factualness' provides no comfort."[66] Consequently, although Hooke might laud "the adding of *artificial Organs* to the *natural*," one might well wonder if this addition did not result in a net loss to a human condition formerly held to be sufficiently well attested to by the senses.[67] Similarly, if the scalpel of William Cheselden might help to solve a question about the nature of vision, known as the Molyneux problem, raised in the second edition of Locke's *Essay on Human Understanding* (1694), the newfangled forceps of Sterne's Dr. Slop— no less closely associated with Lockean theory—would serve to represent the paradoxical darkness that such enlightenment might bring. Le Cat might argue that to an "enlightened anatomist" the unhealthy organs of the sick are "types of microscopes," and he might further maintain that the senses are "machines" that "establish such society as exists between us and almost all the beings of nature";[68] but then the likes of Hoffmann might plausibly suggest

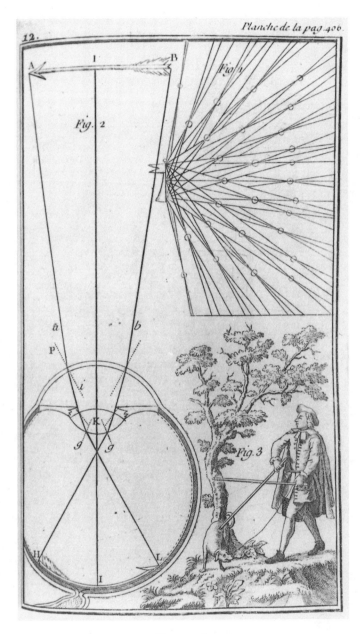

FIGURE 6.
Illustration of vision from Claude-Nicolas Le Cat, *Traité des sensations
et des passions en général, et des sens en particulier* (1739), History of Science
Collections, University of Oklahoma Libraries

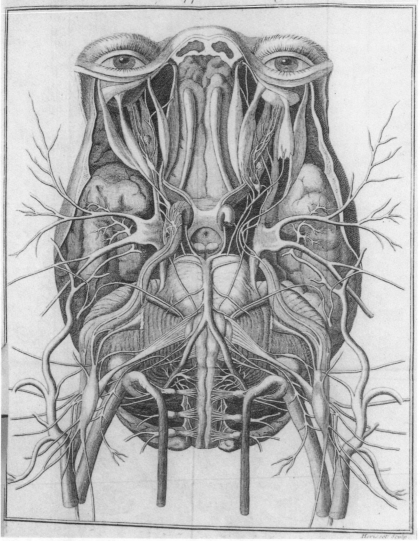

FIGURE 7.
Anatomy of the eyes from Claude-Nicolas Le Cat, *Traité des sensations et des passions in général, et des sens en particulier* (1739), History of Science Collections, University of Oklahoma Libraries

that if one machine is looking at another and considering itself comparatively enlightened, there must yet be darkness somewhere within it.

Writing of modern science in general, Maurice Mandelbaum has described an "opaqueness in the relations between the objects which we perceive and the means by which we perceive them" by pointing out that "belief in the existence of unobservable entities normally antedates the manufacture of the instruments through which we confirm their existence, and our hypotheses concerning the properties of such entities will determine the design of the instruments we build," which, moreover, "we must in many cases regard . . . as possessing an unobserved microstructure of their own."[69] In the eighteenth century in particular, a recognition of this opaqueness was at the heart of any conceivable enlightenment, and for this reason it was natural to consider human experience in terms of the experience of automatons. Perhaps most notably in such moments of extremity as were cited by Diderot, but also in its most ordinary functions, the body of this era was definitively beside itself.

In the first place, one could always imagine finer or different instruments, as did Haller in arguing that if he were given a more powerful microscope, he would be able to establish the truth of preformationism.[70] So the human senses in this era were not simply fused with the organs of animals and with scientific instruments but were also joined to every imaginable future of technology—and thus to histories beyond imagination. No sooner did the testimony of the senses become institutionalized in modern science than the senses became wholly theoretical. In the nineteenth century this situation would lead to the invention of realism as a genre from which an extended sequence of quasi-scientific reconceptualizations of perception would then logically follow: impressionism, expressionism, cubism, and abstraction.

Even as he sought to oppose the autonomy of reason to the image of automatons, Kant recognized this turn of the senses, which led him to suggest that the most important lesson brought to humankind by the "observations and calculations of the astronomers" must concern "the abyss of our *ignorance.*"[71] In the modern world, as the physical ground of human understanding, the senses had become simultaneously historical and imaginary in such a way as effectively to deny the commonplace distinction between these categories. It is precisely because he thought they failed to recognize the broader implications of this situation that Hegel criticized philosophers in the English empiricist tradition. "There are many who believe that they have grasped philosophy more from immediate feeling and intuition than from the knowledge of necessity, and in fact such immediacy of perception is even called reason," he wrote. "In this sense Newton and the English confuse experimental physics with philosophy, so that electrical machines, magnetic appliances, pumps and the like are called philosophical instruments. But surely it is only thought which should be called the instrument of philosophy, and not a mere assemblage of wood, iron, or other materials."[72]

The modern body is definitively beside itself: hence the parallel that Hoffmann set up between himself as narrator of "The Sandman," in which role he writes of feeling compelled to tell this story because it is a disturbance he carries within his senses and in his very blood (25–26), and Nathanael, his protagonist, who tries to relieve his fear of Coppelius by writing a viscerally disturbed and disturbing poem. In the course of this poem, Coppelius is portrayed as removing the eyes of Klara, Nathanael's former beloved, and causing them to jump into Nathanael's breast, where they have time to begin burning before Nathanael in his entirety is thrown into a storm of fire. The ins and outs of the imagery in this poem correspond to those in Hoffmann's environing tale, in which the eye in particular and vision in general are made to figure as the extrusion of viscera into the space of aesthetic representation, mechanical manipulation, social organization, and metaphysical understanding. The eye is shown to be the animal that leads us, compelling us to follow or imitate it, and yet an entity that remains just distinct enough from us so that when we dissect it or mechanically reproduce it, moving outside in or inside out, it is bound always to jeopardize our sense of self-possession, leading to all sorts of uncanny doublings. So Klara is brought to say, in response to Nathanael's fears,

> If there is a dark power that so very fiendishly and treacherously places a thread in our insides, by which it then seizes us and draws us forth into a path of dangers and destruction, into which we would not otherwise have stepped—if there is such a power, it must become our very self within us, as fashioned by our own selves; for only thus would we believe in it and surrender the place that it needs to accomplish all its secret work. . . . It is a phantom of our own ego, whose intimate kinship and deep influence on our temperament throws us into hell or transports us into heaven. (22–23)

The fact that Spalanzani first introduces Olympia to the public by having her give a concert on the piano, in the manner of the famous *Musician* (1773) designed by Henri-Louis Jaquet-Droz, only emphasizes all the more the wondrous connections among metaphysics, history, engineering, and art in the era of Enlightenment.

The horror attendant upon all this business in Hoffmann's tale, then, marks a conventional device of Romantic art, not a perdurable schema of identity formation. Already prepared for by writers such as Swift, Yvon, and Condorcet, this device appropriates the Enlightenment body—fragmented, manipulable, bemusedly monstrous, metamorphic in all its aspects—to serve as a cover for the innovative interior works of bourgeois sentiment.[73] But for the works inside it, there would have been no wonder in Vaucanson's faun, only cheap imitation or charlatanism. By the same token, without the inner machinery of sentiment in Hoffmann's tale, there would be no horror in a young man's love for an automaton—even though by Freud's day this technology of feeling would indeed have moved inside out, becoming a bodily surface fully as conventional to the eyes of a Viennese gentleman as baroque pastoralism had been to Coysevox.

In his reading Freud saw Hoffmann's tale as a representation of feeling, but he failed to see this representation as ideology, and reactionary ideology at that. This tale was designed to represent the normal body of the Enlightenment as pathological and the desire appertaining to it as violently cut off from its proper origins and ends. Although it was commonplace in the eighteenth century to identify both texts and bodies as machines, Freud failed to recognize that Hoffmann's story was a serinette playing a provocative cultural song, mistaking it instead for the voice of nature. Freud saw exactly what Hoffmann's machine would have had him see (this is the brilliance of his interpretation) but nothing of the history that his own vision had incorporated. Thus, even as he identified his interpretive approach as a scientific one, Freud was blinded by a popular Romantic image of technology that Hoffmann had helped to invent. In fact, because he so fully identified with Hoffmann's insistence that the bodily imago must represent a symbolic accomplishment, not a visceral effect of machinery, the scientific references in the tale did not signify at all for him. By way of contrast, "The eye is the dog that leads us," Diderot had written, calmly taking for granted the blindness that is the focus for such histrionics in Hoffmann's tale, just as his physiology regarded "castration"—the metamorphosis of male into female genitalia—as a matter of course.[74]

In this regard, with all due respect to Walter Benjamin, it must be said that technological form does not dictate aesthetics, metaphysics, or politics—even though, as the *Encyclopédie* noted, it may appear to do so, threateningly and dazzlingly. Though there are technologies that shape our ends, any given technological form cannot dictate them because other powerful agencies come into play, such as those of family, class, gender, religion, and nationality. Among these agencies, structural dominance in any event is not predictable in advance because this dominance will be of a nature to be defined and wagered in that event.[75] (This is not even to mention the multiplicity of technologies in the modern world, the irregularities of their distribution, and the vagaries of their applications.) What can be said with some assurance, drawing on the thought of Benjamin and those who have profitably reworked it, is that technological form is bound to be a powerful locus of recursive identificatory modeling for human nature even as this nature is simultaneously articulated through these other agencies. Technological form may be so powerful, in fact, that it might seem to obliterate the multiple differences, conflicts, and contradictions among these agencies. Therefore, it might even seem to promise the advent of something like universal reason, an end to prejudice, or (as in Benjamin's "The Work of Art in the Age of Mechanical Reproduction") a theory of art that could not possibly be appropriated in the service of fascism.

One last feature of Vaucanson's duck becomes relevant here, completing the allegory imaged in Gravelot's engraving. This is the theatrical deceptiveness of its innards. As wrongheaded as they were in calling Vaucanson a charlatan for supposedly having concealed a serinette in his faun, those spectators of whom Condorcet wrote would have been on considerably firmer ground, it turns out, if they had directed their accusation to the duck. In marveling at this creation, they were unwitting participants in what Stafford has described as "the unstable compound of performative experiment and out-and-out chicanery" in "the wider cultural debate over technology and visualization in the Enlightenment."[76] Christophe-Frédéric Nicolaï appears to have been the first to record the deception, reporting in 1781 that the duck in fact excreted a prepared mush already hidden within its body, not the digested remains of the grain it was seen to eat.[77] It was the manufacture of feces, not of song, that had been craftily hidden by Vaucanson. Apparently the deception was maintained as long as it was because audiences were allowed to view the duck's interior in only the most cursory manner, despite Vaucanson's proclamations to the contrary. Thus, while the duck was indeed designed to illustrate contemporary theories of physiology, and did do so through the modeling of its anatomy and actions, it also illustrated something else: the implication of desire, trailing clouds of obscurantism, in what passes for the perception of nature. As if to foretell Blake's account of the instruments and mechanisms of Urizen's universe, which also figure as the shrunken fibers of the human organs of sense, Vaucanson had left the world a lesson in the imaginary nature of nature.

Eighteenth-century philosophes such as Diderot were well aware that this kind of jiggery-pokery is exemplary, not extraordinary, in representations of the body. Benjamin's notion that "the surgeon represents the polar opposite of the magician" simply will not do;[78] the example of Vaucanson, along with the lessons of physicians such as La Mettrie and anatomists such as the Marquis de Sade, tells us why. It was with good reason that Hoffmann compared Coppelius in "The Sandman" not only to Spallanzani, the Italian scientist, but also to Cagliostro, the Italian con man. From the ridiculous Cagliostro to the Kantian sublime and beyond, it would seem that our perceptions must finally depend on a sense of visceral understanding that may be modeled or managed in various ways but that still is bound to remain unimaginable and so profoundly upsetting, and to our contemporary theorists of Turing Machines no less than to an Augustan divine such as Swift.[79]

Toward the end of the eighteenth century, in his *Critique of Judgement,* Kant would follow Vaucanson in representing the nature of nature in terms of the imitation of a bird. He wrote at a time when *serins,* canaries, were still enjoying great popularity in drawing rooms across the Continent. It was a popular pastime to teach them to sing melodies by repeatedly playing the desired tunes on a serinette, as we can see, for instance, in Chardin's *The Serinette* (1751). This was also an era in which avian automatons enjoyed a great vogue not only in adorning serinettes but as part of decorative cages, snuffboxes, clocks, watches, mirrors, and even pistols, among other manufactures. Kant did not explicitly refer to such things in the following passage, but they furnished one of its implicit contexts for his contemporary readership. In arguing that, properly regarded, nature is "subject to no constraint of artificial rules" and "can supply constant food" for one's taste, he wrote,

> Even a bird's song, which we can reduce to no musical rule, seems to have more freedom in it, and thus to be richer for taste, than the human voice singing in accordance with all the rules that the art of music prescribes; for we grow tired much sooner of frequent and lengthy repetitions of the latter. Yet here most likely our sympathy with the mirth of a dear little creature is confused with the beauty of its song, for if exactly imitated by man (as has been sometimes done with the notes of a nightingale) it would strike our ear as wholly destitute of taste.[80]

The effect imagined here as resulting from the discovery of human works inside a bird marks a visceral response to social, cultural, and political possibilities of the sort that were brilliantly communicated by Vaucanson's duck. Kant was concerned with a deception that would break an emotive identification with a bird, and with all this bird was taken to represent in terms of beauty and taste, so as to reveal both nature and aesthetic judgment as manufactured products of human artifice. His defensiveness in this regard was akin to that of Bonnet, who had insisted that one need not fear that artistic productions would "diminish the excellence of the works of nature." Bonnet argued that "while VAUCANSON constructs, with a skillful hand, his artificial duck and, gripped by astonishment and surprise, we admire that bold imitation of the works of the CREATOR, the CELESTIAL SPIRITS smile and see only an infant who cuts out the silhouette of a bird."[81]

Kant, however, had felt compelled to abandon the sort of simple piety to which Bonnet clung for his assurance, and so he did not see Vaucanson in so innocent a guise. Instead, in his *Critique of Practical Reason*, he used Vaucanson's automatons to image the death of free will and, with it, of humanity.[82] That man might be revealed inside the effect of nature, as that a machine might be revealed inside the effect of man, was bound to be a viscerally upsetting prospect to Kant. Like Stahl, who had articulated human will as the faculty by which we are able freely to "appropriate to ourselves" the things of the world or equally to reject things "that we regard as disagreeable and for which human nature feels a certain repugnance, a veritable disgust, in its contact and commerce with them,"[83] Kant could not accept with equanimity this possibility that he might take pleasure in one kind of thing while thinking it something else entirely. For a man of his philosophical temperament, this simple category error would imply that man might be a thing forever consumed in his acts of consumption, continuously assimilated to "other" things (such as the unsublime "woman," for example), and thus deeply deceived in his self-conceptions.[84]

The most telling deception would then be in terms of the human apprehension of the limits of the senses. This was not the case because of the relatively trivial and far more general consideration that the senses are always subject to possible deception. Rather, this had to be a pressing concern because of the metaphysical problem of delimiting sense perception in an age in which machines had taken the place of the senses not only through scientific practice, industrial process, and artistic design but in the very substance of the human body, insofar as it was imaginable. In this context, Vaucanson's deception, in faking the machinery of digestion, is the exact counterpart to the fakery of the nature of song described by Kant. The deceptive bird, singing or defecating, calls attention to an unfathomable dispossession in every moment of apperception. In this moment "the ego, the synthetic unit of apperception," must be recognized as being "in fact the product of, as well as the condition for, material existence," as Max Horkheimer and Theodor Adorno put it.[85] This moment is then the locus of our historical articulation: a spot of time in which self-consciousness is recognized for the technologically based, culturally elaborated, ideologically resonant thing that it is even in and through compelling idealities such as those of space, time, causality, and gender. Such a moment would make it possible, for instance, to imagine the "Kantism without a transcendental subject" of Claude Lévi-Strauss, who would judge that the "so-called songs of birds are on the frontiers of language" while also maintaining that "the dividing line between nature and culture is not identical, as used to be thought, with the lines of demarcation between human and animal nature."[86] In such a moment a mechanical duck can well and truly appear more human than human.

As Vaucanson's works illustrated, the production of song and the production of excrement posed identical challenges to the eighteenth century precisely because the identification of the cultural with the biological product had become a real possibility. In an age of mechanical digestion, one of the central problems of aesthetic judgment must be to distinguish between art and waste—a problem that still presses upon us in the twentieth century despite the instructive examples of artists such as Marcel Duchamp, Salvador Dali, Piero Manzoni, Andy Warhol, John Waters, Kiki Smith, Karen Finley, the metal band GWAR, the collaborative duo of Gilbert and George, David Hammons, and Chris Ofili, all of whom have explored this problem by incorporating excrement into some of their artworks. A makeshift answer to this problem did in fact arise from the network of galleries, dealers, museums, educational institutions, and publications that collectively constituted the invention of the art world, and thus of art in the modern sense, in the nineteenth and early twentieth centuries. This response, however, was never more than a holding action, as one can see in issues of aesthetic theory and practice that remain unresolved in the art world today.

Represented also in the sublime trembling of the boundaries among sex, excrement, and money in the works of Sade, in its greatest scope this problem of distinguishing art from waste matter became the question of how to justify the senses: how to make and maintain qualitatively signifying differences in the world of human sensibility. This was not the old question of justifying the senses before reason but of justifying them before the *limits* of reason. The problem was that these limits would sooner or later come to appear as the orifices of our swirling sensations, orifices that so bafflingly join entrance and exit, self and other, propriety and impropriety, and a host of related and equally slippery oppositions. Yet even as they may baffle us, these limits enable us to perceive why Vaucanson's duck was the very emblem of the modern universe that Kant would feel a visceral compulsion not to enjoy.

FOUR

The Exchange of FLUIDS in the Beau Monde

*L*IKE JACQUES DE VAUCANSON'S androids and the eviscerated ray fish, ready for the pot, painted by Jean-Siméon Chardin, the eighteenth-century city of Bath drew its vitality from the bowels of humanity; and like these other artifacts, this city was a phenomenon distinctively of its time. Despite its long history as a watering place, which extended back to the era of the Roman conquest, many contemporary writers observed that Bath had become a new thing in the eighteenth century. Once a small and unaccommodating resort, it had been refashioned to profit from recent developments in social organization, transportation, tourism, and recreation. It was then prepared to shape and even create the tastes of newly prosperous members of the middling classes, as well as those of the gentry and aristocracy.

No less than Vaucanson's duck and Chardin's painting, then, this Bath was a modern invention. The new nature of the city found popular representation in the image of Beau Nash, its reigning master of ceremonies from 1705 to 1761. In the words of John Feltham's *Guide to All the Watering and Sea-Bathing Places,* "From the time of Elizabeth, this city seems to have been occasionally visited by our sovereigns or some of the royal family; but, notwithstanding its present beauty and elegance, it appears that about the year 1700, it had only one house with sashed windows, and that the dancers did not exceed ten couple." The features of the Bath in which Horatio Nelson sometimes resided and with which Jane Austen assumed her readers would be familiar—the

Pump Room, the Upper and Lower Rooms, the shopping, the dances, the confused crowds—all had originated in just the last century. Hence Feltham's conclusion, which was a commonplace by the time he published his *Guide:* "Whoever was the original founder of *Bath*, to Nash is due the merit of being its restorer."[1]

In its renovated form Bath symbolized the "spa mania" that began in the late seventeenth century and continued throughout the eighteenth not only in England, which saw dozens of watering places newly proclaimed or rediscovered and advertised, but also across the Continent. Théophile Bordeu, an official superintendent of mineral waters in France as well as the physician immortalized in Denis Diderot's *Dream of D'Alembert* (1769), commented that mineral water had "never been so much of an issue as in this century."[2] Sir Walter Scott took account of this historical change in placing his one attempt at a contemporary novel in the manner of Austen and Fanny Burney, *St. Ronan's Well* (1824), at a provincial spa in the opening decade of the nineteenth century. Although it failed to enjoy the success he would have wished for it, this narrative provided an apt caricature of the historical changes for which Bath had become the most prominent model in England. At St. Ronan's Well, a place said to have "got a' its fame in the times of black Popery," modernization began when "a fanciful lady of rank in the neighbourhood chanced to recover of some imaginary complaint by the use of a mineral well about a mile and a half from the village; a fashionable doctor was found to write an analysis of the healing waters, with a list of sundry cures; a speculative builder took land in feu, and created lodging-houses, shops, and even streets."[3]

Like Chardin's painting and Vaucanson's duck, Bath came to be perceived as an embodiment of some of the most vital and specifically contemporary concerns of social life, science, economics, philosophy, and culture. It embodied these concerns in such a viscerally compelling way, in fact, that it came to be a byword for the mixtures of heterogeneous things, dissolutions of boundaries, and confoundings of bodies that were seen as typifying recent historical developments. This historical tendency was especially aggravated, in the case of Bath, by the way in which it made strange bedfellows of medicine and fashion. In a poem occasioned by the prominent placement in the Pump Room, between busts of Alexander Pope and Isaac Newton, of a full-length painting honoring Nash, these categorical confusions in the popular impression of Bath found their expression: "The picture plac'd the busts be-tween / Gives satire all its strength; / Wisdom and Wit are little seen, / But Folly at full length."[4] In this comic form, but also quite seriously, Bath came to represent a provocative challenge to the pretensions of enlightenment in diverse areas of social life. The potential for such satire was built into the very foundations of the place, which made itself a fashionable resort of the beau monde by appealing to its unlovely bowels.

It is virtually impossible to distinguish between the literal and the figura-tive in this matter of the bowels at Bath. In the first place, an immemorial trope had hot springs such as those at Bath originating in "the very bowels of the earth," as in the early-twelfth-century *Gesta Stephani*, or spewing healing waters from "their entrails, full of quicke Brimston," as Edmund Spenser had it in writing of "the boyling Bathes at *Cairbadon*" in the *Faerie Queene* (1590).[5] Familiar as it was, this trope was ritually repeated in the eighteenth century, as when David Kinneir told of the "nice combinations" of minerals with which these waters were "impregnated" as they were "work'd up in the bow-els of the earth." Similarly, in his medical treatise on bathing, Tobias Smol-lett noted the relationship that waters from hot springs bore to "the bowels of the earth" whence they came.[6] Yet this trope was repeated with a differ-ence in the eighteenth century, for the world whose bowels were in question was no longer what it had formerly been conceived to be.

As we can see in the verses that identified Nash with folly, the earth of this time had come under the spell of forces that might be thought superior to the trumpery of any and all ceremonies. These were the forces of the new "me-chanical philosophy," and they promised utterly to transform the under-standing of the bowels of the earth. Of course, there were those who refused to accept the revolutions wrought by this modern philosophy that had New-ton as its greatest philosopher and Pope as one of its most telling propagan-dists. Notably, George Berkeley, whom I discuss in what follows, still clung to some of the more traditional rhetoric concerning the body of the world. Yet it was clear in any case that this body, and its bowels, had been brought into a significantly different relationship to the body of humankind.

In this regard, it is important to reiterate Scott's recollection that water-ing places such as Bath often had legendary histories as spots held sacred to pagan or Christian deities. (Bath's own legend told of Bladud, a leprous youth who was the son of Lud Hudibras, an ancient king of Britain in the lineage of Aeneas; after his illness was cured through an accidental discovery, while he was in exile as a pig herder, that the oozing springs in which the pigs delighted might be medicinal for his flesh as well, he himself became a monarch and the progenitor of King Lear.)[7] One consequence of the English Reformation was a more or less concerted effort to strip these holy wells of their religious associations and, not incidentally, of their suspected role as gathering places for recusants and schemers against the Protestant succession. They were placed instead under the authority of medical science; and despite Christopher Smart's contemporary claim that the waters of Bath "were blessed by St Matthias,"[8] references to Christian belief were more remarkable for their absence in discussions of this resort in the eighteenth century. The healing waters might still be represented as having their ultimate source in the beneficence of God, as in Kinneir's *New Essay on the Nerves* (1739), but their virtues now came to require the testimonies of physicians such as Kinneir, Smollett, and Bordeu.

Treatises puffing the merits of the waters at different locales were accordingly churned out. Like the authors of guidebooks to spas, such as James Schofield, who unabashedly presented himself as being "like the TOUTERS of other public places,"[9] medical men served at once to authenticate and to advertise the waters. An early example of this practice was William Oliver's *Essay on Fevers . . . To Which Is Annex'd, A Dissertation on the Bath-Waters* (1704). This pamphlet boldly proclaimed that "*Bath* is the *Assylum Chronicorum Morborum*, the Refuge for all *Chronical Diseases; Scurvies, Cachexies, Colics,* Old *Aches* and *Pains,* and almost all lingering Diseases that Afflict Mankind, are here very often Cured, *cito, tuto,* & *jucunde,* which in all probability would yield to no Course of Medicine out of it."[10] The general transformation in the conception of spas in this era was perhaps most notably sketched out in Daniel Defoe's *Tour through England and Wales* (1724–26), in which the traveling author showed himself always to be concerned with the nature and vicissitudes of healing springs and wells, the medicinal potential of which he did not doubt, while he was no less determined to reject local legends that stank to him of Romanism or of ignorant antique fable.

The new philosophy now claiming the bowels of the earth for its own could be a very dubious business, as both professional and lay observers were given to remarking. Smollett, for instance, observed that the "diversity of opinions, among those who have laid themselves out for *analysing* Mineral

Waters, cannot fail to perplex and embarrass people who attempt to reason upon the use of them." In the opening of his respected *Essay on the Bath Waters* (1772), immediately after he assented to a medical colleague's judgment that "upwards of a thousand Treatises" had been written on the virtues of mineral waters, William Falconer similarly concluded, "The accounts, however, transmitted by the generality of these Writers, are very little to be depended on, as they are mostly filled with instances of the grossest ignorance, or misrepresentation."[11] The doubts had popular currency as well: in a letter written from Bath in 1766, the Reverend John Penrose commented on the prospects of his own improvement in health by saying that "many other Causes may possibly concur towards it, tho' here the Waters run away with the credit."[12]

It was in this context that the spa physician became a popular stereotype of folly, caricatured for his greed, meaningless jargon, homicidal incompetence, and general quackery. The spa physician was thus abused by his own professional brethren, such as Smollett and Falconer, no less than by other recorders of the contemporary scene, such as Thomas Rowlandson in the series of engravings that he gathered together under the title *Comforts of Bath* (1798). So when Philip Thicknesse devoted the conclusion of his *New Prose Bath Guide, for the Year 1778* to criticism of "advertising Quacks" ("those Men are themselves the very Pests they pretend to destroy") he was not threatening the reputation of Bath but simply repeating common wisdom.[13] In fact, medical men were popularly regarded not only as potential murderers, as in William Blake's characterization of Bath as "the physician and / The poisoner,"[14] but also, more specifically, as cannibals. So Anders Sparrman would turn his vision back to Europe from New Zealand and mention "quacks (of their kind dangerous cannibals in society)" just as the anonymous author of *The Diseases of Bath* (1737) had expressed outrage at "that canibal; man-mangling Brood" of physicians.[15]

Nonetheless, under the dubious aegis of "that *Pandora's* Box—the Faculty,"[16] watering places had been displaced from the purview of sacred legend to the realm of a professionalized scientific discourse. Unto its very bowels, the earth was now to be subject to analysis, as were the bowels of the "Spawers" or "Spaws," as they are termed in Schofield's *Historical and Descriptive Guide to Scarbrough and Its Environs* (1787).[17] We find this change marked in Richard Graves' "comic romance," *The Spiritual Quixote* (1773).

One character's account of the waters—that "the heat of the bath was caused by a constant fire in the bowels of the earth; which had been burning ever since Noah's flood, and would in time burn up the whole world"—is mocked by Opifer, the scientifically minded apothecary, who refers instead to "the operations of *chemistry*."[18] Echoing the views of writers such as Rice Charleton and George Cheyne (who cited Isaac Newton's *Optics* [1704] in support of his position), Opifer is here used to recognize, satirically, how Bath had come to be identified with advanced scientific thought.[19]

In keeping with this transformation in the body of the earth, the manner in which people partook of the waters was reconceived. Defoe took note of this transformation, too, with particular reference to the city of Bath. He called attention to the fact that "whereas for seventeen hundred or two thousand years, if you believe King Bladud, the medicinal virtue of these waters had been useful to the diseased people by bathing in them, now they are found to be useful also, taken into the body; and there are many more come to drink the waters, than to bathe in them." Drinking the waters had not been unheard of before this time, as he could testify from his own experience; but "'tis certain," he concluded, "a modern discovery, compar'd to the former use of these waters."[20] (In this respect it is notable that a treatment based on glasses of water could be calculated, quantified, and organized with a greater appearance of systematicness than was available through the modes of the bathing cure, even though the latter could be complicated enough, given the elaboration of different types of bath—hot, cold, and vapor—together with the option of having the water pumped on a particular part of the anatomy.) Visitors still used the public baths throughout the century, but their popularity relative to drinking the waters in the Pump Room (or elsewhere, in bottled form) continued to decrease. In 1739, Kinneir lamented this change and attributed one aspect of it, a growing disinclination to plunge one's head under water, to the concern felt by fine ladies for their elaborate coiffures.[21] The change, however, was more thoroughgoing in its causes and complex in its significance. Imitating the more expensive baths that the Duke of Kingston had built in 1766, "private" baths were built by the corporation of the city next to the King's Bath in 1788, and Feltham wrote in 1803 that the public baths were then "chiefly used by hospital invalids or by persons of the lower class of life," being "little regarded by people of condition."[22] Readers of Jane Austen's *Persuasion* (1818) may recall that the only character shown actually to be using the baths is the poor, infirm, neglected, and unimpressively surnamed Mrs. Smith.

It would be stretching the point to see this growing preference for an "interior bath" as following inevitably from the general Enlightenment turn toward the inner workings of mind and body. Numerous factors undoubtedly played a part in this change of fashion, as I argue in what follows. Still, we ought not to overlook the symbolism of this change simply because it was overdetermined in its causes and complex in its implications, calling our attention as it does to the increasing privatization of the body, elaboration of decorum, commodification of goods, and professionalization of medicine in this era. Whether or not John Locke had indeed "made the whole internal world his own," as Feltham said when he mentioned his birthplace in the section of his guidebook titled "Walks and Rides Round Bristol" (116), Bath clearly made the insides of man, along with the bowels of the earth, its own. In accordance with these transformations in the body of the world and in the taking of the waters, the insides of human beings were reconceived. The new popularity of drinking the waters not only shifted attention from Bladud's leprous skin to the viscera of the beau monde but also quite literally and dramatically touched upon the body's insides. Previous to a course of the waters at Bath and other spas, it was customary "to cool the body by gentle purges, by a low diet, and, if found necessary, by bleeding."[23] Emetics were sometimes used as well. Moreover, the most obvious effect of drinking the waters, as opposed to bathing in them, was to stimulate the processes of elimination. "For these Waters not only readily dilute, propel, and carry off Collections of impure Humours, lodged in the Stomach and Intestines," Friedrich Hoffmann said in his much cited work, "but likewise admirably promote the Discharge of all peccant, saline, and unctuous Matter by the Conduits of Urine: more subtle and rarified pernicious Particles, by that general Strainer of the Body, the Skin."[24] More than one rural spa in this century failed to prosper, in part, because of the lack of toilet facilities at any convenient distance from the well.[25]

This emphasis on the bowels was given its due in *The New Bath Guide* (1766), a popular satirical romp that made Christopher Anstey famous enough to be deserving of a portrait by Thomas Gainsborough (who set up shop in Bath between 1760 and 1774). In the second of the "Series of Poetical Epistles" that compose Anstey's poem about the B——n——r——d family, Simkin B——n——r——d tells of the doctors he, his sister Prue, their maid Tabby, and their cousin Jenn have seen on the day after their arrival at Bath:

> He determin'd our cases, at length, (G——d preserve us!)
> I'm bilious, I find, and the women are nervous;
> Their systems relax'd, and all turn'd topsy-turvy,
> With hypochondriacs, obstructions, and scurvy;
> And these are distempers he must know the whole on,
> For he talked of the peritoneum and colon,
> Of phlegmatic humours oppressing the women,
> From foeculent matter that swells the abdomen;
> But the noise I have heard in my bowels, like thunder,
> Is a flatus, I find, in my left hypochonder.[26]

One may wonder what Frances Burney's Evelina thought when Lord Orville came to this passage while he was reading Anstey's *Guide* to her at Clifton just after she had visited Bristol Hot Well for her health. (This question must be of more than passing significance to a narrative that Burney presented as an anodyne for "the distemper" and "contagion" generally spread by novels, which "are found to baffle all the elemental art of physic, save what is pre-scribed by the slow regimen of Time, and bitter diet of Experience.")[27] As if this were not sufficient matter for embarrassment, in describing the baths Sim is brought to exclaim, "You cannot conceive what a number of ladies / Were wash'd in the water the same as our maid is." He then advances his ob-servations yet another step by considering where that water might have ended up. "So while little TABBY was washing her rump," he observes, "The ladies kept drinking it out of a pump."[28]

As was only to be expected, some readers found this last couplet difficult to swallow. In his *Guide*, Feltham emphatically denied its verisimilitude ("We are well assured, that the sparkling glass of the drinker is unpolluted with any such defilement"); and more than fifty years after the original publication of Anstey's poem, Pierce Egan, in his *Walks through Bath* (1819), took pains to note that "upon inquiry" it had been determined that the otherwise estimable Anstey was in this case having his fun at the expense of the truth.[29] (Anstey himself, in the epilogue to the second edition of his poem, offered a defense against an imagined audience of "ladies, who n'er could endure / A hymn so *ineffably vile and impure*," which they compare unfavorably to Samuel Richardson's *Pamela* [1740].)[30] Yet this paradoxical turn, in which hygienic refinement appears as grotesque defilement, was by no means peculiar to this moment in Anstey's work. On the contrary, these lines might be taken to sum up the pleasures of eighteenth-century Bath, which all involved a plunge into the contamination of communication.

Despite itself, Defoe's critical remark on the closeness of early-eighteenth-century Bath, "which, more like a prison than a place of diversion, scarce gives the company room to converse out of the smell of their own excrements" (2:168), actually captured the appeal of the place. William Conner Sydney was also having his bit of fun when he described the experience of tasting the waters—"It is perhaps worth recording that while the company were drinking their nauseous draughts, a band of noisy musicians thundered away in the gallery above, doubtless on the same principle that the aid of music was brought in at the sacrifices of Moloch, in order to drown the shrieks of the victims"—but his hyperbole scarcely amplifies the way this experience was popularly represented in the eighteenth century.[31] If Bath and towns akin to it had once been imaged as the sites of miraculous cures, they were now viewed as resorts where one might hope to experience disgust. The anxiety felt by Samuel Pepys in 1668—"methinks it cannot be clean to go so many bodies together in to the same water"—was the attraction that brought visitors in the next century.[32] Following Pepys and Defoe, the author of *The Diseases of Bath* presented this image in a form no less economical than Anstey's when he described one of the baths as "that Jakes obscene; / Whence I come sullied out who enter'd clean." This passage sums up the author's preceding description of the mixed company—"greasy" cooks, sweeps, "Jilts, Porters, Grooms, and Guides," and other "Unwholesome" bodies—who commingled in the waters.[33]

When he came to write his *Life of Richard Nash* (1762), Oliver Goldsmith sought to explain the fascination of such abomination. Anticipating Walter Pater's argument that "the way to perfection is through a series of disgusts," he contended that the "natural gradation of breeding begins in savage disgust, proceeds to indifference, improves into attention, by degrees refines into ceremonious observance, and the trouble of being ceremonious at length produces politeness, elegance, and ease."[34] In other words, he suggested that people were brought to Bath by the opportunity it gave them to recapitulate the natural course of civilization during a vacation of six weeks or so in the fall or spring of the year.

Taken to its extreme, Goldsmith's argument could lead to the Sadean paradox that one best follows nature by violating it, by plunging into its disgusting guts so as to emerge utterly transformed by its elemental processes. To be sure, Anstey's gentle mockery of Richardson may seem as nothing to the Marquis de Sade's brutal parody of *Pamela, or Virtue Rewarded* in *The History of Justine, or The Misfortunes of Virtue* (1797). Similarly, Smollett's mockery of Rousseauian pity in *The Expedition of Humphry Clinker* (1771) may appear to be radically different from Sade's outright contempt for it throughout his writings. If such is the case, however, it is so only because we fail sufficiently to appreciate their shared insight into the desire for disgust that sets all the vital organs of civilization to trembling.

The excremental sense of the world in Smollett's writings is especially interesting in this regard, and nowhere more so than in *The Expedition of Humphry Clinker*. Through every aspect of this narrative, readers are invited to revel in revulsion. Our pleasure in what are presumed to be disgusting mixtures of heterogeneous things is solicited through images of dubious remedies, ruthless romances, distasteful conversations, physical accidents, and disguised identities. This extinction of distinctions extends even to the surface of representation, as in the conflicting accounts of things we get from the irascible Matthew Bramble and his nephew, Jery Melford, and to the level of the signifier, in the missives written by the maid, Winifred Jenkins, whose tortured orthography becomes the unmeaning source of all sorts of comedy and bawdy (as when she writes of Humphry, "He was tuck up for a rubbery, and had before gustass Busshard").[35] Even opinions incidentally voiced in the course of the narrative come to participate in this weltering world of contamination. For instance, when Matthew Bramble warns against the dangers of granting the press unrestrained liberty, he does so by telling of a publisher who was expelled from Venice and who subsequently established himself at Lugano, "from whence he squirted his filth at some respectable characters in the republic, which he had been obliged to abandon" (101).

Spas, however, provide the greatest occasion for dwelling on such matters. The tone is set at the outset of the narrative, when the touring family is at Bristol Hot Well, in a bravura passage in which Melford describes his uncle:

I was t'other day much diverted with a conversation that passed in the Pump-room, betwixt him and the famous Dr. L——n, who is come to ply at the Well for patients. My uncle was complaining of the stink, occasioned by the vast quantity of mud and slime, which the river leaves at low ebb under the windows of the Pump-room. . . . The Doctor overhearing this remark . . . observed, that stink, or stench, meant no more than a strong impression on the olfactory nerves; and might be applied to substances of the most opposite qualities; . . . that individuals differed *toto cælo* in their opinion of smells, which, indeed, was altogether as arbitrary as the opinion of beauty; that the French were pleased with the putrid effluvia of animal food; and so were the Hottentots in Africa, and the Savages in Greenland; and that the Negroes on the coast of Senegal would not touch fish till it was rotten. . . . He affirmed, the last Grand Duke of Tuscany, of the *Medicis* family, who refined upon sensuality with the spirit of a philosopher, was so delighted with that odour, that he caused the essence of ordure to be extracted, and used it as the most delicious perfume: that he himself (the doctor) when he happened to be low-spirited, or fatigued with business, found immediate relief and uncommon satisfaction from hanging over the stale contents of a close-stool, while his servant stirred it about under his nose; nor was this effect to be wondered at, when we consider that this substance abounds with the self-same volatile salts that are so greedily smelled to by the most delicate invalids, after they have been extracted and sublimed by the chemists. . . . In short, he used many learned arguments to persuade his audience out of their senses; and from *stench* made a transition to *filth,* which he affirmed was also a mistaken idea, in as much as objects so called, were no other than certain modifications of matter, consisting of the same principles that enter into the composition of all created essences, whatever they may be. . . . Then addressing himself to my uncle, "Sir (said he) you seem to be of a dropsical habit, and probably will soon have a confirmed *ascites:* if I should be present when you are tapped, I will give you a convincing proof of what I assert, by drinking without hesitation the water that comes out of your abdomen." (18–19)

No matter how much allowance we make for the different conceptions of bodily matters in earlier centuries as compared with our own—remembering, for example, that Louis XIV would ceremoniously receive his courtiers while sitting on his closestool of a morning—this doctor's discourse is clearly intended to rub the noses of Smollett's readers in filth. In doing so, however, it is just as obviously intended not to turn us away from the filth, as it does the doctor's appalled audience in the Pump Room, but rather to draw us into its pleasures. For readers living in a Freudian "climate of opinion," as W. H. Auden termed it, this perverse pleasure is likely to be classified as "infantile."[36] For nineteenth-century readers, a dismissal under a category such as "crudeness" was more likely, as in the terms used in Austen's *Northanger Abbey* (1818) to condemn articles published a century earlier in *The Spectator* ("and their language, too, frequently so coarse as to give no very favourable idea of the age that could endure it").[37] Even though they might touch upon these other classifications, however, the one most at issue for eighteenth-century readers was very different.

To its contemporary audience, the comically disgusting folly of this passage did not arise from the presumed incongruity of a distinguished physician talking like a two-year-old or a peasant. It derived instead from the philosophy of science itself. O. M. Brack Jr. has identified Dr. L——n with Diederich Wessel Linden, a German physician who spent eleven years at Bristol and contributed to the flood of spa writings in this era.[38] As one might gather from the resemblance between this character and some of the Projectors in Jonathan Swift's *Gulliver's Travels* (1726), however, the satire in this passage is directed more at the profession than the man. Matthew Bramble is made to be disgusted and Jery Melford to be delighted by the way this character's discourse takes the modern scientific attitude—in its historical, anthropological, physicochemical, and methodological aspects—to what could seem to be its logical extreme, where it finds its image in the cannibalism of one person consuming part of another's body. This is the extreme that clarifies the significance of that most outrageous couplet from Anstey's poem. Within their images of cannibalism, readers of Smollett and Anstey were invited to observe a distillation of modern society to a self-consuming essence.

Excrement, both animal and human, had long been included not only in various folk remedies but also in the materia medica of professional physicians. It was so commonplace that when Swift mocked Paracelsus, "who was so famous for Chymistry," for having made a perfume of human excrement, his readers might have been forgiven if they failed to understand that this author meant to be satirical.[39] Thomas Willis, one of those who instructed John Locke in medicine, had still listed excrement and urine in his pharmacopoeia in 1674; Locke himself noted the usefulness of such substances in his medical journals; and uses of these and similar materials continued into the eighteenth century.[40] Given this background, and considering that he is identified with an age that saw Thomas Beddoes advising consumptives to cure themselves by living in barns so that they might breathe the salutary flatus of cows, Dr. L——n might seem a figure of satire only in terms of his manners, as distinct from his ideas.[41] Smollett's satire went beyond manners, however, to aim at the doctor's distinctively modern scientific attitude. His attack suggested that this attitude not only breaches the boundaries of politeness and flesh but also violates the very notion of bodies as defined in terms of a hierarchy of distinct species.

When Robert Boyle adopted "that common axiom of naturalists, *corruptio unius est generatio alterius; & è contrà*," he was unwittingly preparing the ground, or the night soil, for this sort of humor in Smollett's works. According to the principles of his corpuscular philosophy, generation and corruption "appear to be but several kinds of alteration, taken in a large sense." In the automaton, "or self-moving engine," of the world, corpuscles can be expected "to become a body, sometimes of one denomination, and sometimes of another," and, in fact, "to associate themselves, now with one body, and presently with another."[42] In such a situation it would be absurd for the natural philosopher to regard excrement as aught but one collocation of corpuscles among others, just as it would be absurd for him to regard cannibalism as evil or even as alien to European sensibilities, as Boyle also maintained.[43] If one extrapolates from the physics of natural philosophy into the overlapping domain of anthropology, then, one might logically come to the conclusion reached by David Hume:

> Those who ridicule vulgar superstitions, and expose the folly of particular regards to meats, days, places, postures, apparel, have an easy task. . . . A Syrian would have starved rather than taste pigeon; an Egyptian would not have approached bacon: But if these species of food be examined by the senses of sight, smell, or taste, or scrutinized by the sciences of chemistry, medicine, or physics, no difference is ever found between them and any other species, nor can that precise circumstance be pitched on, which may afford a just foundation for the religious pas-

sion. A fowl on Thursday is lawful food; on Friday abominable: Eggs in this house and in this diocese are permitted during Lent; a hundred paces farther, to eat them is a damnable sin. This earth or building, yesterday was profane; to-day, by the muttering of certain words, it has become holy and sacred. Such reflections as these in the mouth of a philosopher, one may safely say, are too obvious to have any influence; because they must always, to every man, occur at first sight; and when they prevail not, of themselves, they are surely abstracted by education, prejudice, and passion, not by ignorance or mistake.[44]

From Hume's response, as from Dr. L———n's learned disquisition, it is but a step to *The History of Juliette* (1797). In this novel the Marquis de Sade's heroine declares, "In general, we are confused about the exhalations that emanate from the *caput mortuum* of our digestions; there is nothing unhealthy about them, nothing but what is very agreeable. . . . [They possess] the same guiding spirit as that of [medicinal] simples. There is nothing to which one may accustom oneself so easily as to sniffing a turd; eating it is delicious; it has the piquant savor, absolutely, of an olive."[45] Their conception of modern science had brought Hume, Dr. L———n, and Sade to recognize that ordure is not opposed to order but is rather its indwelling motivation, point of fixation, and source of potential transformation. By extension, they had then recognized that even as science was being constituted as a novel source of technological innovation and economic growth, its empiricist basis was bound also to suggest a phantasmic social equality and anthropological relativism.

In the short run, this suggestion helped to spur on the quarrels over professional legitimation involved in many accusations of quackery. In the long term, it could threaten to dissolve all of culture into nature. The sense of potential equality and relativism generated by the corpuscular, mechanical, or methodological grounds of modern science might then lead logically not only to a reasoned defense of cannibalism but also to an approving nod at the spectacularly grotesque end of Julien Offroy de La Mettrie, who choked to death on a paté almost as if he were destined to symbolize the self-consuming energy of the materialist universe described in his own writings. Certainly the luxuriance of the Sadean drive for sovereignty, which finds its consummation in self-destruction, runs counter to the professed Christianity of Boyle, which included among its tenets an insistence that the human species was spiritually unique in the order of creation. As the works of Smollett and Hume may serve to indicate, though, Sade was by no means aberrant in either the dietary views or the religious and anthropological implications that he drew out of modern science. From the very first—as when William Harvey helped to inaugurate the empirical study of nature and yet called empiricists "shittbreeches"[46]—the development of modern science in the Western world had been fraught with contradictions that were bound to upset the visceral sense through which people were possessed of their bodies and societies.

Furthermore, in the polymorphously perverse way that it draws attention to the body, as in its culminating image of one man drinking the fluids "tapped" from another, Dr. L——n's discourse to Bramble is suffused with the suggestion of transgressive sexuality. In this respect it taps into the popular image of Bath as a place that drew attention to the naked body and gave rise to scandal. This image was given further resonance by the potency this spa's waters were supposed to have in healing women of infertility.[47] At least since the previous century, when the Earl of Rochester satirized the similar reputation of Tunbridge Wells, such cures were joked about as owing more to sexual license than to the wonder of the waters; Smollett drew the same conclusion about Bath in *The Adventures of Peregrine Pickle* (1751).[48]

Nude mixed bathing had long been common in the baths, despite various attempts to stop it; and though the practice seems generally to have ceased by the end of the seventeenth century, the threat perceived in it still lived on. This is why a comedy that turns upon the confusions among mismatched couples at this spa, Thomas D'Urfey's *The Bath: Or, The Western Lass* (1701), opens with an account of a scandalous mad fellow plunging naked into the waters. ("And if there be e're a plump *Londoner* there . . . he's on the back of her in a trice, and tabering her Buttocks round the Bath as if he were beating a Drum.")[49] Defoe said that even under the more decorous conditions enforced under Nash, while "the ladies and the gentlemen pretend to keep some distance, and each to their proper side," they "mingle" nonetheless, "and talk, rally, make vows, and sometimes love" (2:34). As late as 1737 the Bath Council felt the need to proclaim an order "that no Male Person above the age of Ten years shall at any time hereafter go into any Bath or Baths within this City by day or by night without a Pair of Drawers and a Waistcoat on their bodies" and "that no Female Person shall . . . go into any Bath . . . without a decent Shift on their bodies."[50]

In addition to the liberties that might be made possible when men and

women were moving about in water almost up to their necks, the indeco-
rousness of their being subject to the gaze of any passersby was frequently remarked. ("At the pump-room," writes Burney's Evelina, "I was amazed at the
public exhibition of the ladies in the bath: it is true, their heads are covered
with bonnets, but the very idea of being seen, in such a situation, by whoever
pleases to look, is indelicate.")[51] It was but a step from the image of Bath as
a place where bodies were examined, treated, and exposed to the image of
Bath as a place where bodies promiscuously mingled and just one step more
to the image of sexual scandal in this city, which was, after all, famous not
only as a health spa and recreational resort but also as a marriage mart. Thus,
in his romantic comedy *The Bath Unmask'd* (1725), Gabriel Odingsells did not
even bother to make reference to the waters, foregrounding instead the an-
tics of various libertines, gamblers, and sharpers in this flesh market. Even as
late as Austen's *Northanger Abbey* one may see traces of this carnal image of
the city in the threats of scandal that enter into this novel's romantic affairs.
They appear as well in Catherine's first experience of the Upper Rooms,
where she finds herself "being continually pressed against by people," as if in
an overcrowded bath.[52] Scientific, erotic, and social matters were fluidly interrelated at Bath, to say the least; and it is the distilled essence of these matters that composes the fluid decoction Smollett's Dr. L——n forces upon his
audience's attention when he desires to prove his point upon Matthew Bramble's body.

Farcically (in Bramble's outrage) and ironically (in Melford's amusement)
this passage draws attention to the cannibalistic nature of the social structures
wrought through rank, wealth, race, nationality, and culture. It is the spirit of
this perception, at once jaunty and bitter, that makes Smollett's prose such a
pleasure to read. The pleasure Smollett expected to stimulate in his readers
was based on the desire for exploitation—which Sade, again, would press to
its logical conclusion: "the supreme pleasure that comes from the spectacle of
the suffering of others."[53] It is the excremental elimination of this pleasure
that the assembled company cannot accept in the doctor's scientific discourse,
which threatens to eliminate the hierarchical basis of their identities by systematically reducing Medicis, Hottentots, and spawers to the same ground
of objectivity.[54] In order to accept this ground, the company would have to
be "persuaded out of their senses." The presumed enjoyment of the readers of
this passage must then depend on a sense of superiority to both the doctor

and his listeners—and thus on an implicit conviction that the pleasures of exploitation are not really threatened here at all. The order of their senses is reaffirmed by the demonstrable ability of readers to master the fear of being bereft of them. This passage may then be an object lesson in how to create distinction out of disgusting excess or, in short, in how to turn excrement to gold. Civilized manners may then be reaffirmed from the ground up. The doctor's outrageous words may be taken and enjoyed at their face value: as sounds comically signifying nothing of the sort for which spa physicians, like natural philosophers more generally, were popularly mocked in this age. Readers may enter the novel, be dirtied by it, and so become clean.

If the communion imaged here is perverse, in the proposed invasion and symbolic transformation of Bramble's body, it is so—as is the case with perversions generally—only because it is so logical. (We would have a very different kind of comedy if the character venturing to drink the abdominal fluid were actually a child, a clown, or a madman.) The laughable character of the doctor's logic is owing simply to the fact that it gives the fluid exchanges that characterized social life at spas a universalized ideological expression. His revolting conception of things is then designed to be amusing only to an audience that cannot help noticing and yet cannot help denying the implications of this fluidity. Dr. L——n is bound to go beyond all bounds so that Smollett's readers may be assured that appropriate limits to the order of the senses, or of aesthetics, are still in place. It is precisely because he conflates food and excrement, just as he levels Medicis and Africans, that the doctor can be a source of humor to the audience anticipated by this text. In effect, the image of revulsion becomes an antidote to any prospects of rebellion readers might consciously or unconsciously be entertaining.

Dr. L——n is then the anti-Beau through whose image we see the waters swallowing up those who were supposed to be taking them and overrunning in this process all ceremonies, histories, and hierarchies, just as they had threatened to do in Defoe's *Tour through England and Wales*. Through this character Smollett parodies the social conditions implicated in the contemporary production, distribution, and consumption of goods by reducing the signifying differences of rank, wealth, race, nationality, and culture to their material basis in the question of who eats whom—or more precisely, who communicates filth to whom. Social structures collapse into anthropophagical relationships, which in turn are reduced to a coprophagical essence of humanity, just as they were in Anstey's notorious couplet. In both cases the joke lies in the suggestion that the proprieties of society are paradoxically defined by parasites upon it, whose pleasures are profoundly soiled.

Put so concisely, the joke is as unremarkable as it is ultimately unthreatening. It becomes more interesting, however, when it is considered in terms of the more specific meaning it bore in the context of spa culture in the eighteenth century. For what we are drawn to see, in all this reveling in revulsion, is how the exchange of fluids at spas served as a way to confront, explore, and symbolically manage empiricist epistemology as it was disseminated through popular culture and made available to the political motivations of imagination.

To understand this aspect of eighteenth-century Bath, one might compare the character of the pleasure-seeking spawer to the fussbudget character of that modern stoic, Immanuel Kant. Kant also addressed the threat of people being persuaded out of their senses but in a markedly different way, by insisting that all must observe the due limits that philosophy enjoined upon them. For instance, Kant assigned music "the lowest place among the fine arts" because "it plays merely with sensations" and, moreover, does so in a physically invasive way. "For owing chiefly to the character of its instruments," he wrote, "it scatters its influence abroad to an uncalled-for extent (through the neighbourhood), and thus, as it were, becomes obtrusive and deprives others, outside the musical circle, of their freedom."[55] If we remember that in this time music was often considered therapeutic, useful especially in cases of disordered nerves, on account of its mechanical influence on the body, we realize that Kant was making a medical as well as an aesthetic argument.[56] What he proscribed, however, Bath prescribed, sponsoring concerts, employing an orchestra to accompany the drinking of waters in the Pump Room, and insisting upon greeting distinguished new arrivals with a ceremonial ringing of bells despite the predictable complaints about the discomposure this music caused to those already resident in the town, especially those who were actually ill. Persisting in his logic, Kant objected to perfume: "The man who pulls his perfumed handkerchief from his pocket gives a treat to all around whether they like it or not, and compels them, if they want to breathe at all, to be parties to the enjoyment."[57] In contrast, Bath was famed for subjecting its visitors to this equivocal enjoyment, and to such a point that Smollett shows Matthew Bramble passing out at a ball there in response to "a *compound of villainous smells,* in which the most violent stinks, and the most powerful perfumes, contended for the mastery" (63). When James Cox exhibited his automatons in the Spring Gardens at Bath in 1772, he might as well have been deliberately mocking the philosopher who insisted on defining humankind's attainment of maturity through the transcendence of any resemblance to such machines.

In every respect, what the stay-at-home bachelor condemned, the resort of gamesters and sexual adventurers celebrated. The difference could scarcely be more stark if Kant were to be reborn and brought face-to-face with the pulsing neon racket of Las Vegas. Yet this contrast is misleading if it so persuades us out of our senses that we fail to observe how much the stoic philosopher and the fashionable fleshpot had in common. In addition to sharing an interest in the bowels bordering upon obsession, especially in terms of digestion, both felt a pressing need to pay homage to the claims of science while yet guarding against the destructive implications that it might seem to have for traditional social values. What some sought in Kant's critiques others looked for in Bath: a way to manage senses that were being systematically deranged by the new methods, discoveries, and possibilities of modern science. Kant actually showed some recognition of this parallel when he characterized his *Critique of Pure Reason* (1781) as "a true cathartic" that would "luckily purge us of delusion along with its attendant, *viz.,* the attitude of knowing a lot."[58] Kant's method of assigning cognition its limits within sense perception, then, was really more a counterpart than an opponent to the ceremonious methods of Bath; for as we see in the attention to empiricism in *Humphry Clinker* as well as in the attention that Kant paid to matters of fashion, the distinction between science and culture in this period was a precarious one, to say the least.

As previously noted, it was conventional in this era to represent spas as places that united the concerns of science, in the form of medicine, and of culture, in the form of fashionable recreations. Thus, in a 1717 letter written during her journey to Turkey, Lady Mary Wortley Montagu mentioned the hot baths at Sofia as being "resorted to both for diversion and health."[59] Often the former concern was granted priority over the latter, as when Defoe said of Tunbridge Wells that "company and diversion is in short the main business of the place" (1:126). Austen wrote to similar effect in *Persuasion* when she described a moment in which Lady Russell was vexed as much as "a person in Bath who drinks the water, gets all the new publications, and has a very large acquaintance, has time to be vexed."[60] Even writers more concerned to puff the medicinal virtues of the waters would allow that the social life to be found at the spas, in promenades and sightseeing and such, was no inconsiderable contribution to the process of the cures that might be found there. In his book on German spas, for example, J. P. De Limbourg wrote of "the necessity there is for amusement, in order to render the use of these waters successful."[61] Like the apparent contrast between Kant and Bath, however, or like the popular Victorian trope through which certain books were praised for the "instruction and amusement" they promised the reader, the formulation that speaks of "diversion and health" may be a misleading one.

It seems to have become conventional among later historians, as it was among eighteenth-century observers, to regard the supposed concern with health as being most often a vestigial motivation among visitors to the spas of this time. However, although the role of the waters as a mere excuse for indulging in the pleasures of social life is not to be underestimated, to adopt this conventional formulation is to assume an assured knowledge of what social life was at this time, whereas, in fact, it was precisely the character of society that was dramatically at issue in the "vortex of amusement" that was Bath.[62] Moreover, one who adopts this formulation is bound to overlook the nature of a historical situation in which science was so precariously distinguished from fashion, professional discourse from commercial advertising and common gossip, that even medical men such as Smollett and Falconer— and philosophers such as Kant—were forced to struggle with an image of contamination that was no less social and cultural for being thoroughly scientific and material. One would then also be led to overlook the extent to which both fashion and medicine were organized according to political prescriptions and fantasies, as in concerns for the "body politic" of the sort that became evident, for instance, when Berkeley introduced himself into the contemporary discourse on spa going.

In fact, precisely to the extent that it was conventionally reiterated, this rhetorical union of "diversion and health" served continually to reproduce an ideological distinction between social and somatic, political and biological, or phenomenal and real things. This distinction then had the effect of obscuring all the respects in which experience, or the order of the senses, is not the transcendentally regulated basis of social life but rather the organized production of historically specific dispositions of power. (Similarly, the Victorian idiom of "instruction and amusement" served to obscure the erotics and aesthetics of the former and the politics and ever more rationalized organization of the latter.) Rather than telling of a happy union, a simple distinction, or an immemorial tradition, as of the *dulce* and *utile,* the "diversion and health" trope served as an attempt to manage the contamination of communication among all those categories of experience—including rank, wealth, race, nationality, and culture—thrown into question in the modern world that found one of its prominent symbols in Bath.

The term "diversion and health" named a problem to be explored, not an achieved solution. This is why Bramble does not go home, as otherwise might have been expected, after his revolting encounter with the doctor at Bristol. He goes on to Bath, there further to bear witness to the pervasiveness of contamination. "I went into the King's Bath," he writes, "by the advice of our friend Ch——, in order to clear the strainer of the skin, for the benefit of a free perspiration; and the first object that saluted my eye, was a child full of scrophulous ulcers, carried in the arms of one of the guides, under the very noses of the bathers" (44). Recoiling, he seeks a more exclusive spot: "To purify myself from all such contamination, I went to the duke of Kingston's private Bath, and there I was almost suffocated for want of free air" (44–45). In the wake of Anstey's poem, the alternative of drinking the waters provides no relief: "for, after a long conversation with the Doctor, about the construction of the pump and the cistern, it is very far from being clear with me, that the patients in the Pump-room don't swallow the scourings of the bathers" (45). Recourse to a more exclusive source, "the spring that supplies the private baths on the Abbey-green," also fails to divert him from the thought of water "medicated with the sweat, and dirt, and dandriff; and the abominable discharges of various kinds"; for Bramble discovers "that the Roman baths in this quarter, were found covered by an old burying ground, belonging to the Abbey; thro' which, in all probability, the water drains in its passage: so that as we drink the decoction of living bodies at the Pump-room, we swallow the strainings of rotten bones and carcasses at the private bath" (45). He is forced to conclude, "Snares are laid for our lives in every thing we eat or drink: the very air we breathe, is loaded with contagion" (46). His rants on this subject elsewhere in the novel include, for example, a memorable excursus on the water drawn from the Thames to slake the thirst of Londoners. "Human excrement is the least offensive part of the concrete," he notes, adding that this material "is composed of all the drugs, minerals, and poisons, used in mechanics and manufacture, enriched with the putrefying carcases of beasts and men" (119).

Again, as with every such passage in this work, we find within these words a vision of men eating men that might recall Thomas Browne or Thomas Hobbes while also anticipating the likes of Sade. In providing Melford's cheerful vision of things as a foil to Bramble's, as in allowing Bramble to linger no less obsessively on such matters than does Dr. L——n, Smollett takes care to note that the pollution at issue here is only nominally related to what might be classified as the historical realities of public sanitation, or the lack thereof, in the eighteenth century. Bramble does at one point refer to the thwarting of "civil regulation" (121), but in this novel, as in Bath as a popularly recognized modern phenomenon, the pressing question was not one of avoiding pollution as it might be empirically defined. The problem lay in finding a satisfying way to image pollution—physical, social, metaphysical, aesthetic, and otherwise—for bodies under the aegis of empiricism. As Gottfried Wilhelm Leibniz regarded positively, the Abbé Yvon negatively, the proliferation of the machine metaphor in this age, so Melford regards positively, Bramble negatively, the contaminating fluidity of a world now universally and interminably subject to scientific analysis.

Within Smollett's novel, as he further indicates by the friendship he has develop between nephew and uncle, the telling issue is not whether Bramble's nostalgic vision of rural simplicity is to be preferred to Melford's more democratic delight in crowded assemblies and suchlike diversions. The interesting point is what both have in common: the assumption that communication is contamination. Whether for good or ill, both characters take for granted what this novel as a whole is designed to demonstrate, explore, and comedically resolve, which is the essential—and so de-essentializing—fluidity of all modern categories of being. What image can possibly contain this Heraclitean flux, not only in the bowels of humanity and of the spring-spewing earth but in social life in its every aspect, if not the insistence on a power of pollution—and thus of satire—so illimitable as to encompass even the universalized claims of science? It is because it must satisfy this question that Smollett's satire is drawn from and directed to matters that threaten to burst the bounds of literary decorum.

Whether dramatized in terms of Bramble-like disgust or Melford-like urbanity, the politics of pollution was played out through every aspect of the complex alliance of medicine and fashion at the spas of this era.[63] Like Vauxhall and but a few other places, such as the sites of masquerades, Bath was a spot where one expected to mingle with people from all ranks of society.[64] As its waters were said to dissolve kidney stones, among other obstructions to good health, Bath was notorious for attenuating the social distinctions that prevailed throughout most of society. This is why Bramble fulminates against this town in terms that parallel his invective against the amusements of Ranelagh and Vauxhall, those resorts of "this incongruous monster, called *the public*" (88).[65]

Whether they were attributed to the deliberate machinations of adventurers or the inadvertent mistakes of innocents, the striking up of involvements between inappropriately sorted persons was a staple in representations of Bath, appearing in works as disparate as the picaresque tale of *Humphry Clinker,* the comic romance of *The Spiritual Quixote,* and the satirical sketches of Richard Warner's *Bath Characters* (1807). There even came to be a tacit understanding that when acquaintances were made across the divide of social position at Bath or similar places, they were to be forgotten if the persons in question subsequently ran into each other in the metropolis. So Defoe said of Tunbridge Wells, "Here you may have all the liberty of conversation in the world, and any thing that looks like a gentleman, has an address agreeable, and behaves with decency and good manners, may single out whom he pleases, that does not appear engag'd, and may talk, rally, be merry, and say any decent thing to them; but all this makes no acquaintance, nor is it taken so, or understood to mean so" (1:126).[66] In *Northanger Abbey* (which was written around 1797 or 1798), the plot that Austen developed around the social origins and presumed wealth of Catherine Morland was a toying with this well-worn topos, in Bath literature, of the inappropriate introduction. (Catherine's eventual innocence in these terms is secured by a displacement of the threat onto the grasping character of Isabella Thorpe, who functions in this regard in the same way as does Mrs. Clay in *Persuasion.*) The topos was so familiar that it had generated its own reversal long before Austen offered up Catherine as a refreshing ingenue. In the Bath of *The Rivals* (1775), Richard Sheridan had Captain Absolute masquerading as the humble Ensign Beverley to suit the romantic notions of Lydia Languish; and before the public unmasking of Jack Griskin, the "beau-sharper" of Bath in Francis Coventry's *History of Pompey the Little* (1751), this character boasts, "'Tis very fashionable . . . for ladies to fall in love with highwaymen now-a-days . . . and I believe I could not do better than let [my fiancée] know that I have returned from transportation."[67]

"So liable as every body was to meet every body in Bath," as Austen put it, one was forced to conclude that people came to this place out of a desire for the very contamination they would nonetheless profess to abhor. Austen recognized this folly with a philosophical smile: "As soon as divine service was over, the Thorpes and Allens eagerly joined each other; and after staying long enough in the Pump-room to discover that the crowd was insupportable, and that there was not a genteel face to be seen, which every body discovers every Sunday throughout the season, they hastened away to the Crescent, to breathe the fresh air of better company."[68] As Austen showed, the seeming paradox of a desire to be disgusted is not really a paradox at all. It is rather the digestive trope of a social body for which the processes of incorporation and expulsion are necessarily interdependent.

This trope was institutionalized in the charity hospital that was opened in Bath in 1742, which was designed to receive the poor from all over Great Britain and Ireland but which denied entry to local residents. "The poor of this city are excepted," said *The New Bath Guide*, "because it was supposed that they might enjoy all the benefits of this water at very moderate expence, and be accommodated in their own houses."[69] The speciousness of this explanation did not go unremarked at the time—"Is not this a Shame?" wrote Thicknesse[70]—but such reasoning was in keeping with the demands placed upon those poor who were deemed eligible and yet could gain admission only if they satisfied a stringent application procedure. (This included the demand for a written letter of recommendation from their local physician, a parish certificate, and three to five pounds of "caution money," among other things.) The ban on local residents acted to discourage impoverished citizens of the nation from resettling in Bath for the medical help to be found there, and the admission procedures assured that only the "respectable poor" would be able to stay even temporarily. One could not ask for a better example of the logic that binds together what is accepted and what excepted in the articulation of the body politic.

So one entered the bowels of Bath, there to be crowded and pressed against and threatened with contamination, in order to suffer, test, and reestablish the image of society. As a cleansing of the impurities of bodies required that those bodies be analyzed even unto their innermost bowels, so did the refreshment of society at Bath require that the insides of society be examined and regularly purged. This was what Anstey had recognized: that just as the pleasures of paradox cannot be quarantined from the logical scandal they pose, no more can the proper state of the body be removed from the exploration of anxieties over social confusion and contamination.

This recognition was equally embodied in the modern history, the social experience, and the popular image of Bath. As the waters there had been professionalized by virtue of being brought under the aegis of "the Faculty," or its resident physicians, so its social life had been professionalized under Beau Nash, the official master of ceremonies and thus the physician prescribing to the social body. The counterpart to the local balneologists' instructions as to how, when, where, in what quantities, and with what other nostrums to take the waters was Nash's satirical code of decorum—"Rules By General Consent Determined"—which was publicly posted in 1742. (It is not clear whether Nash himself actually wrote this text, but it was popularly attributed to him.) The rules dealt with topics such as appropriate dress and the times at which balls were to conclude, on which questions the master of ceremonies was famously inflexible. (He did not hesitate to rebuke even the most distinguished visitors if they transgressed one of his edicts.) Although Nash had earlier led a successful effort to eliminate the wearing of swords and thus the prospect of duels, his code is notable more for its intent to manage pollution than for the specifications, trivial in themselves, of dress, schedules, and comportment. A striking emphasis is placed, though, on the condemnation of rumormongering—a condemnation further reinforced through a note following the list: "*N.B.* Several men of no character, old women and young ones of questioned reputation, are great authors of lies in this place, being of the sect of *Levellers*."[71]

In itself this emphasis is unsurprising, for the scandal retailed at Bath was another commonplace in eighteenth-century representations. Sheridan's *School for Scandal* (1777) appears to have been developed, in part, from notes titled *The Slanderers—A Pump-Room Scene;* and we may recall that when Arabella first appears in the Pump Room in Charlotte Lennox's *The Female Quixote* (1752), she finds that therein "every new Object affords a delicious

Feast of Raillery and Scandal."[72] This commonplace becomes more interesting, however, when one considers how closely this fear of an unchecked and debasing proliferation of words represents, on the level of intimate social relations, the puffery involving dubious scientific claims for which the spas were already notorious by midcentury. Once again, as Anstey so economically indicated, the dirtying of the beau monde (through scandal) and its cleansing (through the medicinal use of waters) can be seen as processes violently, paradoxically, yoked together. The paradox is only heightened if one remembers that the master of ceremonies in question here began his career as a professional gambler and continued to earn his living in that fashion until he was inhibited by the Acts of Parliament against gambling passed in 1739 and 1745.

Although gambling was always ceremoniously condemned in popular representations of Bath for the scandal to which it gave rise, as in plays such as Odingsells' *The Bath Unmask'd*, novels such as Burney's *Evelina*, or other works such as Goldsmith's *Life of Richard Nash*, it provided much of the impetus for the development of modern Bath, as well as for watering places on the Continent. (Hence the zeugma with which one of Richard Warner's "Bath characters" describes Lady Orange: "She came hither to console herself on the loss of her *first husband* with Bath-waters and *cassino*.")[73] It is notable in this respect that Nash himself was something of an upstart and adventurer and, as the mockery that accompanied his growing celebrity indicates, was recognized as such even as he won acceptance into the highest ranks of society. In his biography, Goldsmith went so far as to make Nash's rise a parable for all the puffery in contemporary social life: "How many little Things do we see, without merit, or without friends, push themselves forward into public notice, and by self-advertizing, attract the attention of the day."[74] Here the upholder of ceremony might even be seen as a trickster figure who confused the very categories of order and disorder that he made his subjects pledge to uphold. Similarly, while appearing as a symbol of early modern life, Bath could also symbolize a fluidity in this life that cannot be captured in conventional distinctions such as those between science and fashion, health and pleasure, or ceremony and chance.[75]

Given this fluidity, it seems only logical that the cannibalistic man of science and the trickster master of ceremonies should be brought into the company of a quack metaphysician. At the very height of Bath's popularity, Bishop Berkeley came forward with *Siris: A Chain of Philosophical Reflexions and Inquiries Concerning the Virtues of Tar-Water, and divers other Subjects connected together and arising One from Another* (1744). It was Berkeley's genius as a metaphysician to comprehend the current fashion of taking the waters and point by point, as it were, to offer a philosophical alternative that reasserted the claims of religion over those of empirical science.[76] If the prevailing fashion generally required that those seeking the benefit of the waters should go to a particular spa, since those who touted these resorts were understandably concerned to emphasize the advantages of taking the cure on the spot, Berkeley would provide a recipe for a healing water that could be taken anywhere. If spas were also extending themselves in the form of commodities, as evidenced by the marketing of bottled waters both in England and abroad ever since the seventeenth century, Berkeley would propose a cheap generic alternative to the brand names being sold. If taking the waters was thus becoming a thoroughly commercialized affair, with the commodity in question being packaged through an increasingly systematized cooperation among local authorities, business people, and physicians, he would recommend a water so simple to manufacture as to be all but impervious to commodification—as people might note in comparing it also to expensive medicines such as Joshua Ward's "Pill and Drop."[77] If spas placed the seeking of health within an extraordinary context that always threatened to break out in scandal, his alternative would encourage people to stay right where they were, away from the shops and the theaters and the other accoutrements of the beau monde, with the most humble among them receiving the same cure as the most distinguished. If the cultural direction embodied in the taking of waters tended to exalt civilized artifice in all respects—so that it was all but inevitable that someone like Robert Whytt, the famous professor of medicine at Edinburgh, would try to concoct an artificial spa water[78]—Berkeley's elixir would be suggestive of an ancient and precritical conception of nature rooted in folk medicine.

Most important of all, if the taking of waters brought the body of the world and the viscera of humanity within the realm of physical science, thus making possible the logical extreme of Smollett's Dr. L——n, Berkeley would bring them under the power of a spirituality that extended beyond the tradition of local holy wells to comprehend all of nature in its conception. ("If physicians think they have a right to treat of religious matters," he wrote with perhaps a touch of peevishness, "I think I have an equal right to treat of medicine.")[79] Whereas Dr. L——n might appear as the progressive anti-Beau, effectively destroying all ceremoniousness through his relentless materialism, Berkeley was the reactionary anti-Beau, effectively destroying all professionalism through his relentless idealism.

Berkeley deliberately sought to popularize tar water, which was made from the resin of evergreens, as a preferable alternative to the cures sought at watering places. He compared it, for instance, with the "fine volatile spirit in the waters of Geronster, the most esteemed of all the fountains about Spa," while noting that the prescription of tar water had the advantage, among others, of being "under no restraint either as to diet, hours, or employment."[80] He also presented it through a systematic contrast to medical procedures—salivations, bleedings, and purgings—popularly resorted to at the time. Most generally, even as he granted high praise to scientific men such as Newton, he presented the very conception of tar water as an antidote to the new mechanical philosophy popularly associated with such figures. "In strict truth," he wrote, "all agents are incorporeal, and as such are not properly of physical consideration. The astronomer, therefore, the mechanic, or the chemist, not as such, but by accident only, treat of real causes, agents, or efficients" (*Siris*, 118). From this premise, albeit by a formidably circuitous route that included personal testimonies, accounts of experimental treatments, and invocations of figures such as Plato and Heraclitus cheek by jowl with respectful references to the likes of Newton, Boyle, and Hermann Boerhaave, he came to the conclusion that tar water was probably nothing less than a cure for all ills. "I freely own that I suspect tar-water is a panacea" ("Letter," 175), he wrote. A concoction virtually anyone could manufacture by pouring off the liquid from the sedimented tar left after one had mixed a certain quantity of resin with a given measure of ordinary water, "this water of health (as it may be justly called)" would be comparable "even to the balm of Gilead" (*Siris*, 53, 38).

Berkeley's claims may seem bizarre today, but they were by no means extreme by the standards of his time. Friedrich Hoffmann had earlier written of mineral water as "the nearest of any thing in Nature to what has been so much searched after, an universal Medicine," and Alexander Hunter would follow many others in opining that "there are few Diseases incident to the human Body which may not be palliated, or totally removed, by the judicious use of water."[81] Berkeley, in other words, judged the popular mind very well; and as A. A. Luce and T. E. Jessop have commented, "The response to Berkeley's publication of his remedy was instant and sensational. The drinking of tar-water became a vogue. The collection and publication of cures was undertaken by his friend Prior. The *Dublin Journal* began its printing of reports in March 1744, and the *Gentlemen's Magazine* in June. By June there was a 'Tar-water Warehouse' in St. James's Street, London" (*Siris*, viii). Berkeley's editors go on to note that prominent figures such as Princess Caroline tried the new remedy, which was already advertised abroad, in Germany, in 1745. Moreover, readers of Charles Dickens' *Great Expectations* (1860–61), a novel whose events are initially set around the beginning of the nineteenth century, may recall that the fad of tar water still had some currency even at that date in the provincial town where young Pip grew up, with consequences that proved very discomfiting not only to this protagonist but also to his Uncle Pumblechook.

Dr. L——n was presented by Smollett as one who would persuade people "out of their senses," and this sort of persuasion was Berkeley's avowed aim as well:

These disquisitions will probably seem dry and useless to such readers as are accustomed to consider only sensible objects. The employment of the mind on things purely intellectual is to most men irksome, whereas the sensitive powers, by constant use, acquire strength. Hence, the objects of sense more forcibly affect us . . . and are too often counted the chief good. For these things men fight, cheat, and scramble. Therefore, in order to tame mankind, and introduce a sense of virtue, the best human means is to exercise their understanding, to give them a glimpse of another world, superior to the sensible, and, while they take pains to cherish and maintain the animal life, to teach them not to neglect the intellectual. (Ibid., 150)

In keeping with the governing metaphor for life in this age, Berkeley conceived of the world in terms of "perpetual oscillations" that "operate without ceasing on all things that have life" (ibid., 77). In his conception, air is the "elastic and restless element" in which all bodies have their being. "By this same air fire is kindled, the lamp of life preserved, respiration, digestion, nutrition, the pulse of the heart, and motion of all the muscles seem to be performed" (77–78). This atmosphere "is no distinct element, but a mass or mixture of things the most heterogeneous and even opposite to each other," including things as sensibly distant from each other as the macrocosm and the microcosm. "Small particles in a near and close situation strongly act upon each other, attracting, repelling, vibrating," he wrote. "Hence divers fermentations, and all the variety of meteors, tempests, and concussions both of earth and firmament. Nor is the microcosm less affected thereby. Being pent up in the viscera, vessels, and membranes of the body, by its salts, sulphurs, and elastic power, it engenders colics, spasms, hysteric disorders, and other maladies" (80). In this air we see the instrumentality of the "vital spirit of the world"; for as Berkeley insists, "We have no proof, either from experiment or reason, of any other agent or efficient cause than mind or spirit" (82–83). It is the mixing together within this living atmosphere of every heterogeneous thing that can logically account for the possibility of a humble substance, tar water, proving to be a panacea. As at watering places, but on a much different scale, the only problem is one of confronting and eliminating disgust, which in this case is associated with "the grosser nauseous resin" ("Letter," 177).

Berkeley's conception of tar water is neither more nor less of a folly than Dr. L——n's paean to filth and Beau Nash's ceremonious rationalization of the substance of social life at Bath. It does no violence to the contingencies of history to say that given the modern pleasures of Bath, in which science and taste were symbolically united, there is a certain Greimasian inevitability in the conjoined appearance of a Nash (in whom taste appears without science), Dr. L——n (science without taste), and tar water (neither taste nor science). Simply to put it thus, however, would be to overlook the extent to which science and taste, in the historical circumstances of this age, were mixed up in discourses through which bodies, manners, disgust, and deities, among other things, were put into circulation. More specifically, the interrelated figures of Bath, Nash, Dr. L——n, and tar water illustrate the fluid exchanges in this time between the categories of science and aesthetics. After all, if Berkeley's pretense of scientific reasoning was more tropological than inductive in its logic, the reasoning of the spa physicians was no less derived from a theological and cultural heritage. Similarly, the figures of Nash and Dr. L——n differ on the grounds of taste and science only if we fail to observe the rigorous method of the former and the sensuous solicitation of the latter. Therefore, the point-by-point contrasts between tar water and the waters of Bath may just as well be taken to indicate how "water" in both cases was less a thing of physical properties than a phantasm invested with the life of contemporary anxieties and desires.

In the case of tar water, this last consideration especially demands attention. Berkeley distinguished his balm not only from the waters at spas but also from alcohol, and more specifically from the gin drunk by the common people. No doubt it is impossible to distinguish digressions from the presumptive main narrative among all the fantastic rhetorical wanderings that compose *Siris;* but even if one could do so, no digression would appear where Berkeley pauses to remark, "The public virtue and spirit of the British legislature never shewed itself more conspicuous in any act than in that for suppressing the immoderate use of distilled spirits among the people, whose strength and numbers constitute the true wealth of a nation." He added by way of explanation, "To prove the destructive effects of such spirits with regard both to the human species and individuals, we need not go so far as our colonies, or the savage nations of America" (*Siris,* 67). The centrality of his concern with the political economy of water is made clear through the extensive use he made, by way of recommending his concoction, of accounts of its value in preserving the health of slaves. With one of his publications, he went so far as to append "a solemn affidavit of Captain Drape at Liverpool; whereby it appears that of 170 negroes seized at once by the small-pox on the coast of Guinea one only died, who refused to drink tar-water, and the remaining 169 all recovered, by drinking it, without any other medicine, notwithstanding the heat of the climate, and the incommodities of the vessel."[82]

Whereas the fluid exchanges at spas offered a chance to gamble with social distinctions that was no less exciting and socially productive for being utterly disgusting, Berkeley's tar water was meant to be pure. In this character it was supposed to eliminate the instabilities and uncertainties that would otherwise accompany the growth and reproduction of society. Through tar water he could hope to reassert spiritual control over all bodies but especially those of Africans and common folk, even unto their very bowels. He thus sought to reaffirm the security of an order in which black and lower-class bodies would prove healthy enough to give themselves up to the cannibalistic exploitation so enjoyed by those who had power over them. In this regard, at least, the church divine was as candid in representing his pleasures as was his contemporary, the Marquis de Sade. By way of contrast, we may recall that Matthew Bramble took care to include, among the objects of his scorn at Bath, "clerks and factors from the East Indies, loaded with the spoils of plundered provinces," and "planters, negro-drivers, and hucksters, from our American plantations, enriched they know not how" (36). We may also care to note that in 1792, the same year in which the *Bath Chronicle* published an anti-Jacobin declaration from the "Association for Preserving Liberty, Property, and the Constitution of Great-Britain Against Republicans and Levellers," the Corporation of Bath refused to lend its support to a citizens' petition to abolish the slave trade.[83]

Berkeley's writings were ostensibly devoted to a substance that could never be turned into a luxury item and that was meant to displace spa waters, spirituous liquors, and the medicines of apothecaries. The fact that these writings should nonetheless be explicitly dedicated to the purpose of commodifying human bodies should give us pause when it comes to the use of categories such as science, aesthetics, and morality in referring to eighteenth-century social life. If it seems almost predictable that the popular image of a universal defilement through the Bath waters should meet its match in Berkeley's image of a universal purification through tar water, the pathetic anxieties and filthy desires embodied in the latter may at least serve to remind us not to be overhasty in our evaluation of the characterization accorded the former. The exchange of fluids in the beau monde at Bath in the eighteenth century was a most curious cultural experiment in the articulation, organization, and revision of ideological categories whose mixing was bound to arouse disgust at the time, and the most notable outcome of this experiment may have been the obsessively reiterated confession that taste is a form of consumption ultimately derived from the pleasures of exploitation.

True, as often as it was reiterated, this potentially revolutionary lesson was dissimulated so as to make the cannibalistic logic of culture seem merely natural. Sheridan recognized a cognate point in his prologue to *School for Scandal:* "Needs there a School this modish art to each you? / No need of lessons *now* the knowing think: / We might as well be taught to eat, and drink."[84] The value of Bath, however, lay in its power to bring one to recognize the desire for disgust that lives in the very bowels of every professed object of knowledge, valued form, and categorical imperative. Although this recognition is nothing like a panacea for human ills, perhaps it is not taking things too far

FIGURE 8.
Thomas Gainsborough, *Portrait of Mrs. "Perdita" Robinson* (1781–82), reproduced
by permission of the Trustees of the Wallace Collection, London

to suggest that without it, we would not have had certain works of art that might still contribute a great deal to the health of our social life if they were to be more fully appreciated. These would include, for instance, Gainsborough's scandalously bold *Portrait* of Mrs. "Perdita" Robinson (1781–82), who looks so calculatingly at the viewer (fig. 8); Austen's sly portrait of Catherine Morland, the young lady who "cannot speak well enough to be unintelligible";[85] and Berkeley's sublimely self-indicting portrait of the divine spirit.

CANNIBALISM, *Trade, Whatnot*

OCTOBER 5, 1773, was a pleasant day for Captain James Cook, who was on board the *Resolution* at its anchorage by Tongatapu, one of the Friendly Isles. Writing in his journal, he could afford to indulge his sense of humor:

> The different tradeing parties were so successful to day as to procure for both Sloops a tollerable supply of refreshments in concequence of which I gave the next morning every one leave to purchase what curiosities and other things they pleased, after this it was astonishing to see with what eagerness every one catched at every thing they saw, it even went so far as to become the ridicule of the Natives by offering pieces of sticks stones and what not to exchange, one waggish Boy took a piece of human excrement on the end of a stick and hild it out to every one of our people he met with.[1]

The record of this incident may still cause readers to smile, and in part because the boy's action would not seem to call for any translation. It appears to offer us something universal, perhaps the seed of an allegory, and of a strikingly modern allegory at that. (Karl Marx would explicate its structure in the course of explaining the fetishism of commodities, Sigmund Freud in analyzing money as an unconscious equivalent to feces, Ferdinand de Saussure in contemplating the arbitrariness of the signifier, Jean Baudrillard in cele-

FIGURE 9.
Portrait of a New Zealander, from John Hawkesworth, *An Account of the Voyages Undertaken by the Order of His Present Majesty for Making Discoveries in the Southern Hemisphere* (1773), History of Science Collections, University of Oklahoma Libraries

brating the inauthenticity of simulacra.) Surely it is this universal quality that helps explain why Cook found the boy amusing rather than threatening or insulting—although we might note that the captain was given to self-deprecation at other times as well. Five months earlier, for instance, he had written about the consequences for New Zealanders (fig. 9) of "a commerce with Europeans and what is still more to our Shame civilized Christians." He commented, "We debauch their Morals already too prone to vice and we interduce among them wants and perhaps diseases which they never before knew and which serves only to disturb that happy tranquillity they and their fore Fathers had injoy'd" (175). Having given such dark reflections their due, he was able to laugh at himself in this light moment of mutual understanding with the waggish boy.

This is one of the more attractive episodes in the life of the captain, whose biographies would need tell of many others that are repulsive. The contributions to our understanding of the human race made by "the immortal Cook," as Johann Friedrich Blumenbach called him, met with an appropriately ambiguous apotheosis when he was killed by natives of Hawaii.[2] On the one hand, he could be uncompromising in telling of the depredations wrought by voyagers such as himself: "If any one denies the truth of this assertion let him tell me what the Natives of the whole extent of America have gained by the commerce they have had with Europeans" (175). On the other, he could be absolutely brutal in his treatment of the natives of foreign lands, as became especially clear during his third voyage.

Yet this contradictory logic of identity may itself appear to have something universal about it, at least in the modern world. We may sense this in the fame Cook has enjoyed from the eighteenth century to the present day, as well as in the widespread popularity of all sorts of tales that turn on the mystery of character. Drawing readers to mystery rather than heroism, marvels, fatality, or sin marks a distinctively modern turn in European narrative form that originated in the late eighteenth and early nineteenth centuries; and if we wish to understand its peculiar attraction, we need to reconsider the impression that we might immediately understand the allegory of a boy holding up a piece of excrement on a stick.

To this end, consider a scene described by Bartolomé de Las Casas in a work written more than two centuries before Cook's second voyage:

If . . . pagans speak blasphemously about the Christian religion not out of contempt and hatred of religion but out of anger toward Christians by whom they have been maltreated and injured, that is, with lawful cause, such persons are not blasphemous. Such is the case of the Indians in the province of Jalisco, where, in order to ridicule priests and Christians, the Indians would lift a little cake over their heads with both hands in imitation of the practice of Christian priests, who immediately after consecrating the body of Our Lord Jesus Christ show it to the people. For they do not know what the Christian priests show for adoration is the body of Christ. Nor do they do these things from contempt but from a desire for revenge, when they burlesque the acts of those whom they have found by experience to be totally cruel enemies, for they think that the religion of these very evil men reflects their way of life.[3]

In contrast to the intentionally travestied object of trade, we have here the unintentionally desecrated object of religion; instead of humor, a spirit of revenge; in lieu of immediate understanding, a polemical insistence on miscommunication; and so where there might otherwise be an enjoyment of the uncircumscribed moment, an anxious search for historical context. Yet the two narratives remain so similar that these differences might seem to tell of wrenching identities between matters of economy and theology, pleasure and loss, sensation and reason, or immediacy and alienation. In other words, the structural similarity between the two incidents might seem almost to demand a Hegel to come forth and mediate their differences while explaining as well those aforementioned contradictions in the thoroughly modern character of Captain James Cook.

If we are to find our way to the dialectic of Gottfried Wilhelm Friedrich Hegel, however, we must begin with the issue of cannibalism. This issue is crucial to the writings of Las Casas and Cook even in passages such as those I have just quoted, where it is not literally present. In these passages the question of cannibalism is turned back upon Europeans through the mockery of the excrement (which is treated like something sacred) and of the consecrated bread (which is made to seem valueless). Between the turd, which evidently has come from a human body, and the host, which supposedly has become a divine body, the issue of humanity's borderlines is joined.

Above all else, what unites these two scenes is their dramatic challenge to the rituals of consumption peculiar to Europeans. In both cases the ultimate challenge is to the assumed difference between the cultural incorporation of things through trade and the physical incorporation of things through the mouth. As against the offering of "sticks stones and what not" by the other jokers, which invites the sailors to see themselves as being indiscriminate in their desires, the boy's offering of excrement is a more pointed gesture. It is not a markedly random object that he holds forth but one that recalls the human body and its processes of nutrition and digestion.[4] Similarly, even if Las Casas is correct and not simply diplomatic in his argument that the Jalisco Indians held no profane intent, their gesture was definitely a pointed one. Even if they could not possibly have understood the doctrine of transubstantiation associated with the Spaniards' totem, we must at least credit the Indians with an intuitive recognition of a fetishism vital to the cultural body of the colonizers. Their gesture defined the most distinctively European foodstuff as immediately imitable, utterly lacking in distinction, and so nothing other than what the Indians made part of their flesh as a matter of course, without all the ceremonial folderol.

So these elevations of parodic objects confront us with the ethnographic moment: the encounter with radically challenging difference that virtually defined the Enlightenment and that was popularly represented, for instance, in Montesquieu's *Spirit of the Laws* (1748). John Locke helped to set the pattern when he appealed to anthropological variety, especially in terms of cannibalistic practices, to support his argument in favor of a conception of reason based upon experience.[5] In the eighteenth century this ethnographic moment would become so crucial to the propagation of enlightened reason that philosophers would end up being popularly identified as apologists for cannibals—and this long before the Marquis de Sade sought to demystify the concept of cannibalism in works such as *Aline and Valcour* (1793).

William Shakespeare had foretold this moment through the anagrammatic name of Caliban, whose allegory of communication would also fit the encounters of the conquistadors with the Jalisco Indians and of Captain Cook's crew with the Maoris. ("You taught me language," Caliban famously tells Prospero, "and my profit on't / Is, I know how to curse.")[6] In this moment the simplicity of a commander's smiling reaction to a waggish native must also come to bear the complexity of response articulated by persons such as Las Casas or, say, Louis-Ange Pitou, in his *Penal Voyage to Cayenne in the*

Two Americas and among the Anthropophagi (1805). Describing how he and his fellow transportees were jokingly "baptized" as their ship crossed the equator, Pitou wrote, "Each baptized individual paid the price with a forced laugh: this constraint is the image of the horrors committed in Peru, where the sun of Cuzco reluctantly illuminates the tombs of the Incas and of the two million Indians slaughtered by the Europeans."[7] In this ethnographic moment a mere blink of an eye may turn treasures into trash, commodities into fetishes, and Christians even into monstrous cannibals—if such a being as the cannibal could actually be imagined.

As it happens, in a narrative of exploration that preceded Cook's, *A Voyage to Guinea, Brasil, and the West-Indies* (1735), John Atkins had argued that cannibalism was simply unthinkable. Some of his statements to this effect were reasoned criticisms of the extant reports of this behavior, as when he supposed that "the Accusation every where has probably proceeded from *Fear* in some, to magnify the Miracle of escaping an inhospitable and strange Country, and from *Design* in others, to justify Dispossession, and arm Colonies with Union and Courage against the *supposed Enemies of Mankind.* Conquest and Cruelty, by that means go on with pleasure on the People's side, who are persuaded they are only subduing of brutish Nature, and exchanging, for their mutual Good, SPIRITUAL for TEMPORAL INHERITANCES."[8] This criticism recalls the bitter reproach offered by Las Casas in his *History of the Indies* (ca. 1559): that the accusation of cannibalism "is the language of the Spaniards, and of those who record their horrible exploits, to defame all those nations of the world so as to excuse the violence, cruelty, robbery, and slaughter that they have committed."[9] Some of the other arguments in Atkins' *Voyage,* such as his remarks upon the role that dubious translations may have played in reports of cannibalism, also foreshadow the criticisms of scholars in our own day who regard cannibalism as a myth.[10] More fundamentally, however, Atkins maintained that the very idea of cannibalism ought to be sufficiently discredited by one's recognition that "the Charge carries the highest Reproach on Humanity, and the Creator of it."[11]

Atkins was not alone in denying the existence of cannibalism in this time. Cook complained of those who doubted the accounts of this practice among the New Zealanders, which had been published in John Hawkesworth's official record of his first voyage, and William Wales, the astronomer assigned to the *Resolution* on Cook's second voyage, remained skeptical even after his first introduction to New Zealand.[12] As an educated man of science, Wales felt that proper evidence was wanting, whereas others were simply inclined to agree with Atkins' commonsensical suspicion of travelers' tales. (So Francis Coventry had one of his characters in *Pompey the Little* [1751] describe his return to London from Jamaica, where he had been transported as a felon: "But as I landed without a farthing of money in my pocket, I was obliged to beg my way up to town in the habit of a sailor, telling all the way the confoundest lies—how I had been taken by pirates, and fought with the *Moors*, who were going to eat me alive, and twenty other unaccountable stories, to chouse silly women of a few half-pence.")[13]

Although they represented a minority viewpoint, these sorts of denials carried a certain cogency within the popular representation of cannibalism in this era, which became remarkably nuanced as writers sought to anticipate and accommodate objections. Explorers, scientists, historians, missionaries, and novelists—Daniel Defoe no less than James Cook and the Abbé Raynal—all sought to establish the verisimilitude of their accounts by demonstrating that theirs was a painstaking judgment in this matter. As evidence, they drew marked distinctions among reports of cannibalism (with eyewitness experience coming to hold canonical authority); among savage peoples (the majority of whom were said not to indulge in this practice);[14] among the cannibal lands (to some of which the practice was said to be indigenous, in others a corruption spread from neighboring parts); among the groups within cannibal societies (only some of which, such as warriors or priests, were said actually to partake of human flesh); and among the causes of this practice (such as revenge, hunger, a specific taste for human flesh, or some combination of these or other motives). Early in the next century, at least one writer was even capable of observing that the same locale could find cannibalism both embraced and abhorred.[15] In casting a critical eye on reports of cannibalism, this writer and his predecessors in the eighteenth century helped to keep the stereotype of the cannibal uncertain in its application and implications. This uncertainty did not make it any less a stereotype, but it did force Europeans to entertain the possibility that it might ultimately turn around and ridicule them, as in Jonathan Swift's "Modest Proposal" (1729), Voltaire's *Candide* (1759), or James Gillray's anti-Jacobin engravings of the 1790s (figs. 10 and 11).[16]

The consequences of this reversal would prove to be significant, to say the

FIGURE 10.
James Gillray, *Un petit Soupèr, al la Parisiènne* (1792), reproduced by permission
of the Trustees of the British Museum, London

least. The crucial figure here is Michel de Montaigne, whose essay "Of Cannibals" (1580) laid out the grounds for thinking through this reversal, and in
such a telling fashion that no one since has been able to improve upon it. He
elaborated a form of discourse that would still prove rich in possibilities four
centuries later, as in the fiercely proud and yet endlessly ironic assumption of
cannibal identity in Aimé Césaire's *Notebook of a Return to the Native Land*
(1939–56). Jacques Attali's use of the image of cannibalism as a master trope
for social relations, as exemplified especially in the history of medicine, is another recent extension of Montaigne's work.[17]

In the popular representation of cannibalism, Montaigne helped to construct a second tradition, complementary to but distinct from that set out by
Las Casas. Whereas Las Casas expressed outrage, Montaigne responded with

FIGURE II.
James Gillray, *To the worthy Members of the Society and the* CROWN & ANCHOR (1793),
reproduced by permission of the Trustees of the British Museum, London

irony. Cannibalism under his pen became an occasion for urbane social criticism and philosophical reflection. The former is well represented by his conclusion, after a description of cannibalism among Brazilian warriors, "I think
there is more barbarity in eating a man alive than in eating him dead; and in
tearing by tortures and the rack a body still full of feeling, in roasting a man
bit by bit, in having him bitten and mangled by dogs and swine (as we have
not only read but seen within fresh memory, not among ancient enemies, but
among neighbors and fellow citizens, and what is worse, on the pretext of
piety and religion), than in roasting and eating him after he is dead."[18]

Like Jean de Léry, the Protestant missionary who had urged that his readers should not "abhor so very greatly the cruelty of the anthropophagous—

that is, man-eating—savages" on the ground that among Frenchmen there were some "even worse and more detestable,"[19] Montaigne began with a comparative weighing of sins. He went even further, however, in that the philosophical musings accompanying his criticism take all of history within their compass, from ancient Greek philosophy to the pharmacopoeia of contemporary medicine. "Indeed, Chrysippus and Zeno, heads of the Stoic sect, thought there was nothing wrong in using our carcasses for any purpose in case of need, and getting nourishment from them; just as our ancestors, when besieged by Caesar in the city of Alésia, resolved to relieve their famine by eating old men, women, and other people useless for fighting. . . . And physicians do not fear to use human flesh in all sorts of ways for our health, applying it either inwardly or outwardly." This history having been established, social criticism and philosophy could then be combined, and cannibals could be shown as philosophers. So Montaigne recounted an anecdote about the three Tupinamba from Brazil who came to the French court at Rouen in 1562. "They had noticed that there were among us men full and gorged with all sorts of good things," he wrote, "and that their other halves were beggars at their doors, emaciated with hunger and poverty; and they thought it strange that these needy halves could endure such an injustice, and did not take the others by the throat, or set fire to their houses."[20]

The ironic reversals for which Montaigne codified the pattern would be echoed throughout the eighteenth century. Their most notable manifestation was in the opposition between noble and evil stereotypes of savages, as in the distinction between the Abaquis and the Rouintons in the Abbé Prévost's *The English Philosopher, or the History of Mister Cleveland* (1731). It is important to recognize that this was always a false opposition, one bound within Montaigne's patterns of irony, through which each figure could be brought to support and confirm the other's identity. The fact that these two images obeyed the same fundamental logic is evident, for example, in the ease with which they cohabited in eighteenth-century texts, such as the *New Voyage to the South Seas* (1783) by Julien Marie Crozet.

At one point in his narrative Crozet cites the writings of Cook, in addition to his own experience of an incident in which a number of Frenchmen were killed by some New Zealanders, as testimony to the reality of cannibalism. He then launches into an angry screed that damns cannibals and philosophers together:

Behold these natural men so praised by those who do not know them and who freely grant them more virtues and fewer vices than those men they are pleased to call artificial because education has perfected their reason! As for me, I maintain that among all the animals of creation, there is none more ferocious and dangerous to man than the natural and savage man; I would much prefer to encounter a tiger or a lion, because I would be distrustful of them. I speak in accordance with what I have seen.

Engaged since my childhood in the profession of navigation, I have never been able to enjoy the happy leisure that allows for the study and the contemplations by which philosophers are formed; but I have travelled through the greater part of the globe, and everywhere I have seen that where this world was not aided and perfected by good laws, by a good education, it was the prey of force and treachery, as much among the natural men as among the animals: I have seen that reason without culture was but a brutal instinct, more ferocious than that of beasts.[21]

At this point Crozet's editor, Alexis de Rochon, feels obliged to interrupt the text so as to provide the opposing, revisionary view. "In the account he gives of the massacre of the French in New Zealand," he notes, "M. Croizet [*sic*] does not assign any cause to this deadly event. It is impossible, however, to conceive that any entire people should be made up of monsters who slaughter, in cold blood and without any motive, strangers to whom they had accorded hospitality. I know very well that these savages are anthropophagous; but there is an immense distance between that execrable custom of feasting on the bodies of their enemies and the treachery of which they are accused."[22] He then goes on to provide a historical context for the incident that spurred Crozet's wrath. He describes an encounter two years earlier between some New Zealanders and a different French vessel, whose captain—after some friendly intercourse and trading—decided to avenge the theft of one of the ship's boats by setting fire to the natives' boats and, for good measure, their village. In terms worthy of Las Casas, the editor then proceeds to defend what he regards as the childlike innocence of the natives as against the violence and thoughtlessness of Europeans. Similarly, in quoting the foregoing passage from Crozet's *New Voyage*, Anders Sparrman, a botanist who had accompanied Cook on one of his voyages, chose to omit Rochon's words but provided in their stead an extenuating comment of his own. He referred his readers to "the barbarism of [their] European forefathers" (even as he spoke of his delight over "the news of the establishment of an English mission for the civilisation and conversion of the New Zealand Heathens").[23]

Just as there is no contradiction, historically speaking, between Montaigne's statements that cannibals are unquestionably barbarians and that they are philosophers, the apparent opposition between the narrative voices of Crozet, on the one hand, and Rochon or Sparrman, on the other, is really nothing of the sort.[24] In this regard it is notable that Denis Diderot, for example, could syncretize the noble and the evil savage in his *Supplement to the Voyage of Bougainville* (1773–74). This work takes note of cannibalism, in a ho-hum sort of way, as a thoroughly rational mechanism of population control. Similarly, we have a surfeit of historical evidence that Cook could feel great sympathy for natives, could thoughtlessly murder them, and could notice himself engaged in both actions while yet feeling no incoherence within himself—while feeling only hope for the future.

As when he wrote of the natives of Tana in the New Hebrides, Cook recognized full well that this apparent contradiction between the noble and the evil savage was actually an irony faithfully serving his culture. "Thus we found these people Civil and good Natured when not prompted by jealousy to a contrary Conduct," he commented, going on to explain that theirs was

> a conduct one cannot blame them for when one considers the light in which they must look upon us in, its impossible for them to know our real design, we enter their Ports without their daring to make opposition, we attempt to land in a peaceable manner, if this succeeds its well, if not we land nevertheless and mentain the footing we thus got by the Superiority of our fire arms, in what other light can they than at first look upon us but as invaders of their Country; time and some acquaintance with us can only convince them of their mistake. (*Voyage*, 493)

In Montaigne's essay as in Swift's "Modest Proposal," Crozet's narrative, Cook's journals, Joseph Conrad's *Heart of Darkness* (1899), and works still being produced in our own time, such as Francis Ford Coppola's *Apocalypse Now* (1979), the opposition between the noble and the evil savage is the instrument of irony that enables philosophically inclined Westerners to imagine that they are taking an honest look at the profound mystery of their selves.

I do not mean this statement simply to be dismissive. In the first place, I am not so naïve as to conceive of an honesty that does not begin in imagination; and in the second, the critical force in Montaigne's conception of cannibalism cannot be reduced to the imperial forces represented by the likes of Captain James Cook. Nevertheless, the ironic view of cannibalism was always bound to remain somewhat obtuse, and not only because Montaigne's humane social criticism might be commandeered to serve the comfortable self-deprecation of someone like Cook. It remained obtuse because even in its most striking reversals, this ironic vision was still stuck with the originary identification of cannibalism with barbarism.

The problem was obvious. After all, Montaigne himself had noted that the real issue was never whether acts of cannibalism had actually taken place. His doubting contemporaries, like Atkins in the early eighteenth century and William Arens in the late twentieth, were perfectly willing to allow that this act had been known to occur under certain rare and extreme conditions, such as those of imminent starvation. Defined minimally as the consumption of human remains by other humans, cannibalism was certainly thinkable. The real issue was how to deal with the tendency shown by the concept of cannibalism, once it was allowed to be thinkable in any case, immediately to overrun its own borderlines in all cases until nothing coherent, nothing literal, was left either of the act or of the flesh that was its nominal object. Instead of "Does it happen?" the more pressing question was "What does it mean?" In this respect it paralleled the image of the machine in the Enlightenment, which was not provocative because it represented a determinate meaning but rather because it did not—and so might threaten even to assimilate all things to itself. The nature of the cannibalistic act seemed perfectly clear right up to the point at which it was actually imagined to have been committed, at which moment the capacity of language to turn upon itself, to curse the source of its own indoctrination, would begin to become all too apparent.

That we still dwell within this problem of the thinkability of cannibalism is evident from the fact that all the major theoretical positions on this topic that are being maintained today were already well established in the eighteenth century. As the debunking of William Arens has its counterpart in the reactions of Wales and Atkins, so it is with the materialist anthropology of Marvin Harris (who sees cannibalism as a utilitarian response to nutritional need) and the structuralist anthropology of Claude Lévi-Strauss and Marshall Sahlins (who regard it as at once constitutive of and constituted by symbolic cultural distinctions). Whether explicitly, as in the work of Lévi-Strauss, or implicitly, these approaches take their origins from eighteenth-century speculation. One of the first questions in the minds of students of cannibalism in the eighteenth century was whether it could be blamed on necessity or must rather be attributed—as in Johann Reinhold Forster's account of Cook's second expedition, *Observations Made During a Voyage Round the World* (1778)—to the structuring of a particular society. With an eye for cultural logic that seems entirely modern, John Liddiard Nicholas, in his 1817 *Narrative of a Voyage to New Zealand*, even noted that "the same superstition which disposes [the New Zealanders] to respect with the most scrupulous veneration the dead bodies of their friends, acting conversely, impels them to gorge themselves upon the mangled remains of their hostile opponents."[25] In pointing to such prefigurations I would not wish to minimize the many differences between contemporary discourses on this topic and those established two centuries ago, but I do mean to describe a limitation, perhaps an unavoidable limitation, in the positions established within anthropology today.

These positions, which tell of the ideological fantasy, the biological necessity, or the cultural value of cannibalism, reveal as much about the categories of thought with which scholarship has been stuck since the Enlightenment as they do about the topic presumed to be in question. Although contemporary anthropological studies on this topic have certainly brought us considerable knowledge through their empirical research and formal analyses, they have done so by turning away from the historical drama of the issue of cannibalism, which utterly confounds the categories of fantasy, need, and value. Consequently, they have turned away as well from the most powerful representations of cannibalism with which we have been gifted, which are those of Las Casas, Defoe, Sade, and—desperately determined as he was not to let this problem of the thinkability of cannibalism endlessly repeat itself through the categories of fantasy, need, and value—Hegel.

Las Casas is especially important in this regard. Frantic to stop the slaughter of the natives of the New World, he was driven to formulate the question of cannibalism in a way that subsequent writers could not help but confront, whether or not they had any awareness of his precedence. To counter apologists for the conquistadors and colonizers, he put forth the argument that the nature of cannibalism is far from self-evident. Indeed, he argued that for all intents and purposes cannibalism is entirely metaphorical. As he portrayed it, the act cannot be literally defined because its nature demands comparison, or contextualization, even when the testimony bearing upon it comes from eyewitnesses, those exemplars of truth in the modern world. So he wrote of the apologists for European empire, while referring to one of the popular allegations of how cannibalism was practiced, "It is as if they held all the peoples of the New World shut up in cages or slave pens and would want to cut off as many human heads as are usually sold each day in the markets for the feeding and nourishment of the populace," adding, "I suggest this as a comparison" (*Defense*, 27–28).

Wherever it addressed the accusation of cannibalism, the defense of the Indians put forward by Las Casas grew out of his insistence that this act cannot be defined and cannot even occur in isolation. He does not simply conclude that one must turn a critical eye on reports of cannibalism, questioning the motives and understanding of the supposed witnesses and committing oneself to the responsibility of ascertaining exactly how, when, where, and why this behavior in fact takes place. Although this sort of questioning does have its importance in his writing, he does not think that it goes far enough. More importantly, he maintains that one must always measure the evil of this dubiously attested act against the incontrovertible facts of the responses that have been made to it. "For not all of them eat the flesh of the innocent," he writes of the natives of the New World, "but only the rulers or priests, who do the sacrificing, whereas war brings the destruction of countless innocent persons who do not deserve any such thing" (191). It then stands to reason that the authorities "should most carefully consider the tumult, sedition, killings, arson, devastation, and furor of the goddess of war that necessarily attend the prevention of this evil" (188). Moreover, one must evaluate cannibalism in terms of the fundamental conditions of language, human understanding, and behavior and thus come to recognize the extent to which violence enters into all imaginable acts of communication, even in their most idealized forms:

> Let us put the case that the Spaniards discover that the Indians or other pagans sacrifice human victims or eat them. Let us say, further, that the Spaniards are so upright and good-living that nothing motivates them except the rescue of the innocent and the correction of the guilty. Will it be just for them to invade and punish them without any warning? You will say "No, rather, they shall send messengers to warn them to stop

these crimes." Now I ask you, dear reader, what language will the messengers speak so as to be understood by the Indians? Latin, Greek, Spanish, Arabic? The Indians know none of these languages. Perhaps we imagine that the soldiers are so holy that Christ will grant them the gift of tongues so that they will be understood by the Indians? Then what deadline will they be given to come to their senses and give up their crimes? They will need a long time to understand what is said to them, and also the authority and the reasons why they should stop sacrificing human beings, so that it will be clear that evils of this type are contrary to the natural law.

Furthermore, within the deadline set for them, no matter what its length, they will certainly not be bound by the warning given them. . . .

Now, I ask, what will the soldiers do during the time allowed the Indians to come to their senses? . . . Even the presence of the Emperor would not restrain them from thievery and bloodshed for more than two days. (217–18)

Because "there can be cases in which it is lawful to eat human flesh, for example, necessity and extreme hunger" (218), cannibalism as an accusation cannot concern the eating of human flesh per se. Its object must rather be the violence of war, torture, or sacrifice said to attend upon or prepare for this practice. The very attempt to define cannibalism, then, confronts us with the infinite abstraction of violence. Violence thus conceived cannot be limited to a specific people's character but must rather be judged in terms of a range of behavior in which Spaniards and other Europeans are no less implicated than the Indians. "Making its decision with prudence, the Church will at times take up arms, at other times it will overlook [such provocation]. For circumstances sometimes make what is just in itself be unjust" (188).

Whereas the irony of Montaigne extenuated the crime of the cannibal, the outrage of Las Casas challenged the coherence of this very word. In his polemics the literal instance of cannibalism can be defined only through this word's immediate and potentially illimitable metaphorical extension. It follows that far from being the defining basis of this act, human flesh can have no propriety in and of itself. No wonder Diderot and Sade in the eighteenth century, like Freud and Lévi-Strauss in the twentieth, associated cannibalism with incest.[26] In both cases the commonplace understanding of the term must prove incoherent because it fails to distinguish between the acts of stig-

matizing and of conceptualizing the phenomenon in question. The name of
the thing turns out to be an overdetermined act of repulsion, its definition a
complex masquerade of revulsion, and thus its entire conceptualization an allegory of the violent exchanges across borderlines within any articulation of
cultural identity. It is only out of the drama of such violence, it seems, that
people come to their senses.

In the eighteenth century it became possible to see the fascination with
cannibalism as a displacement and disavowal of the European consumption
of human flesh that was most grievously carried out in the slave trade but also
in myriad forms of exploitation, colonialism, enforced dependency, hierarchy,
and, as William Blake would say, Christian mercy. If Alexander Pope could
seem blissfully oblivious to the equivocal parallelism in his line, "What war
could ravish, Commerce could bestow,"[27] not all were so blind. Referring to
the Spanish conquest of Peru, "Societies then devour societies!" Raynal wrote
in his widely read *Philosophical and Political History of the Establishments and
Commerce of the Europeans in the Two Indies* (1770). He imagined a monument
built to Las Casas that would show him interposing his body between American and Spaniard, presenting his chest to the sword of the latter so as to save
the former, with the inscription "IN AN AGE OF FEROCITY, LAS CASAS, WHOM
YOU SEE, WAS A BENEFICENT MAN."[28] If this appreciation ignored, as is usual
with monuments, the more dubious qualities of Las Casas—such as his support for slavery in certain circumstances—Raynal's outrage at slavery in particular and European depredations in the New World in general was clear
enough and included French actions within its compass, as well as those of
Spain and other countries. Similarly, when he turned his attention to commerce and consumption, Claude-Adrien Helvétius wrote, "No barrel of sugar
arrives in Europe that is not stained with human blood."[29] Given this background, Nicholas was actually adopting a rather mild position when he wrote
of New Zealand, "The detestable trade in human flesh is carried on in this
island; but when we consider that it has been suffered to exist so long in civilized Europe, and might still be the disgrace of Britain, had not a Wilber-
force been found to proclaim its enormity, and break the fetters of an afflicted
race, shall we wonder that cannibals should be insensible to injustice, nor feel
any compunction in making a traffic of that body which they would not hesitate to devour!"[30]

The differences among Raynal, Helvétius, Nicholas, and others who addressed this issue may certainly be interesting in their own right, but the crucial point in the present context concerns the development of a widespread recognition of a profound dubiety in the definition of cannibalism. No matter how successfully it was avoided by most eighteenth-century writers other than Sade, one logical conclusion was that far from being barbarous, cannibalism was actually demanded by civilization. A comment made by Sahlins, who in this case echoes Freud, is apropos: "It would be difficult to agree with the Christian missionary, who on partaking the Lord's Supper with a small group of Marquesan converts, thought he was witness to a remarkable religious change, since only a few years before these inveterate cannibals had been eating the flesh of their fellow men: . . . "They were now sitting at the feet of Jesus, and in their right minds, eating and drinking the emblems of that body which was broken, and that blood which was shed for man.'"[31]

Not all missionaries were so obtuse. In 1757, for instance, the rather more cagey Pierre Roubaud sensed that it might not be wise to bring his religion's sacraments into close juxtaposition with the cannibal feast he had just witnessed. He reported, "After having consulted together [with the other missionaries who were present], we all deemed that the respect due to the sacredness of our mysteries did not permit us to celebrate, in the very center of barbarism, the sacrifice of the Lamb without spot; and the more so, as these people, devoted to the most grotesque superstitions, might take advantage of our most solemn ceremonies in order to make them the substance, or even the ornament, of their juggleries."[32] Yet both these accounts may serve to suggest that cannibalism is commonly termed unthinkable only because it is all too thinkable, all too compelling, as an image for the fundamental nature of social life.

To some extent, as the pertinence of the passage from Sahlins would indicate, this insistence that cannibalism is never "literal" is in keeping with its representation in contemporary anthropological theory. Donald Tuzin, for example, has described cannibalism as, "inter alia, a device through which the unthinkable (eating people) gives form to the otherwise inconceivable substance of the relationship to oneself and to the supernatural. Paradoxically, then, the symbolic office of cannibalism depends upon its being thought of as 'unthinkable.'"[33] Broadly speaking, this formulation fits with Lévi-Strauss's analysis of myths in which "a certain form of cannibalism [is] the precondition of civilized nourishment"—myths that may involve, for instance, a human being committing "an act of cannibalism against the vegetable king-dom."[34] Similarly, Sahlins has summed up the "cultural sense of cannibalism" as "the concept of it as set by its place in a total cultural scheme, which gives it a differential value in relationship to other categories or concepts."

For these and many other anthropological theorists, cannibalism has never been and cannot be literal except within the metaphor of one's own kind, which in its turn must of necessity be delimited within specific cultures or cultural institutions. Before it can hope to be an act of the human organism, cannibalism must have found its place within the values, beliefs, associations, and rituals of a particular social organization—for as Sahlins says, "cannibal-ism is always 'symbolic,' even when it is 'real.'"[35] It was precisely because he considered that Jean-Paul Sartre had failed sufficiently to appreciate this les-son that Lévi-Strauss thought it necessary to correct the former's *Critique of Dialectical Reason* (1960), and through just the kind of metaphorical exten-sion that had been established as a trope of social criticism by writers such as Las Casas, Montaigne, and Swift. "The price . . . paid for the illusion of hav-ing surmounted the insoluble antinomy (in such a system) between self and other," he wrote, "consists in the assignment, by historical consciousness, of the metaphysical function of the Other to the Papuans. In reducing these lat-ter to the condition of means, just the thing to satisfy its philosophical ap-petite, historical reason gives itself over to a sort of intellectual cannibalism, which, to the eyes of the ethnographer, is much more revolting than the other sort."[36]

Ultimately, however, the direction of the argument made by Las Casas dif-fers from that of these contemporary theorists no less than it does from the biological functionalism of Harris and the psychological fundamentalism of Arens. For the premises of structuralist or symbolic anthropology, which rest upon the determination of coherent cultural borderlines, get consumed by the image of cannibalism that Las Casas and Montaigne bequeathed to the En-lightenment. This image served to body forth the violent instability of all such borderlines, whether they be in theory, on the ground, or in the flesh.

In this respect it is the confusion in the writing of Las Casas, the desper-ately redundant multiplication of defenses, that is most notable. He failed to define cannibalism in the manner of our contemporary anthropologists, neatly and summarily, not because his reasoning was less systematic than theirs but because it was more so. He saw cannibalism not as an ethnographic issue but as one that was universal, and so much so that it would finally lead him to identify universality with self-contradiction or paradox ("For circumstances sometimes make what is just in itself be unjust"). This turn in his writing paid due obeisance to Christian tradition, which could always find a sacred authority for paradox in the person of Jesus Christ, among other places. At the same time, however, this paradox went beyond the boundaries of tradition into a visceral sense of violence systematically excluded from much of the more disciplined reasoning of our contemporary theorists.[37]

The politics of his rhetorical context obliged Las Casas to address cannibalism in relation to natural law and theories of just war and, more broadly, in the terms of Christian doctrine. Within and beyond these contexts, his reasonings all sought to uncover a hysteron proteron, a reversal of cause and effect, in the representation of desire. First, in the place of native peoples who were termed savages because of the abominable nature said to be evident in their eating of human flesh, he put Spaniards whose acts of violence were so abominable as to make them more cannibalistic than those so called. Thus far his approach resembled Montaigne's ironic reversal. Las Casas then took the further step of suggesting that the accusation of cannibalism must be regarded as a confession on the part of the European. In the portrayal of Las Casas ("I suggest this as a comparison"), the cannibal is not the cause but the effect of the European's endlessly mendacious and voracious desire. In other words, Las Casas sought to divert his readers' attention away from the formal definition of cannibalism and toward its historical figuration, in which it becomes imperative to recognize the workings of European desire. In doing so he anticipated the way cannibalism would be transformed, in the eighteenth century, by an attention to its eroticism that went well beyond the conventional imagery that Henry Fielding, for example, exploited in *Tom Jones* (1744) to compare the appetites involved in eating a meal, reading a book, and rogering a maid. In Voltaire's *Candide* (1759), in fact, to qualify as a cannibal one need do nothing but desire to live, for such desiring proves to be self-consuming, leading us "to caress the serpent that devours us."[38]

Although reports of cannibalism can be traced to the beginnings of recorded history, as in Herodotus, they took on a new character in the wake of the European explorations and conquests in the fifteenth, sixteenth, and seventeenth centuries. With the heroic exception of Las Casas, the writers who first described cannibalism in the New World, such as Bernal Diaz de

Castillo and Bernadino de Sahagún, simply took for granted its repulsiveness.[39] This attitude still allowed for a wide range of responses, from the bland observation that Hernán Cortés made of his native supporters in the aftermath of one of his battles—"that night, our allies supped well, because they cut up all those whom they had killed and captured to eat"[40]—to the excited title of Hans Staden's account of his experiences in Brazil, *True History of a Country of Wild, Naked, Ferocious Man-Eaters in the New World of America* (1557). In the narratives of missionaries and voyagers this range of responses would continue into the eighteenth century. In this century, however, a new era in the Western representation of cannibalism began to take form as the sheer accumulation of narratives, in the contexts of increasing overseas trade, religious proselytization, and imperial expansion, led writers to reflect upon the perverse attractiveness that the image of the cannibal had come to hold for their societies. The implicit contention in the arguments developed by Las Casas, that the cannibal was a figure of European desire, here became explicit. In this era cannibalism was transformed from a behavioral category into a nexus of desire. Sex between Europeans and the peaceful Tahitians had taken place in the context of and as a part of commerce, and there was a growing recognition that the European encounter with the supposed cannibals of New Zealand and other lands was also a matter of trade. In fact, it had become clear that whatever else they might be, cannibals were being merchandised as objects of consumption.

An incident illustrative of this state of affairs occurred during Cook's second voyage and, paradoxically, served to convert William Wales from an agnostic on this topic to a true believer. In June of 1773, Wales had written that despite popular preconceptions to the contrary, not "the least signs" of "this most detestable Practice" had come before his eyes. Describing the gestures through which the sailors heard natives tell of their revenge upon their enemies after battles, he argued that this supposed evidence for cannibalism "was shewn by signs which every one will allow are easily misunderstood." True, for anything he knew to the contrary, these signs "might mean they Eat the Man they had just killed; but is it not as likely that after the Engagement they refreshed themselves with some other Victuals which they might have with them?" Wales added, "I did not see one out of the many who went through those Massacres, who did not stop before he made the sign of eating; or that did it before some of us made the sign, as if to remind him that he had forgot that part of the Ceremony. This circumstance is brought as a proof both that they are, and that they are not Caniballs" ("Journal," 790). Wales even went so far as to point out that on the evidence said to have been witnessed on the *Resolution*'s companion ship—a native bearing a decapitated head—David might have been adjudged a cannibal in the aftermath of his set-to with Goliath.

On November 23, 1773, however, Wales made a new entry in his journal: "I have this day been convinced beyond the possibility of a doubt that the New-Zeelanders are Cannibals." He proceeded to describe an incident in which some natives were found with the head that once belonged to a boy on whom, Wales was told, they had been feasting. "Thus far I speak from report" is his scrupulous comment, but then comes the eyewitness observation, which is supposed to be definitive. "To convince us also, another Steake was cut off from the lower part of the head, behind, which *I saw* carried forward, broiled, and eaten by one of them with an avidity which amazed me, licking his lips and fingers after it as if afraid to lose the least part, either grease or gravy, of so delicious a morsel" ("Journal," 818).

What Wales did not observe, even though it is recorded in his journal and so presumably was equally before his eyes, is that this act of cannibalism took place entirely within the framework of the sailors' incitement to it. Unlike Las Casas and the editor of Crozet's narrative, unlike even himself in his earlier attention to the ambiguities that can enter into gestures in a context in which the relation between question and response, or cause and effect, is unclear, he overlooked the dramatic setting of this scene. This head was first met with "on shore at a place where many of the Natives generally dwelt to purchase Curiosities" and where other body parts were also scattered. It was sold to one of the ship's officers after this officer declined to prove himself a man-eater even though he was spurred on by one of the natives, who "with great gayety struck his spear into one lobe of the Lungs" and held it close to the Englishman's mouth. The native's act of cannibalism then took place only after the head was brought on board the *Resolution*, broiled in the ship's galley, and offered to him ("Journal," 818–19).[41] Moreover, according to Sparrman, when Cook later showed up he "caused a further piece to be roasted and eaten by a native, so that he also was an actual witness of cannibalism, a thing which was doubted in England by many so-called philosophers."[42] In other words, cannibalism finds its source here in a context of institutionalized trade between the New Zealanders and Europeans, and the act itself figures in this setting as another item of trade—as witness how the native raises flesh on a stick to mock the ship's officer before a second native accepts the reversal of this challenge and eats some of it.

Another observer of this incident, Johann Reinhold Forster, noticed precisely this aspect of this scene (as did his son and assistant, Georg). Referring to the battle that had produced the corpse from the head of which the steak was then sliced, he commented, "I am afraid we are the innocent causes of this war." He went on to explain, "For having bought up all the Curiosities & green Stones, the Natives in the Sound were possessed of, & hearing us constantly ask for more and offering various things, which tempted their desires; They went I believe in quest of them among their neighbours, who they knew had a great many left, & killed several of them in order to possess themselves of these things which are so much coveted by the Europeans." What is more, his account of the reactions of the Europeans to this scene effectively serves to dissolve the concept of cannibalism: some are said to have responded with laughter, others as if "their bowels were acted upon as by a dose of Ipecacuanha," still others with an expression of feeling "for that unhappy creature that fell a sacrifice to these Savages," and he himself with "several very pertinent reflexions on the subject."[43] The diversity of these visceral reactions, which threatens to confound the writer's reasonings with tears, excrement, and laughter, also threatens to expose the causes at issue here as being "innocent" only in an insufferably pettifogging sense of that term.

This innocence once lost, out of the image of cannibalism we may see that of capitalism emerge, and with a vengeance.[44] Raynal went so far as to reflect that given the relatively stable and economically advanced state of Europe at the time of his writing, "only the discovery of a new world could furnish aliments for our curiosity."[45] It is notable in this regard that this richly signifying head from Cook's second voyage appears to have been purchased by Richard Pickersgill, third lieutenant on the *Resolution,* for the express purpose of preserving it in spirits so that it might be placed in the anatomical collection of Dr. John Hunter, the eminent London surgeon.[46] No wonder Sparrman no sooner concluded his statement about Cook's eyewitness proof of cannibalism than he cited diverse testimonies of this practice among his European contemporaries as well as among Mexicans, Brazilians, North Americans, Sumatrans, Africans, and peoples of antiquity.[47]

Other narratives of this era, such as Sydney Parkinson's *Journal of a Voyage to the South Seas* (1784), provide further evidence of how well the New Zealanders appreciated the Europeans' taste for cannibalism. "The natives also brought us several human bones on board," wrote Parkinson, "and offered them to sale, sucking them in their mouths, and, by the signs which they made to us, evinced that they thought human flesh delicious food. One day, in particular, they brought four skulls to sell; but they rated them very high."[48] The commerce in such bones of contention had already been well established at the time of Cook's first voyage, as Hawkesworth's account made clear: "The people here brought us out several human bones, the flesh of which they had eaten, and offered them to sale; for the curiosity of those among us who had purchased them as memorials of the horrid practice which many, notwithstanding the reports of travellers, have professed not to believe, had rendered them a kind of article of trade."[49] Moreover, throughout his writings, as when he described Pedro de Alvarado's conquest of Guatemala, Las Casas had long before noted how it might come to be that cannibalism among "natives" would in fact prove to be an act inspired by Europeans and thus one bearing "the royal seal of approval."[50]

Given this background, Cook's sentimental plaint for the condition of the New Zealanders—"we interduce among them wants and perhaps diseases which they never before knew"—proves to be thoroughly confused in its motivations. Is this expression of sympathetic feeling not also a form of laughter, of visceral revulsion, of self-serving reason? What tone should we attribute to this sentimental affection of the body when we see how Cook and his crew, fervently desiring to catch hold of the real thing at last, ended up grasping nothing but some whatnot that each had blindly held out to his one hand with his other? Or when the proof supposed to be a matter of eyewitness perception turns out to be an item of trade between peoples that was created out of dramatic role-playing on both sides? ("We fool each other," Raynal wrote, in describing how the natives engaged in trade with Europeans must laughingly attribute the same "imbecility" to the latter as these others do to them, "or rather neither one or the other of us is fooled.")[51] Here it becomes especially crucial to remember that, as Anthony Pagden puts it, "accusations of cannibalism have always gone both ways."[52] For instance, in his *Interesting Narrative of the Life of Olaudah Equiano or Gustavus Vassa, the*

African (1789), Equiano testified to his fear, when he was dragged into slavery, that he would be "eaten by those white men with horrible looks, red faces, and long hair." In his *Travels in the Interior Districts of Africa* (1795–97), Mungo Park reported similar reactions among the natives he encountered.[53] The least of the conclusions to be drawn in these circumstances is that for Wales to regard the event he witnessed as a New Zealand custom, pure and simple, was no less absurd than it would have been for Cook to regard that boy as being dead serious when he put excrement on a stick and offered it up as if it were something of pure fantasy, need, or value.

It would seem that none of these adventurers had ever read *Robinson Crusoe* (1719), or at least had not read it with profit; for from beginning to end, *Robinson Crusoe* pursues the recognition that Europeans eat cannibals. The historical question of the originary incitement to and participation in any particular incident of cannibalism here becomes secondary to the more fundamental question of the meaning of this term in any case. It was Defoe's genius to suggest that cannibalism is nothing more or less than society with the middleman cut out: unmediated sociality. In this novel the image of cannibalism confronts us with the contradiction at the heart of all systematic ethicopolitical reasoning: the terrible banality of the fact that the logic of self-preservation is bound to be articulated at the expense of designated others whose survival will not be held so dear. Set one Adamic individual into relation with another, as in the parable of the lord and the bondsman that Hegel would develop in his *Phenomenology of Spirit* (1807), and communication immediately becomes a question of consumption. It is as if the reign of appetite Thomas Hobbes imagined as the state of nature were to be taken in its narrowest and most literal sense, and hence at its most fantastic. This state of things is wonderfully set forth when Crusoe first sees a footprint on the isle he has claimed as his own and immediately leaps to the conclusion that it might indicate the presence of Satan or (what he considers an even worse possibility) a cannibal. "How strange a Chequer-Work of Providence is the Life of Man!" he exclaims. "To Day we love what to Morrow we hate . . . for I whose only Affliction was, that I seem'd banished from human Society . . . [so] that to have seen one of my own Species, would have seem'd to me a Raising me from Death to Life, and the greatest Blessing that Heaven it self, next to the supreme Blessing of Salvation, could bestow; *I say*, that I should now tremble at the very Apprehensions of seeing a Man, and was ready to sink into the Ground at but the Shadow or silent Appearance of a Man's having set his Foot in the Island."[54]

To render the question of one's own species as coterminous with the question of cannibalism is effectively to destroy any matter-of-fact understanding of either term. If it is to be at least minimally coherent, the concept of cannibalism depends upon the prior assurance of a concept of the species. The journal attributed to James Matra takes note of this point in offering reflections on the evidence of cannibalism witnessed on Cook's first voyage: "I would however hope, for the honour of mankind, that this savage practice has been produced among them only from the grossest depravation of human nature; for in its primitive state I should be sorry to believe it would feel no repugnance at a meal, which brutes will not make on the bodies of their own species."[55] It is precisely this assurance of the species, however, that Crusoe finds unavailable in the "Chequer-Work" of Providence.

Crusoe continues to use the word *cannibal,* as he does the word *Providence,* as if they still must signify. Yet the implications of his first encounter with the sign of another being, a being seemingly human and yet uncertain not only in species but in ontological status, becomes even more disturbing as the novel proceeds. Crusoe turns out to be the middleman in a society of one— or perhaps two—in either case, in a society without middlemen. Therefore, he is brought to recognize the autocannibalism of humankind and to experience in his own person the dissolution of categorical distinctions among fantasies, needs, and values. So he writes, "In the middle of these Cogitations, Apprehensions and Reflections, it came into my Thought one Day, that all this might be a meer Chimera of my own; and that this Foot might be the Print of my own Foot . . . and that if at last this was only the Print of my own Foot, I had play'd the Part of those Fools, who strive to make stories of Spectres, and Apparitions; and then are frighted at them more than any body" (124).

His subsequent judgment that the footprint was real will prove a distinction without a difference to Crusoe, for every step that he might take to define and resolve the threat of cannibalism in the world around him will reflect back on his own desires and on his status as a son of European history. He is a son all the more exemplary for the prodigal errancy that took him out of the security of the middling rank of life so as to cast his identity into the closed circuit of adventurer-merchant-slave-colonist-slaver-king-bourgeois gentleman. Surveying the landscape of his world, he finds that it will not suffer itself to remain fixed before his eyes but instead must appear as the unstable and ultimately incoherent map of desire that is entirely his own and yet again not his at all:

> As long as I kept up my daily Tour to the Hill, to look out; so long also I kept up the Vigour of my Design, and my Spirits seem'd to be all the while in a suitable Form, for so outragious an Execution as the killing twenty or thirty naked Savages, for an Offence which I had not at all entred into a Discussion of in my Thoughts. . . . But now . . . my Opinion of the Action it self began to alter. . . . What Authority, or Call I had, to pretend to be Judge and Executioner upon these Men as Criminals, whom Heaven had thought fit for so many Ages to suffer unpunish'd. . . . How do I know what God himself judges in this particular Case. . . . They do not know it to be an Offence, and then commit it in Defiance of Divine Justice, as we do in almost all the Sins we commit, They think it no more a Crime to kill a Captive taken in War, than we do to kill an Ox; nor to eat humane Flesh, than we do to eat Mutton. (133–34)

What is more, he finds inscribed in his desires the history of the Spanish conquest of the New World, with devastating consequences to his sense of his own species, not to mention his nationality and religion. Reflecting further upon his hostile intent, he writes, "In the next Place it occurr'd to me, that . . . this would justify the Conduct of the *Spaniards* in all their Barbarities practis'd in *America,* where they destroy'd Millions of these People, who however they were Idolaters and Barbarians, and had several bloody and barbarous Rites in their Customs, such as sacrificing human Bodies to their Idols, were yet, as to the *Spaniards,* very innocent People" (134).

With this turn in Crusoe's thinking, the way Defoe adapted one of the urtexts of his novel, the history of Alexander Selkirk, becomes especially interesting. As recounted in the narrative of Woodes Rogers, *A Cruising Voyage Round the World* (1712), the story of Selkirk said nothing of his having felt a fear of cannibals during the period that he was a castaway on the island of Juan Fernandez. What he did say he had feared was being captured and enslaved by Spaniards to work in their mines in the New World.[56] In splitting this fear of enslavement and economic exploitation at the hands of Spaniards into two halves—a narrative background that still recalled Selkirk's and a foreground in which this mariner's fear of the Spanish was turned into Crusoe's terror of being eaten by cannibals—Defoe perfectly anticipated the nature of Captain James Cook and other modern characters. We see in this example how the mystery of modern character serves to divert attention from events of destruction and war so that these events may seem to represent an aberration of human identity, not the historical mechanism of its social and cultural formations. The psychology and aesthetics of mystery consume the historical politics of mastery.

The appearance of contradiction that makes modern characters so fascinating is just this mystery of transubstantiation. The bloody lines of historical violence are retraced as a psychology of desire said to be wrought through the teleology of each and every individual's flesh. By reducing the issue of cannibalism to the question of the cannibal within every human being, this transubstantiation makes it possible for theory to discipline violence, bringing it under categories—such as those of anthropology, psychology, and philosophy—that can offer it a civilized home. Thus it is that a contributor to the *Encyclopédie* (1751–65) could quite comfortably allow that once upon a time "most peoples ate human flesh." This judgment would be echoed in the works of other writers, such as Cornelius de Pauw, who became one of Sade's favorite sources.[57] One of the more extreme examples of this naturalizing of historical violence, which anticipates the writings of Thomas Malthus, appeared in a work by Jean-Baptiste-René Robinet, *Of Nature* (1761). If it were not for the population control that nature provides in the forms of disease and war, Robinet argued, we would all be thrown into the cannibalistic desperation of people starving in ships becalmed at sea. "It costs humanity much less to kill an enemy in the heat of an action," he observed, "than to slaughter a parent or friend in cold blood so as to feed on his bloody limbs!"[58] In these words Robinet suggested that politics is just cannibalism by other means, and yet his frankness in drawing this connection was undercut by his attribution of this violence to the nature of things. The irony is that a confession of bloodthirstiness in this form might actually strengthen one's confidence in the progress of enlightened civilization.

In writing of his experiences on Cook's second voyage, Forster would reproduce this enlightened attitude in assuring his readers that cannibalism "must after some time be laid aside as a custom which is inconsistent with itself."[59] His argument was that this custom must logically lead, whether through losses in battles or repeated victories, to the recognition "that a living man is more useful than one that is dead or roasted" (214). In his scientific manner he differed from Crusoe in his approach to the world, and so he sought to illuminate those workings of Providence that Crusoe had felt obliged to leave as a mysterious "Chequer-Work." Nevertheless, he still followed this predecessor in taking cannibalism as a basis on which to construct a providential history through a general psychology of desire that could equally comprehend the peoples of New Zealand and those "who are used to live in better regulated societies, where, for many years backwards, anthropophagy has been in disuse." He concluded,

If we examine the whole economy of their societies, we find that their education is the chief cause of all these enormities. The men train up the boys in a kind of liberty, which at last degenerates into licentiousness . . . [and] this naturally brings on an irascibility, which, in the men, cannot brook any controul, action or word, that can be construed, according to their manners and principles into an affront, or injury; inflamed by passion, they are impatient to wreak their vengeance. . . . They know not where to stop . . . and the corses of the slain immediately serve to glut the inhuman appetites of the conquerors. When the bounds of humanity are once passed, and the reverence due to the bright image of divinity, is conquered by frenzy, the practice soon becomes habitual, especially as it is reckoned among the honours due to the conqueror, to feast upon the wretched victims of savage victory; add to this, that a nation which has no other animal food, than a few stupid dogs and fish, will soon reconcile themselves to human flesh, which, according to several known instances, is reputed to be one of the most palatable dishes. (212–13)

To be sure, many in this era would not share in Forster's confidence. Edward Gibbon, for instance, was notably less in earnest when he suggested that the cannibalism attested to among the ancient Scots and Picts might offer grounds for optimism in regard to those peoples currently deemed savage. "If in the neighbourhood of the commercial and literary town of Glasgow a race of cannibals has really existed," he wrote, "we may contemplate in the period of the Scottish history the opposite extremes of savage and civilised life. Such reflections tend to enlarge the circle of our ideas, and to encourage the pleasing hope that New Zealand may produce in some future age the Hume of the Southern Hemisphere."[60] Moreover, the ironies developed over the past four centuries could be labyrinthine: it is not going too far to suggest that some readers of Hume in this time thought *him* the savage holding up a piece of human excrement on a stick and mocking, among other things, the elevation of the host and the bright image of divinity in man. Be that as it may, to see Defoe's fiction as a vital context to Forster's science is to recognize that in both forms of writing, cannibalism had been situated among human customs and thus assimilated to a psychology of the species. It had been moved out of the realm of incomprehensible savagery and into the realms of natural history and education. (In this regard, the ease with which Crusoe permanently cures Friday of his cannibalistic tastes, simply by giving him some roasted young goat to eat [166], anticipates Forster's faith in inevitable progress.) The old rhetoric would still appear—"unnatural," "inhumane," and so on—but in a context that drove this language to interrogate, challenge, and even curse the authority presumed to found it. So Cook would be brought to conclude of the New Zealanders, "Notwithstanding they are *Cannibals*, they are naturaly of a good disposission and have not a little share of humanity" (*Voyage*, 578). Similarly, Forster emphatically insisted, against polygenetic theories of human origin, that "all mankind, though ever so much varied, are, however, but of one species" and, indeed, "are descended from one couple" (*Observations*, 175).

This attitude was generalized in one of the recurrent features in the travel narratives of this era: the European's encounter with a disgusting foreign diet. In many instances this was dog meat (to which, however, most explorers seemed to accommodate themselves rather easily).[61] In any case, the gastronomical outrage came to be placed on a continuum with human flesh, which, after all, as everyone ritually acknowledged, would sometimes be a dish to which civilized persons would turn. (So Crusoe is brought to reflect, after seeing a European vessel and imagining that its men might have been swept away when they attempted to land on his island in one of the ship's boats, "that perhaps they might by this Time think of starving, and of being in a Condition to eat one another" [146]). At times such references appear very self-conscious, as when John Martin inserts a footnote in his account of the adventures of William Mariner in order to correct the assumption that the Pacific islanders' habit of eating raw fish is "revolting": "If we eat the oyster raw, why not other fish?"[62] As it happens, in noting this example Martin truly ought to have been self-conscious, for he was reiterating the starting point from which Robert Boyle had set out to challenge the common view of cannibalism. In "Upon the Eating of Oysters" (1665), Boyle had added to the arguments popularized by Montaigne—as of the diversity of customs and the relativity of cruelty—an emphasis on nature as physically conceived. "To count [cannibals] so barbarous merely upon the score of feeding upon man's flesh and blood," he said, "is to forget, that woman's milk, by which alone we feed our sucking children, is, according to the received opinion, but blanched blood." He also emphasized the use of human flesh (known as "mummy") in medicine, as well as the forms in which his readers—in devouring oysters whole, for instance—commonly made excrement part of their diets.[63]

Like his emphasis on excrement, Boyle's identification of nursing with cannibalism went rather further than others were prepared to go. Nonetheless, attention to raw or unusual animal foods does run through travel narratives in this era as a kind of leitmotif telling of the comprehensibility, and even hinting at the allure, of the eating of human flesh. This sense of cannibalism as belonging to a gastronomic continuum was also disseminated through popular works whose settings were far removed from the New World. In Tobias Smollett's *Adventures of Peregrine Pickle* (1751), for instance, we are told of a physician who observes "that the Negroes on the coast of Guinea, who are a healthy and vigorous people, prefer cats and dogs to all other fare." This character then goes on to make the commonplace reference to "several sieges, during which the inhabitants, who were blocked up, lived upon these animals, and had recourse even to human flesh, which, to his certain knowledge, was in all respects preferable to pork; for, in the course of his studies, he had, for the experiment's sake, eaten a steak cut from the buttock of a person who had been hanged." Repulsed, two of his auditors run out of the room, so violently jostling each other "that both were overturned by the shock, which also contributed to the effect of their nausea, that mutually defiled them as they lay."[64] This nausea, however, tells of something other than simple disgust. As it reworks a scene from *Don Quixote*,[65] this conclusion is but the punch line to the set-up of the whole scene: Peregrine's effort to lead his companions to suppose that unbeknownst to themselves, they had just been dining on cat meat. The joke is on the fleeing men, whose disgust at the doctor's words, which led them to mutter "Cannibal" and "abomination" as they were about to make their disastrous exit, marks them out as deserving victims rather than civilized Christians. Smollett's readers are led to identify neither with the doctor nor with these men but rather with the structure of Peregrine's joke, in which disgust appears as the locus of excitement, pleasure, and exuberant cultural invention.

Here again *Robinson Crusoe* is exemplary. From his presentation of that first encounter with the footprint on to the end of the narrative, Defoe goes to great lengths to show his protagonist's attraction to that which he must consider utterly revolting. Crusoe implicates himself in the violence of cannibalism as both subject and object, showing himself to be attracted both to the image of eating human flesh and to that of being eaten. The first tendency shows itself in the hyperbolic certainty with which he feels the threat of cannibalism before and beyond all evidence—in this respect acting again as an exemplary figure of modern Western man. This tendency is further shown in his reaction to this imagined threat, which takes the form of obsessive fantasizing about the prospect of being eaten by cannibals and equally about the possibility of a murderous revenge that he himself comes to see as imitative, in its irrational bloodthirstiness, of the very practice to which he pronounces himself so viscerally opposed. "It would take up a larger Volume than this whole Work is intended to be," he says, "to set down all the Contrivances I hatch'd, or rather brooded upon in my Thought, for the destroying these Creatures, or at least frightening them, so as to prevent their coming hither any more." He adds, "This Fancy pleas'd my Thoughts for some Weeks, and I was so full of it, that I often dream'd of it" (132). His position does vacillate, as when he sees evidence of a cannibal feast and forgets all his previous cautions: "Nor did I consider at all, that if I kill'd one Party, suppose Ten, or a Dozen, I was still the next Day, or Week, or Month, to kill another, and so another, even *ad infinitum*, till I should be at length no less a Murtherer than they were in being Man-eaters; and perhaps much more so" (144). Despite his occasional reversions to an attitude of unthinking hostility, however, it still may seem logical to close readers of his adventures that there should come a moment in his feverish imaginings when he turns full circle and willingly offers himself to be eaten.

This moment occurs when Crusoe parleys with a mariner from a Spanish vessel that has suffered a mutiny near his island. He who had "turn'd away [his] Face from the horrid Spectacle" of a cannibal feast, who had even been on the point of fainting until "Nature discharg'd the Disorder from [his] Stomach" (129), now constructs a narrative for himself in which he welcomes the prospect of being devoured. "I told him it would be very hard," he writes, "that I should be the Instrument of their Deliverance, and that they should afterwards make me their Prisoner in *New Spain,* where an *English* Man was certain to be made a Sacrifice . . . and that I had rather be deliver'd up to the *Savages,* and be devour'd alive, than fall into the merciless Claws of the Priests, and be carry'd into the *Inquisition*" (190).

Although this admission of desire is presented as a hypothetical next-to-worst case, this qualification is a flimsy excuse for Defoe's protagonist once again to luxuriate in the image of being eaten. That this is so is evident not only from the ambivalence that has complicated Crusoe's relation to cannibalism from its first mention in this narrative but also from the way this ostensibly figurative and extreme comparison has been made dramatically necessary by his entire history, which brings him into such intimate dependence on the enslaved cannibal, Friday. This revolution in his identifications was established when his meditations on Friday led him into the indigestible question of "why it has pleas'd God to hide . . . saving Knowledge from so many Millions of Souls, who if [he] might judge by this poor Savage, would make a much better use of it" than Europeans had (163). Given this recognition, Crusoe's excited fantasies of murder, like his restorative discharge at the remains of the cannibal feast, may even come to seem a form of sexual release— and so we are well on our way to Sade's allegories of desire.

Defoe established a ground for the understanding of cannibalism that further developed the arguments made by Las Casas. Whereas Swift's "Modest Proposal" and Voltaire's *Candide* followed the lines of representation codified by Montaigne, in which the image of cannibalism is made a source of urbane irony, Defoe portrayed it as a nexus of desire. This is such desire as Atkins glimpsed, though only with puzzlement, in one of the authors he discussed: "*La Hontan,* or some other *French* Translation I have read, talking of *Canibals* bordering on *Canada,* flies into a strange *Gallicism,* and makes them commend the Flesh of a *Frenchman* (sad Partiality) in Eating, as of finer Taste than that of an *Englishman.*"[66] Going beyond the example of Las Casas, Defoe let this recognition of the physical excitement of the cannibal scenario stain every page of his work. Crusoe's fluid anxieties, fantasies, dreams, wishes, confusions, and inconsistencies all seep into one another to suggest an erotics of cannibalism natural to humankind in general, despite all the disavowals that hem it about.

Defoe thus prepared the ground for works such as Heinrich von Kleist's *Penthesilea* (1807), which would insert male and female figures into the cannibal dialectics of the master and the slave. Elaborating a fatal harmony between kisses and bites, love and war, this drama brings Penthesilea to meditate over the body of Achilles, slain by her hand:

> Think how often it's the case,
> with her arms wound around her darling's neck, a woman
> says she loves him, oh, so much she's ready
> to *devour* him for love. But then when it
> comes down to it, the poor fool finds
> she's had a bellyful of him already.
> Well, my darling, that was not my way.
> You see: when I wound *my* arms around your neck
> I did exactly that, devour you.
> I wasn't such a mad one as might seem.[67]

This is also the territory that Joseph Conrad would resituate in the Congo, where Marlow, as if he had heard of the boast of that Frenchman mentioned by Atkins, at one point comes to worry that his flesh might not look appetizing to his cannibal workmen.[68] Around this same time Freud would turn this territory into the ground of psychoanalysis, in which cannibalistic behavior is fixed as the first stage of erotic development and therefore as a regressive tendency in both the individual and the species. Whether directly or indirectly, in Freudian theory we see the influence of Defoe, Forster, and other eighteenth-century theorists of cannibalism, just as contemporary anthropological theory finds its groundwork in the speculations of this era.

In terms of the topic of cannibalism, Freud's reliance on the presumed coherence of the species is comparable to the anthropological reliance on the cultural boundary. Just as the cultural boundary may seem inadequate to the undisciplined questions raised in the writings of Las Casas and further developed by Defoe, so may the coherence of the species seem more wish than reality in the context of this heritage as it ripened into the work of the Marquis de Sade. Las Casas came to the brink of imagining a world in which the species would be rendered incoherent by differences of language: a world in which the incalculable duration necessary for full communication to take place would forever be cut short by violence. In the aftermath of the genocidal Spanish conquest that Las Casas so futilely sought to end, Defoe imagined a world in which violence did not so much divide as define the human species. He made violence appear so definitive, in fact, that the determination of the concept of the species had to be deferred to an ultimately inexplicable Providence; a concomitant "secret Communication between those embody'd, and those unembody'd" (*Crusoe*, 138); and a pragmatic determination, no less resolute for being rationally and spiritually unaccountable, to keep the upper hand over all those with whom one might happen to fall into company, be they cannibal or Christian or both.

In Sade's writings, then, communication of the sort for which Las Casas struggled and mastery of the kind desired by Crusoe are simply treated as the fantasies that they acknowledge themselves to be in any case. The implications of this acknowledgment are traced out to their logical conclusions, one of which is that the very notion of the human species, much less of a model of desire or development proper to it, is patently absurd. As Noirceuil puts it in *The History of Juliette* (1797), the idea of fraternity is founded on nothing but "a rationalization as futile as would be that of the lamb to the wolf: *You should not eat me, because I have four feet like you*" (*Juliette*, 8:174). He goes on to say, "The sentiment of humanity is chimerical; it can never restrain passions any more than needs, as one sees in the sieges in which men mutually devour each other" (8:186).

In Sade's writings those things held on high in the exchanges between Europeans and cannibals—excrement, host, and human flesh—are treated as one. Like the anthropological categories of value, fantasy, and need, these objects of trade, transcendence, and anatomy are represented in such a way that the categorical distinctions among them utterly dissolve together with the concomitant borderlines of culture and human nature. In place of *Robinson Crusoe's* closed circuit of character, which erodes the distinctions among adventurers, merchants, slaves, colonists, slavers, kings, and bourgeois gentlemen, we meet with an even more claustrophobic closed circuit of money, sex, and food. The foreign cannibal that Las Casas and Defoe had turned into the cannibal within here becomes a general condition of cannibalism in nature that leaves the world *sans loi* and *sans foi,* if not exactly *sans roi*—for all that remains as a differentiating principle is a drive toward sovereignty that knows no bounds either within or without humanity.

In this world the cannibal feast is the best of all possible meals. In the words of one of the characters in Sade's *Juliette,* "What a mistake it is to despise this flesh! There is none more delicate or better in the world, and savages have good reason to prefer it to all others" (9:292–93).[69] Minski, the giant Russian cannibal, praises not only the taste but the nutritive value of this food:

> It is true that the extreme quantity of human flesh on which I nourish myself helps greatly to augment and thicken the seminal matter. Anyone who tries this regime will assuredly triple his libidinal powers, even aside from the force, the healthiness, and the freshness this nourishment provides for in itself. I am not talking to you of my own approbation: it should suffice you to know that once one has tasted it, it is no longer possible to eat anything else, and that there is not one meat of animals or of fish that can compare to this. It is simply a matter of vanquishing the initial repugnance; that barrier having been cleared, one can no longer restrain oneself. (*Juliette,* 8:559–60)

Even those who do not go as far as Minski are bound to discover, in Sade's world, that the uncertain line between kisses and bites so completely gives way as to make risible the notion of any act that does not logically tend toward the universal imperative of cannibalism.

As he always insisted, Sade had good warrant for this identification of cannibalism and philosophy. For instance, as Susan Meld Shell has noted in writing of one of Kant's early treatises, *Dreams of a Spirit Seer, Elucidated by Dreams of Metaphysics* (1766), "Kant's reason for rejecting Descartes's identification of the soul with a specific portion of the body is as follows: if one were to locate the soul in a specific place, one could no longer distinguish it with certainty from the raw ground stuff of bodily natures. . . . In that case the idea jokingly proposed by Leibniz 'that we may be swallowing in our coffee atoms destined to become human lives' would 'no longer be a laughing matter [*Gedanke zum Lachen*].'"[70] It is this extended sense of carnal appetite, which Kant also made literal in his image of unsanctified sexual intercourse, that Sade embraced. What is more, Sade did, after all, manage to make it a laughing matter, noting that the sanctimonious turning away from this appetite was always made in the name of the greatest cannibal of all, the Christian God who devours his children with a Saturnian relish. "The *vampire* sucks the blood of corpses," he wrote, "God causes that of men to run, both of them prove chimerical upon examination: is it wrong to lend the one the name of the other?" (*Juliette*, 8:46n).[71]

Sade did not cite Kant, but he did seek to align his writing with that of predecessors such as Hobbes, Montesquieu, and La Mettrie.[72] True, his references to their work are as unsystematic as is his conception of human physiology, which combines vitalism, materialism, the Cartesian theory of animal spirits, the Hallerian doctrine of irritability, and vague assumptions about electricity and the ether. To call this undisciplined hodgepodge philosophy might then seem to be dignifying it far beyond its deserts. However, just as the work of Las Casas might be seen as challenging the premises of the contemporary discipline of anthropology, and the work of Defoe those of psychoanalysis, so may Sade's appear as a challenge to the disciplining of philosophy. In appropriating the name of philosophy for cannibalism, in making cannibalism not only the ideal gastronomical but also the exemplary intellectual act, Sade ventured to think of what philosophy might be without the dignity of mastery—which, as Las Casas and Defoe had made clear, is another name for what gets called humanity. Stanley Cavell, the well-known contemporary philosopher, may still be correct in one of his statements relevant to this topic—"So I gather that no one is in a position to say what the right expression is of our knowledge that we are strung out on both sides of a belly"[73]—but Sade did at least demand that any philosophy worthy of the name must confront this frustration.

Moreover, Sade's representation of cannibalism arose out of an eighteenth-century context in which cannibalism had become, in the popular sense of the word, a philosophical matter. Although his fiercely aggrieved tone was distinctively personal, Crozet was typical of this era in his identification of philosophers as persons who threatened to turn cannibalism into a nonissue. The cannibal had come to signify the lengths to which philosophers would go in their refusal to accept the common sense and gut feelings of ordinary human beings. In some cases, as in Sparrman's narrative, this involved an identification of philosophers as those who were skeptical that such a thing as cannibalism existed. More generally, especially in the second half of the eighteenth century, the case was put in an even more extreme form. The philosopher was he who would go so far as to find the cannibal not simply explicable or pardonable but rational in his tastes. All those travelers' tales, voyages, colonial narratives, and missionary reports, together with the cases, both real and compulsively imagined, of the behavior of starving persons, had been distilled into this popular impression of the philosopher as the cannibal's apologist. "Since more numerous facts, more impressive testimonies, and more authentic accounts have dissipated the doubts" about the reality of cannibalism, Raynal wrote, "we have seen philosophers who would try to justify this practice of savage peoples. . . . They have thought that it is a matter of indifference whether a cadaver should be devoured by a man or by a vulture."[74] It was this sort of characterization that prepared the way for the libertine and materialist philosophe in Nicolas Réstif de la Bretonne's *The Perverted Peasant Girl* (1787) to compare himself to "the most barbarous of anthropophagi"—an accusation he goes on to dismiss on the grounds of its crudeness, not of its inaccuracy.[75]

The likes of Léry, Montaigne, and Boyle lay behind this image of the philosopher, although in this time it came to be most closely associated with the name of Voltaire. So widespread was this image that we may find the passages on this subject from Raynal's history and Crozet's narrative mirrored in the journal of a common midshipman, serving on Cook's first voyage, who alluded to Voltaire when writing of the natives of New Zealand:

> Perhaps they thought, like a celebrated philosopher, that it was as well to feed on the bodies of their enemies, (for by their own accounts they eat no other) as to leave them to be devoured by crows. . . . Some gentlemen, who never left their own homes, have ventured, on the strength of speculative reasoning, to question the veracity of those travellers who have published accounts of cannibals in Africa and America; treating as falsehoods every relation, which, from their ignorance of human nature, appears to them improbable: but let them not indulge the same freedom on this occasion; the fact will be too well attested to be rendered doubtful by their visionary impertinent objections.[76]

Even more worriedly, Hawkesworth, too, addressed this rapprochement of cannibals and philosophers. Perhaps envisaging a more educated audience for his work than the one contemplated by Crozet and the anonymous midshipman, he felt it impossible simply to dismiss the argument of "some who wish to appear speculative and philosophical, that whether the dead body of an enemy be eaten or buried, is in itself a matter perfectly indifferent; as it is, whether the breasts and thighs of a woman should be covered or naked; and that prejudice and habit only make us shudder at the violation of custom in one instance, and blush at it in the other." Reasoning in the same way as Raynal did, he still found cause to oppose this behavior: "it may safely be affirmed, that the practice of eating human flesh, whatever it may be in itself, is relatively, and in its consequences, most pernicious."[77] The fact that such an unexceptional English mind felt pressed to concede this much ground to the name of philosophy, however, helps to indicate just how normal Sade was in his identification of cannibalism with philosophical demonstration. One might scorn this state of things, in the manner of Crozet; treat it gingerly, as Hawkesworth and Raynal did; or take it as the ground for ruthless criticism of "a philosophical age" characterized by general war and destruction, in the manner of De Pauw.[78] But wherever one might turn, the connection was unavoidable.

In *Aline and Valcour,* Sade enthusiastically brought forward this identification through the parallel figures of a "cannibalist European" and a "black philosopher" who are met by one of his protagonists in the course of various adventures in Africa. The former asserts that "it makes absolutely no difference whether it is the entrails of the earth or those of man that serve as the sepulcher to the disorganized elements" of human flesh after death; the latter explains the absurdity of the Catholic doctrine of transubstantiation. The result is to establish the seemingly irrefutable lesson that "anthropophagy is certainly not a crime" but rather a "practice indifferent in itself" (*Aline et Valcour,* 5:198, 59, 4:198n). Just as Sade aligned himself with philosophers in this fashion, he joined with Smollett in rewriting that same farcical scene from *Don Quixote* in which Don Quixote and Sancho Panza vomit on each other. In Sade's version this scene is all about the erotic ecstasy that two characters feel in discharging the contents of their bellies into each other's mouth—a point pressed even further in the following scene, in which a monk has his meal "thrust into the open cunt of his dulcinea" in preparation for its consumption.[79]

In promoting his philosophical attitude, Sade sought further to assert his normality through a favorite narrative device: the list of anthropological and historical precedents for various soi-disant crimes that all converge upon the image of cannibalism. One such list, which is put into the mouth of the pope in a conversation with Juliette, mentions that "the New Zealanders and many other peoples eat their enemies" and then accords an equivalent mention, in the same list, to the conquistadors excoriated by Las Casas and Crusoe. "Who could number the Indians sacrificed by the Spaniards in their conquest of the New World?" (*Juliette*, 9:192–93), the pope asks rhetorically. Here as elsewhere in *Juliette*, none other than Captain James Cook is cited as one of those providing the evidence for the argument at hand.[80] It is only logical, then, that after encountering the members of a sentimentally perfect peasant family—the domestic equivalent to the noble savages of Tahiti—Juliette should compare herself to "the Caribes," from whose encounters with Europeans we get the very name of the cannibal, when she describes the immense pleasure she took in destroying this family. "And so behold what murder is," she says: "a bit of disorganized matter, some changes in combinations, some molecules broken and plunged back into the crucible of nature, which in a few days will render them into another earthly form—and where then is the evil in that? If I take life from one, I give it to another: where then is the harm that I do him?" (8:399).

In his hodgepodge of history, anthropology, theology, philosophy, science, and literature, in which characters, even when they are not literally eating each other's flesh, are forever defecating, vomiting, pissing, bleeding, and ejaculating in each other's mouths, we find Sade working his way through to the logic of excrement, host, human flesh—whatnot—raised up in any articulation of culture. Thus, describing her orgy in St. Peter's with the pope, whom she would also and not incidentally disengage from considerable wealth, Juliette says, "Once the host was consecrated, the acolyte carried it over the platform and respectfully deposited it on the head of the papal cock; as soon as he saw it there, the fellow stuck it in my ass. . . . Sodomized by the Pope, the body of Jesus Christ in my ass, O my friends, what pleasures! It seemed to me that never in my life had I enjoyed myself so much. We fell back exhausted in the midst of the divine objects of luxury that surrounded us, and the sacrifice was completed." A new mass is celebrated a bit later, after some refreshment and regrouping; and this time, "carried on the most beautiful cock in the room, the host was introduced into the ass of the Holy Father," who subsequently sodomizes and sacrifices a fourteen-year-old boy.

"Finally this scoundrel, drunk with luxury, tore out the heart of that child and devoured it as he spilled his seed" (9:206–7).

In contrast to the image of the machine in the Enlightenment, in its potentially endless proliferation of identifications, the image of cannibalism tended to incorporate all identifications, beginning and ending with its own. The machine might press its image upon plants, animals, organs, humans, and everything else in the universe; the cannibal swallowed the distinctions among such things. In place of the recursive identificatory modeling provided by the machine, we have the progressive destruction of identity imaged through the cannibal. The machine is the technological abstraction of the cannibal; the cannibal, the sensuous realization of the machine. Through their techno-organic conjuncture the Enlightenment would nourish later figures such as Alfred Jarry, the creator of *Ubu roi*, founder of pataphysics, and inspiration to the cultural movements of dada and surrealism.

The machine, which could suggest the imaginary closure of ideology, also served to represent the visceral displacements at the heart of any experience of identity. Correlatively, the image of the cannibal bodied forth the potential dissolution of humanity while yet making it possible to imagine a teleology of mastery extending from the psychology of individuals to the history of all civilizations. (In the case of Sade, the result is that his critique of colonial exploitation as cannibalism tends to be undone by his own exploitation of cannibalism as eroticism.)[81] Like the noble and the evil savage, which worked together to secure the self-reflection of Europeans, the sublimely modern machine and the inconceivably primitive cannibal were fundamentally as one in the Western imagination. Beyond the Enlightenment, their conjuncture would reappear not only in Jarry's work but also in the dog-eat-dog world of the late-nineteenth- and early-twentieth-century movement of naturalism, in which organic nature is typically portrayed as a man-eating machine.

Blithely abusing the very evidence that he cites, which would suggest that cannibalism generally is a limited, ritualized, systematic practice, and taking the European consumption of cannibals to its logical extreme, Sade drives his characters to eat disgust. In doing so he forces into view the incoherence internal to the very concept of cannibalism, which depends on an impossibly narrow conception of "eating" and an impossibly broad conception of one's "own kind." The world is then made visceral in its every dimension, with no ultimate distinctions between exteriority and interiority.[82] Because a drive for sovereignty animates absolutely everything, throughout every level of its being, no object can save itself from falling into the (non)category of whatnot, as at the meal Juliette enjoys at the end of a murderous orgy: "And there, naked, smeared with semen and blood, drunk with luxury, we carried our ferocity to the point of mixing our food with bits of flesh pulled by our hands from the bodies of those unfortunates on the table. Gorged with murder and shamelessness, we finally fell on top of each other in the midst of the cadavers and in a deluge of wines, liqueurs, shit, semen, bits of human flesh. I do not know what we became" (*Juliette*, 9:324). The quintessential Sadean setting may then be found, as in *The Hundred and Twenty Days of Sodom* (ca. 1785), "in the depths of the entrails of the earth" (13:48). Similarly, the quintessential Sadean carnal act may be revealed as one that kills two individuals by viscerally binding them to each other: "One fellow extracted the entrails of a young boy and a young girl, put the entrails of the boy in the body of the girl and those of the girl in the body of the boy, then sewed the wounds back up, lay them back to back within a structure that contained them, and having placed himself between the two of them, watched them die" (13:411).[83]

This is where Hegel comes in and proves himself no less concerned than Sade to illustrate the knowledge of the mouth, the teeth, the tongue. For Hegel, wisdom begins with the act of consumption:

> We can tell those who assert the truth and certainty of the reality of sense objects that they should go back to the most elementary school of wisdom, *viz.* the ancient Eleusinian Mysteries of Ceres and Bacchus, and that they have still to learn the secret meaning of the eating of bread and the drinking of wine. For he who is initiated into these Mysteries not only comes to doubt the being of sensuous things, but to despair of it; in part he brings about the nothingness of such things himself in his dealings with them, and in part he sees them reduce themselves to nothingness. Even the animals are not shut out from this wisdom but, on the contrary, show themselves to be most profoundly initiated into it; for they do not just stand idly in front of sensuous things as if these possessed intrinsic being, but, despairing of their reality, and completely assured of their nothingness, they fall to without ceremony and eat them. And all Nature, like the animals, celebrates these open Mysteries which teach the truth about sensuous things.[84]

According to Hegel, the dialectic of reason can be described as incorporation in every aspect of existence. So he describes how the individual achieves his "formative education" by "devouring his inorganic nature, and taking possession of it for himself" (16). Similarly, Hegel says of "human law in its universal existence" that it "*is, moves,* and *maintains* itself by consuming and absorbing into itself the separatism of the Penates, or the separation into independent families presided over by womankind" (287–88).

In the *Aufhebung* we find the expression of this teleology of consumption articulated at every level of being from that of the least inorganic particles of matter to the mind of God. Famously untranslatable, *Aufhebung* is usually paraphrased as a process in which something is at once canceled and raised higher or taken over and yet preserved. In effect, it is the progressive world-making movement of desire that Freud would seek to decompose into the distinct mechanisms of introjection, condensation, sublimation, and idealization, among others. If we attend to the way Hegel's writings sought to synthesize the intertwined figures of the machine and the cannibal that had so dominated the human image in the age of Enlightenment, however, the *Aufhebung* might more aptly be termed the motormouth of his philosophy, and the labor of the negative its autocannibalistic principle. Such a description is not fanciful, or at least no more fanciful than the figures of speech favored by Hegel himself. As he put it in his *Encyclopedia of the Philosophical Sciences in Outline* (1817), "The abstract process of living individuality is the process of inner formation in which the organism converts its own members into a nonorganic nature, into means, and feeds on itself. Thus it produces precisely this totality of its self-organization, so that each member is reciprocally the end and the means, and maintains itself through the others and in opposition to them. It is the process which has the simple feeling of self as a result."[85]

On the one hand, the activity of reason is completely comparable to the mechanistic process of eating. "Just as the instinct of the animal seeks and consumes food, but thereby brings forth nothing other than itself," he writes, "so too the instinct of Reason in its quest finds only Reason itself" (*Phenomenology,* 157). Even in animals, however, this "mechanical seizure of the external object is only the beginning of the unification of the object with the living animal." We must recognize that the activities of consuming and digesting food disrupt "the generality and simple self-relation of the living

[175]

organism" so as to manifest the dialectical interrelation of that which is posited as being internal and external (*Encyclopedia*, 191–92). In human beings as distinct from animals, this process must prove radically divisive. "The animal finishes up with the feeling of self. The instinct of Reason, on the other hand, is at the same time self-consciousness; but because it is only instinct it is put on one side over against consciousness, in which it has its antithesis. Its satisfaction is, therefore, shattered by this antithesis" (*Phenomenology*, 157).

Whereas eating fulfills human beings insofar as they are animals, reason fulfills them only by eating away at them in the very moment of their apparent satisfaction and so propelling them forward. It is because of this argument that Hegel would object to the theory of medicine popularized in the eighteenth century. He saw it as being based on "formal and material relationships" and as aiming "to reduce all differences in the organism to the formalism of a merely quantitative differentiation, involving increase and decrease, strengthening and weakening." He insisted that medicine instead must recognize that "the absolute form, the concept and the principle of life, has for its soul only the qualitative difference which consumes itself in itself" (*Encyclopedia*, 189). In accordance with this reasoning, in Hegel's most famous allegory the agency of the future is found to lie within the slave, who is destined to triumph over the master because the latter can feel satisfied while the former cannot. The self in the initial stages of self-consciousness "relates only negatively to the selfless object and the object is thereby merely consumed" because "desire is in its satisfaction always destructive and selfish." This satisfaction is bound to contradict itself, however, leading to the "struggle for recognition and subjugation under a master," which in its turn leads to "the substance of all true spiritual life, of the family, the fatherland, the state, and of all virtues,—love, friendship, bravery, honor, fame" (*Encyclopedia*, 220–22).

Whereas Sade's writings followed the line of representation epitomized by Las Casas, in which cannibalism ceases to be barbaric in and of itself, Hegel's writings, in which the brutality of cannibalism becomes a starting point for critical reflection, followed in the tradition set forth by Montaigne. As the historical outrage of the Bishop of Chiapas was brought to a perverse conclusion in the furious orgies imagined by the Divine Marquis, the unpretentious irony of Montaigne was brought to a perverse conclusion in the systematic exposition of the labor of negativity imagined by Hegel. Sade so fully identified the cannibal with the philosopher as to put the former in the position of teaching the latter his business; Hegel so fully identified the cannibal with the philosopher as to make the existence of the former completely insignificant in any creation in which the latter exists. In the introduction to his *Lectures on the Philosophy of World History* (ca. 1830), Hegel established this point in reference to the character he ascribed to Africans:

> Cannibalism at once strikes us as utterly barbarous and revolting, and we instinctively reject it. But we cannot speak of instinct in the case of human beings, for such reactions have a spiritual quality about them. All men who have progressed even to a limited extent in consciousness have respect for human beings as such. In an abstract sense, we may well say that flesh is flesh, and that what we eat is simply a matter of taste; but our powers of representation tell us that this is human flesh, identical with that of our own bodies. The human body is of an animal nature, but it is essentially the body of a being capable of representation; in short, it has psychological associations. But this is not the case with the negroes, and the eating of human flesh is quite compatible with the African principle; to the sensuous negro, human flesh is purely an object of the senses, like all other flesh.[86]

Accordingly, Hegel argued that although slavery was unjust, it was proper that it should be ended only gradually, as Africans became sufficiently cultured to deserve their freedom. "Since human beings are valued so cheaply," he wrote, "it is easily explained why *slavery* is the basic legal relationship in Africa. The negroes see nothing improper about it. . . . The lesson we can draw from this condition of slavery among the negroes . . . is the same as that which we have already learnt in the realm of ideas: namely that the state of nature is a state of absolute and consistent injustice" (ibid., 183–84).

Hegel did not fail to observe what might be called the Sadean phenomena of nature. In his *Philosophy of Nature* (1830) he noted that "in many animals the organs of excretion and the genitals, the highest and lowest parts in the animal organization, are intimately connected: just as speech and kissing, on the one hand, and eating, drinking, and spitting, on the other, are all done with the mouth."[87] Whereas Sade sought to lose himself in this compossibility, however, Hegel labored to universalize himself through it. So he argued,

The *depth* which Spirit brings forth from within—but only as far as its picture-thinking consciousness where it lets it remain—and the *ignorance* of this consciousness about what it really is saying, are the same conjunction of the high and the low which, in the living being, Nature naïvely expresses when it combines the organ of its highest fulfillment, the organ of generation, with the organ of urination. The infinite judgment, *qua* infinite, would be the fulfillment of life that comprehends itself; the consciousness of the infinite judgment that remains at the level of picture-thinking behaves as urination. (*Phenomenology*, 210)

In the present context, the most striking feature in both cases is the assumption that nothing, whether human or otherwise, can prove alien to philosophy. For in this sense of things philosophy forgets that cannibalism had never been and could never have been anything other than an item of trade. In other words, it forgets that cannibalism is an act that presupposes and yet denies the borderlines of self and other. (It is this historical amnesia that made imperative the revisionary understandings of philosophy made possible through Marxist, anthropological, and psychoanalytic theory.) Through the historical issue of cannibalism we can see that the boundaries of the Hegelian philosophical concept, like those of culture and identity, can be articulated only through a dramatic struggle over signs, territories, and bodies. Cannibalism is imaginable only in and through the self-dividing articulation of cultural, psychological, and conceptual borderlines: through a positing of sameness that must subvert itself in the excessiveness of its every assertion. Given this recognition, we may be brought to see the justice in Blake's description of Los, that figure of fierce creative hope, laboring to build Golgonooza, the city that would be the redemption of culture: "Striving with Systems to deliver Individuals from those Systems; / That whenever any Spectre began to devour the Death, / He might feel the pain as if a man gnawd his own tender nerves."[88] Here as elsewhere, Blake identified cannibalism with the spectral powers of abstract reasoning, experimental philosophy, and moral law because he intuited a crucial flaw in modern accounts of reason such as Kant's. Even though they were meant to save reason from war and to raise it above the state of nature characterized by Hobbes in terms of "injustice and violence," these accounts demanded a sense of universality that could be assured only through the disavowed perpetuation of violence, injustice, and war.[89]

Hegel laid the groundwork for historicizing subjectivity that would be taken up, in various forms, by Karl Marx, Friedrich Nietzsche, Freud, Lévi-Strauss, Jacques Lacan, and Michel Foucault. In pressing the philosophical concept into the service of history, though, he also suggested that its cogency depended upon a dynamic subjectivity: that it could live only so long as it continued to eat its own otherness. In this way Hegel effectively forecast the postphilosophical condition of philosophy today, in a world in which the very distinction between subjectivity and history has proved impossible to maintain. He forecast this postphilosophical condition, despite himself, because he so ably demonstrated the extent to which the rigor of the concept was implicated in the violence of jealously defined families, religions, economies, and nations. Following a very different method, Sade came to a similar conclusion, which he proclaimed with a frantic cheeriness that must seem rather less obscene than it is commonly considered to be if it is compared with the viciously racist forms in which Hegel condemned, and so yet celebrated, the inhumanity of cannibalism.

So just as the historical expression of cannibalism may be seen as challenging the cultural borderline fundamental to the discipline of anthropology and the delineation of the species crucial to psychoanalysis, it may also be seen as challenging the coherence of the concept in and of philosophy. We may see this challenge in the mocking resemblance between the writings of these disparate figures: in the mad Catholic apostate's pornography and in the pious Protestant professor's theodicy. As both of them traffic in the image of the cannibal and obsessively seek to convert it to themselves, we see the very concept of the concept dissolve into the drama of an imaginary first encounter between individuals representing different cultures. Someone, philosopher or cannibal, raises something on high: what is it? It may seem recognizable, if one can trust one's senses; but what is it *really?* And can he be serious? Does he understand what he is doing? And where is there an end to the violence that beseeches us in absolutely necessary questions such as these?

SIX

KANT
Comes to His Senses

*C*ONSIDER THE KISS. Consider it as a sign and seal of our making. Think of all the circumstances in which a kiss might prove that we have come to our senses—and then imagine how at a crucial moment, *not* to be kissed must be the hero's despair, the metaphysician's nightmare, and a total loss of power for the lover of literature. Only imagine: but for a kiss, any sense of assurance in our experience of the world might vanish. Searching for starry skies above and a moral law within, we might meet with nothing but utterly repulsive sensations that would leave us writhing in self-disgust.

This is how Thomas De Quincey imagined things when he contemplated the death of Immanuel Kant. Dwelling on the image of Kant's last kiss, he also remembered the immortal scene of Captain Thomas Hardy, on board the *Victory* at the Battle of Trafalgar, bent over the dying form of Admiral Horatio Nelson—and he might well have been remembering the girls and crocodiles whose kisses he had shared with his readership over the years. In fact, he might have been thinking through the entire history of kissing. For this image of Kant appears in a footnote in one of De Quincey's more obscure essays, but still it communicates a feeling for questions of culture with which he was preoccupied throughout his life and through which we are still trying to feel our way today.

To appreciate why the English Opium-Eater was so moved by the farewell kiss of the Sage of Königsberg, we must glance back over Western cultural history so as to see something of the assumptions and implications that are conveyed in a kiss. In any such survey what we will find is that in popular imagination, and not only in the imagination of children, the kiss is perceived as an act that establishes human life.

Following classical precedent, Augustine pictured God's breath raising humanity's progenitor *de limo,* from slime. This image of the divine kiss of life can be said to have been sustained by every kiss before or since insofar as it has communicated any sense of transcendence.[1] Such is the case even when this transcendence appears in terms other than those of religion, such as the codes of courtly behavior, genteel manners, or sentimental love. It makes a certain kind of sense that a momentous pursing of the lips could render slime sublime, creating Adam, just as it made sense for those who considered themselves the descendents of Adam to believe that in ceremonious circumstances, they could consecrate the earth by kissing it. This is the case even though, and especially because, "to kiss the earth" has been an expression for death. With the power to bless primeval slime, the contemporary earth, and all sorts of other things from time immemorial to the present day, kissing is at once a statement and an enactment of transcendence. Historically, one might kiss everything from books and rods and the sores of lepers to brides and bones and the frogs of fairy tales. In doing so, one marked them with the sign of civilization and symbolically sealed them within the assurance of humanity's self-possession.

So despite the diversity of its occasions and kinds, the kiss always maintains something of that sense of creative, transformative power marked out by Augustine. If a kiss is any sort of kiss at all, it is an act in which we must imagine that slime is sublimated: that something base is turned to something higher. Were it not so, the kiss would lose its coherence as a gesture, and we would have to speak of lips bumping against some object in the way that a stray elbow might.

To draw out this defining teleology is not to deny the complexity of kissing. This act most certainly can and has communicated many disparate intentions. My argument is simply that this particular usage of the mouth must be minimally defined not only as a definitively cultural act but also as a culturally defining act. To borrow the term from Marcel Mauss that was further elaborated in the work of Michel Foucault, this technique of the body marks a generative boundary of both the human organism and cultural organization. Not by itself, of course, but in keeping company with a host of other bodily rituals, the kiss kisses us into being.

Given the pervasiveness of kissing in Western culture throughout recorded history, I must trust that the foregoing is sufficiently obvious and uncontroversial. Still, one can picture the lips tightened into a grimace of disgust with which some readers might greet a comment offered by Sigmund Freud: "Contact between the mucous membranes of the lips of the two people concerned, is held in high sexual esteem among many nations (including the most highly civilized ones), in spite of the fact that the parts of the body involved do not form part of the sexual apparatus but constitute the entrance to the digestive tract."[2] In desublimating the nature of the kiss, however, Freud was not doing anything particularly uncommon. (That he retained the rhetoric of "highly civilized nations" offers us this assurance.) Kissing would never have had any meaning in the first place if the kiss did not always carry the possibility that it might turn out to be utterly disgusting. Popular tradition has always recognized as much, as when Absalon in Chaucer's *Miller's Tale* finds himself kissing Alisoun's ass instead of the lips he had expected. *Three Essays on a Theory of Sexuality* (1905) was certainly a remarkable book in other respects, but there was nothing unusual in what Freud pointed to in the mouth: the intimacy between the sublime values of civilization and the slimy viscosity of the body's viscera. As he always noted, this intimacy was no less recognized in cultural tradition than the supposed transcendence afforded by the kiss. It was not for nothing, after all, that medieval theologians labored through some rigorous reasoning in order to establish the fact that nasal mucus had no place among the joys of prelapsarian paradise.[3]

As Freud suggested, kissing is one of the civilizing perversions that transform sexual into cultural reproduction, and as such it is always liable to be represented as a perversion pure and simple. It may come to figure as the perversion of philosophy or as the perversion that *is* philosophy, for the slime above which it raises humankind is still the unstable ground of humanity's being. It is an unhuman stuff that participates in the definition of all human organizations, as in the mucous membranes that connect the mouth and nose and other bodily orifices and so suggest a commutative relation among them.[4] In its slippery communications among orifices, as well as in its indeterminate status in relation to the digestive processes that establish identity by distinguishing aliments from excrements, mucus comes to be imagined as a living memento of the slime of imaginary origins. It is a substance that unsettles identity: an "other" matter within the "self." Therefore, it has to be transubstantiated if a kiss is still to be a kiss.

This is the situation on which Francisco Goya's *Caprichos* (1799) (fig. 12) and *Sueños* (1797–98) are based. In these engravings, the wanton anastomosis of orifices imaged through toils identified with witches—farting, eating, vomiting, and sucking—represents an anxious theory of what must ensue when the intimacy between sublime values and slimy materiality goes awry. Popularly thought to cannibalize infants, witches upset the sacred icon of the mother nursing her child so as to suggest an ineradicable violence, eroticism, loss, waste, and disgust in this icon's design.[5] Whereas kissing as Freud presents it is a perversion of biological functions that generally goes unrecognized as such, a sacred perversion that transforms the body of mere animal functions into the form of civilized values, Goya's witches pervert this perversion. They return the mouth to its connection with the anus and thus to destruction and waste in place of creativity and humanity. (For all his differences from Freud, Goya did not neglect to draw out the attraction, the sexual excitement, of the turn toward this imaginary "other matter" of slime.) Whereas the kiss, the phantasmic ostension of the buccal orifice, is supposed to sign and seal bodies over into their transcendence in the form of culture, Goya's nightmarish visions disperse the body of culture back through the messy materialities of its sexual and social multiplicity.

Obviously, the undoing of the kiss need not necessarily take the form assigned it by Goya. His witches bespeak the ins and outs of the particular culture in which he lived, and for that reason their doings can help us to understand some aspects of the images produced by his contemporaries, Kant and De Quincey; they do not speak to every image of the kiss. Yet the visceral turn bound up with the immemorial tradition of the kiss may bring us to recognize that when it comes to kissing, there actually is no forever, no immemorial tradition, and no transcendence. This turn suggests that the kiss supposed to unite us to other people or things in the world is equally destined to divide us. In other words, it suggests that a kiss is not a timeless ritual but a fantastic historical event. This visceral turn of the mouth will be with us as long as we are people who practice the act of kissing. That is why we find the early-nineteenth-century body of Goya's designs and the early-twentieth-century body of Freud's *Three Essays* still being reconsidered today, for in-

FIGURE 12.
Francisco Goya, from *Caprichos* (1799), The Metropolitan Museum of Art,
Gift of M. Knoedler and Co., 1918

stance, in the body articulated in Kiki Smith's artwork (figs. 13 and 14). In these works the body's nature is characterized through precarious falls of hair, dangling organs, excoriated flesh, and extruded bones, tears, feces, semen, blood, and milk—"All the life that happens between the tongue and the anus."[6]

Even though I write of historical specificity, it might seem anachronistic to jump from Goya to Freud and Smith in this manner. One of the effects of kissing that must be taken into account here, however, is its visceral power to signify temporal transcendence. This is the aspect of kissing that calls for us to consider it in relation to and as philosophy.[7] Kissing certainly is a specifically cultural and historical practice, but it will have been appropriate for me to suggest this move between Goya and Kiki Smith if I enjoy any success here in arguing that the relation between philosophy and kissing has never been contained by particular historical bodies. Or at least this movement will then have been no more disturbing than the imaginative movements that we in fact find at the very heart of history, that sticky subject.

Because the kiss is an attempt to sum up the historical body, to reassert and reenact its imaginary identification with the origins of transcendent cultural form, the form in which we imagine any given kiss is liable to plunge us into all the agonizing divisions in the historical experience of cultures. This is precisely what happens when De Quincey dwells on Kant's last kiss. He recalls Nelson, for example: a one-eyed, one-armed, long-suffering hero shot through the left shoulder and fallen, half-paralyzed, begging for relief from his pains, with but a few breaths left before he will find himself embalmed in a cask of brandy for the voyage home. (As it happens, a bottle of this embalming liquid would then end up in a museum located on Queen Square in the city of Bath.) In addition, of course, there is Kant: an erstwhile sage now "tolerated among the living only because of the animal functions [he] performs," dreadfully enfeebled in body and mind, barely able to remain seated even when propped up like a doll at his once beloved dinner table.[8] Then there is the writer himself, a quite small and very thin man forever troubled by digestive problems, the possessor of a deformed right shoulder, a visionary who was to be blind in his left eye for the last twenty years of his life. In other words, in De Quincey we meet the diminutive possessor of "a base, crazy, despicable human system," who at the age of thirty-six already was un-

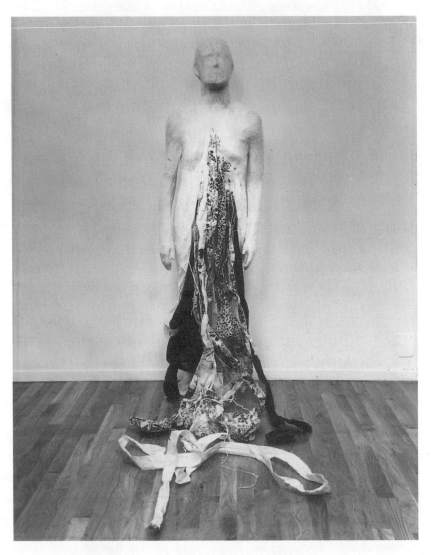

FIGURE 13.
Kiki Smith, *Untitled* (1993), Courtesy Anthony d'Offay Gallery, London,
and by permission of the artist

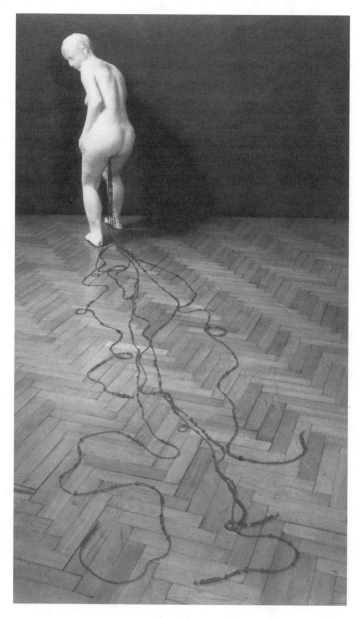

FIGURE 14.
Kiki Smith, *Train* (1993), Courtesy Anthony d'Offay Gallery, London,
and by permission of the artist

able to conceive of "a more worthless body than his own,"[9] at the age of forty-two striving to preserve the culture vital to the kiss *in extremis:*

> The pathos which belongs to such a mode of final valediction is dependent altogether for its effect upon the contrast between itself and the prevailing tone of manners amongst the society where such an incident occurs. In some parts of the Continent there prevailed during the last century a most effeminate practice amongst *men* of exchanging kisses as a regular mode of salutation on meeting after any considerable period of separation. Under such a standard of manners, the farewell kiss of the dying could have no special effect of pathos. But in nations so inexorably manly as the English, any act which for the moment seems to depart from the usual standard of manliness becomes exceedingly impressive when it recalls the spectator's thoughts to the mighty power which has been able to work such a revolution—the power of death in its final agencies. The brave man has ceased to be in any exclusive sense a man: he has become an infant in his weakness: he has become a woman in his craving for tenderness and pity. Forced by agony, he has laid down his sexual character, and retains only his generic character of a human creature. . . . Everybody must remember the immortal scene on board the *Victory,* at four P.M. on October 21, 1805, and the farewell, *"Kiss me, Hardy!"* of the mighty admiral. And here again,—in the final valediction of the stoical Kant, we read another indication, speaking oracularly from dying lips of natures the sternest, that the last necessity . . . is the necessity of love, is the call for some relenting caress, such as may stimulate for a moment some phantom image of female tenderness in an hour when the actual presence of females is impossible.[10]

As De Quincey portrays it, the deathbed conflated from the stories of Kant and Nelson is a scene of beautiful pathos and sublime inspiration.[11] Especially in the latter regard, the absence of women is indeed a necessity; for as De Quincey construed it, the modern sublime was characteristically English (however tolerant of German metaphysicians) and definitively masculine.[12] In that case, however, even to say "English and masculine," in the company of De Quincey, must have been to commit a pleonasm. As surely as one might jest of girls that philosophy "is not their *forte,*"[13] it had to be said that the sublime, "in contraposition to the Beautiful, grew up on the basis of *sexual* distinctions,—the Sublime corresponding to the male, and the Beautiful, its anti-pole, corresponding to the female."[14] If maintaining this commonplace masculine aesthetic were to require some contortions in one's storytelling, was not our lover of literature to be man enough, for all the pronounced infirmities and addictions of his "crazy body," to do his duty? After all, this was the man who professed delight in volunteering his corpse to surgeon's knives and to "the last indignities which the law inflicts upon the bodies of the worst malefactors" (*Confessions* [Masson ed.], 472).[15]

Having long identified himself with both Kant and Nelson (of which more anon), De Quincey drew the occasion for bringing them together from the primary text he was loosely translating in his account of Kant's final days. This was *Immanuel Kant in seinem letzten lebensjahren* by Andreas Christoph Wasianski, who had been Kant's secretary and companion at the end of his life. In describing Kant's last kiss ("Profound compassion made me shudder inwardly; again he offered me his pallid lips"), Wasianski also recalled the only other time he had found Kant kissing him or anyone else, a few weeks before his death. At that time, he noted, Kant seemed to have been completely out of touch, with no awareness of his own actions. He judged the situation to be different on this second occasion, however, when the kiss followed Wasianski's inquiry as to whether Kant recognized him. "After weighing all the circumstances," Wasianski wrote, "I am tempted to take this last offering as a real sign of a friendship now almost ended by death (Nach allen Umständen zu urteilen, bin ich in Versuchung, sein letztes Anerbieten für ein wirkliches Zeichen der, durch den Tod nun bald geendeten Freundschaft, zu halten)."[16]

The reality Wasianski located in his own desire, as led forth by "temptation," was relocated by De Quincey in a "call" from Kant's own body, from Kant himself, as one now led beyond mortal categories of identity by "the necessity of love." Through this displacement De Quincey offered us a compelling image of the cultural apparatus in which kissing made sense to him. Grossly adumbrated in terms of masculinity and Englishness, this image is more complexly sketched out in the transformations of shuddering to knowing—temptation to necessity, desire to recognition, question to response—that are rendered sublime, or at once obliterated and consecrated, in his image of Kant's farewell kiss. The implication of De Quincey's description is that the design of one's entire culture is at stake in every act of kissing, on which philosophy in particular may depend for the ultimate sign of its power to signify.

De Quincey's image of Horatio Nelson demanded no less of him than did the image of Kant. Nelson's death had been immediately and widely publicized in many forms, but accounts soon came to rely on the reporting of William Beatty, originally published in 1807 as the *Authentic Narrative of the Death of Lord Nelson*. Beatty had been the surgeon on HMS *Victory*, Nelson's flagship at the Battle of Trafalgar. His version of events did indeed include the tender request to Captain Hardy that immediately passed into popular legend along with Nelson's valedictory, "Thank GOD, I have done my duty." It also included something more. In this case, what De Quincey had to suffer himself to edit out included the admiral's fear that his body might be thrown into the sea (he does not appear to have offered an opinion on immersion in brandy); Nelson's repeated, impatient complaints of discomfort; and his reiterated concerns for the future welfare of his daughter Horatia and his beloved Lady Hamilton. In Beatty's account, in fact, the words immediately preceding "Kiss me, Hardy" are "take care of my dear Lady Hamilton, Hardy; take care of poor Lady Hamilton."[17]

As De Quincey appreciated rather too well, these preceding words could not hope to stimulate the organs of culture as those following them would. Such was the case even though Hardy was not actually present at the moment of Nelson's death, despite what the popular image of the farewell kiss and many paintings and reproductions of the scene would seem to indicate. (The admiral's fallen body had forced Hardy to attend to other duties.) Furthermore, as De Quincey may not have known but certainly might have inferred, Nelson had often anticipated his own death. Therefore, we have good reason to surmise that the staginess of his dying request for a kiss, which proved so effective in the public's imagination, was not simply inspired by the moment. With all these circumstances taken into account, in De Quincey's isolated and spontaneous occasion of transcendent pathos we must be tempted to see the messy body of historical tradition dispersed among tormenting absences, impatiently desiring petitions, suffering cries for succor ("drink, drink, drink" [45]), and anxious repetitions of unsatisfying ritual formulas—not to mention the more general circumstances that took Hardy away from the moment of death and most of the period leading up to it: the battle in which, on the *Victory* alone, fifty-five seamen were killed and more than a hundred wounded.

Just as he appropriated Kant's kiss from its context in willful fantasy, De Quincey displaced Nelson's from its environment of distracted, dismembered, frazzled, bloody theatricality. To say so is no reproach, of course. My purpose here is not to belabor the obvious point that De Quincey followed in the steps of others, such as Benjamin West, who had glamorized this scene. (West is said to have explained his deliberate inaccuracy in placing the dying Nelson on the quarterdeck of the *Victory*, rather than in its cloacal cockpit, through an allusion to his *Death of General Wolfe* [1771]: "Wolfe must not die like a common soldier under a Bush, neither should Nelson be represented dying in the gloomy hold of a ship, like a sick man in a Prison Hole.")[18] Because I follow De Quincey so far as to take it for granted that a kiss is perforce a fantastic historical event, my desire is rather to examine this passage, in which he is conjoined with Kant and Nelson, for what it can tell us of the sublime mucus that joined the modern body—"still agitated, writhing, twisting, palpitating, shattered"[19]—to the philosophy of culture. In other words, I am concerned to examine how it is that the few yards of gut between the human mouth and anus could have become a theoretical realm in which the progress of all of culture and history might be articulated.[20]

Colloquially, the experience of coming to one's senses is opposed to taking leave of them. Yet in these expressions there lurks an antinomy of ordinary language from which there might seem to be no escape. For to come to one's senses means to come out of them, as by rising above their illusions, even as to take leave of one's senses means to be enthralled by them, as when they tumble over one another in their haste to lend themselves to some passing siren's ravishment. To come to one's senses is commonly taken to mean that one has triumphed over them and so degraded them to an insignificant position in relation to reason and other guiding agencies. Strictly speaking, then, in coming to one's senses, one loses them, just as in leaving them, one abandons oneself to them. Accordingly, insofar as we seek to speak logically from within the limits of sense experience, our discursive forms must come to us as if from beyond it; to be aesthetically moved, our senses must not stir; to judge anything with taste, we must not let that thing pass our lips.

Fortunately, philosophy can offer us a way out of these proliferating para-doxes—or a number of outlets, actually, all conjoined by the mucus of the sublime. In this regard, Kant offered himself as physician as well as meta-physician. In his *Anthropology* (1798) and other writings, he showed a strong interest in matters of nourishment and especially in the question of digestion, recommending, for example, lively conversation at meals as a tonic to the bowels. In fact, the metaphysical implications of digestion were just as cru-cial for Kant as those of impotence were for Tristram Shandy.[21] Moreover, as a self-diagnosed victim of chronic stomach and liver complaints throughout his adult life, which were aggravated by the constipative effects of chronic opium use, De Quincey so fully shared this concern with Kant that he felt the limits of space and time to be negligible barriers against his ability to ex-ercise his nosological skills on the late philosopher. Correcting what he took to be Wasianski's erroneous diagnosis, he argued that "the cause of Kant's death was clearly the general decay of the vital powers, and in particular the atony of the digestive organs" ("Last Days of Kant," 366n). The conclusion is significant beyond its immediate context, for in Kant's writings, as in De Quincey's, the solution to paradox is peristalsis.[22]

This is in keeping with the governing images for sensibility in this age. These images all focused on some kind of rhythmic motion, whether one was addressing the manifest tremblings in a lady of cultured sensibility or the in-visible vibrations of the nerves in one's body. In the eighteenth and nineteenth centuries, as analyzed by physiologists such as Jean-Baptiste van Helmont, George Ernst Stahl, Théophile Bordeu, Johann Friedrich Blumenbach, and Julien Offroy de La Mettrie, tonic movement was seen as crucial to the "an-imal economy," as the contemporary idiom had it, of the body. (Stahl, signif-icantly, was singled out for admiring mention as a pioneer of modern natural science in the preface to the second edition [1787] of Kant's *Critique of Pure Reason*.)[23] Tonic movement was seen as vital to specific organs, especially the intestines, but also to more fundamental elements of the body, including the nerves and even individual cells. Such was the attractive and repulsive prin-ciple of "excitability" that John Brown, a Scottish physician highly praised by Kant, claimed as the essence of life.[24] An emphasis on this kind of oscilla-tion, or on what Jean-François Lyotard has termed "a *vibrato*, inclusive of the viscera," in Kant's writings, was commonplace.[25] "The body ceaselessly trem-bles, quivers, agitates itself, even down to the innermost of its least particles," wrote Bordeu. He added that "these quiverings are unceasingly modified and controlled to maintain the regularity and order of its functions, and they are completely subordinated to the principle of sensibility that controls all." Similarly, although proceeding from assumptions about the nature of life very different from those held by Bordeu, La Mettrie would write of "this oscillation that is natural or proper to our machine, and with which every fiber and, so to speak, every fibrous element is endowed."[26] There were, of course, many differences of opinion over various aspects of these oscillations, such as those that Blumenbach, another important influence on Kant, addressed in regard to the nervous system;[27] but the visceral *vibrato* was ubiquitous.

Isaac Newton's *Optics* (1704), in which vision and hearing were represented in terms of vibrations, was an influential source of this ubiquitous image, as was his *Principia Mathematica* (1687). The concluding words of this latter work offered a conjecture that "all sensation is excited, and the members of animal bodies move at the command of the will . . . by the vibrations" of "a certain most subtle Spirit," which are "mutually propagated along the solid filaments of the nerves, from the outward organs of sense to the brain, and from the brain into the muscles."[28] David Hartley's influential doctrine of vibrations took its cue primarily from Newton, although also from Locke and Boerhaave, among others;[29] and these sorts of vibrations left their impress on writings as diverse as Sterne's *Tristram Shandy* (1759–67), Bishop Berkeley's *Siris* (1744), and Georg Wilhelm Friedrich Hegel's *Phenomenology of Spirit* (1807). Tristram says that he has written his work "in order, by a more frequent and more convulsive elevation and depression of the diaphragm, and the succussations of the intercostal and abdominal muscles in laughter, to drive the gall and other bitter juices from the gall-bladder, liver, and sweetbread of his majesty's subjects." His visceral concerns are related to those of Berkeley, who explained the healing power of tar water in terms of "perpetual oscillations" acting in the world. The conceptions of both of these figures were then sublated, as Hegel would have it, in the movement of his dialectic, "the immanent rhythm of the Notion."[30] The metaphor would still prove compelling long after the end of the eighteenth century: in George Eliot's *Mill on the Floss* (1860), for instance, *vibrating* plays a crucial role in describing bodily fibers, matters of perception, and consciousness in general.

Given this context, it is no wonder *The Critique of Judgement* finds Kant attending to jokes as well as to sublime natural vistas, with his apprehension of the one couched in terms closely resembling those that recommend the other. Like the effects of music, the workings of jokes are characterized in terms of a play of the mind conjoined with an "oscillation of the organs," a "rapidly succeeding tension and relaxation." Kant writes,

> For supposing we assume that some movement in the bodily organs is associated sympathetically with all our thoughts, it is readily intelligible how the sudden act . . . of shifting the mind now to one standpoint and now to the other, to enable it to contemplate its object, may involve a corresponding and reciprocal straining and slackening of the elastic parts of our intestines, which communicates itself to the diaphragm (and resembles that felt by ticklish people), in the course of which the lungs expel the air with rapidly succeeding interruptions, resulting in a movement conducive to health.[31]

Similarly, in the "soul-stirring sensations" (1:116) of the sublime, which is to be distinguished from superstitious fears by its status as a cultured moral perception, we come to our senses by feeling the limits of sensibility shuddering within us. This is a sensation such as that which Wasianski reported having felt at the approach of Kant's lips—such lips as might be said to have reached their sublime apotheosis in the mouth that floats in the skies of Man Ray's *À l'heure de l'observatoire: Les amoureux* (1932–34). In this kind of sublime moment, imagination proves an outrage to itself, the senses are gripped by a supersensuous standard that is no less demanding for being ultimately baffling (thus preparing the way for Franz Kafka's meditations), and we are shaken into a consciousness of consciousness. "The mind feels itself *set in motion* in the representation of the sublime in nature," says Kant. "This movement, especially in its inception, may be compared with a vibration, i.e., with a rapidly alternating repulsion and attraction produced by one and the same Object" (1:107). The paradoxical "negative pleasure" of the sublime, "being brought about by the feeling of a momentary check to the vital forces followed at once by a discharge all the more powerful" (1:91), mightily invigorates us by rushing us past our concerns with such petty matters as personal health. As would De Quincey with the figure of Nelson, Kant therefore looks to the heroic soldier in times of war as an emblem of the sublime, in contraposition to effeminate institutions whose manners would "degrade the character of a nation" (1:113).

To be sure, Kant was determined to distinguish his theory from the laudable but more narrowly physiological aesthetics of Edmund Burke, just as he was generally concerned to insist that the invigoration of the sublime be recognized as a matter of the mind above all else. Much as Maine de Biran would argue that eighteenth-century physiologists had failed to honor Albrecht von Haller's distinction between irritability, which was muscular, and sensibility, which appertained to spiritual self-consciousness, so was Kant concerned to keep muscles, even those of heroic soldiers, within their proper bounds.[32] Otherwise, he argued, the stirring up of seemingly sublime emotions "comes to no more than what the Eastern voluptuaries find so soothing when they get their bodies massaged, and all their muscles and joints softly pressed and bent" (*Critique of Judgement*, 1:126). In other words, the sublime then turns out to be just such feminizing slime as De Quincey found, in his opium nightmares, in his passive acceptance of the Oriental kiss of a crocodile.

It seemed necessary, then, that in the same movements through which he established the intellect by dutifully shrinking before the limiting encasement of the supersensible, Kant should multiply his normative conception of the body and thrust it forth into every imaginable breach of such limits. These reciprocal movements were necessary in order to define his limits against the paradoxes that would split them wide open if foreign or female bodies, of the sort of which Kant was contemptuous—ritually, jestingly, convulsively contemptuous[33]—were ever actually to make sense. These shuddering transformations of the philosopher's definitively masculine body were absolutely vital to ensure that modern civilization would progress and reproduce itself. In effect, they were needed to save this civilization from having to recognize any truth in Denis Diderot's argument that the limits of the senses are sadomasochistically defined. Diderot argued that "it is the nature of the sublime to penetrate us in an extraordinary manner" and that "the model of all sublime things can be found in the image of beautiful, half-naked women serving us a delicious drink in the bloody skulls of our enemies."[34]

Quintessentially modern in its rigorous empiricism, categorical universalism, and presumptive Eurocentrism, the human body of Kant's philosophy is also the multiplicity of forms spread throughout the imaginable universe through its masculine defenses and aggressions. In its militancy on behalf of the idealized culture with which it is identified, this is not one body but many, all of which are continually pressed into service to plug the gaps, or to cover

over the orifices, that are opened in reason whenever it comes to recognize the uncivilized "other matter" that lives both within and without it.[35] We may note, for example, that while Kant rejected Georg Forster's argument for multiple human origins, which had the African and Asian races being generated out of "sea slime,"[36] he did so without prejudice to Forster's assumptions about the inferiority of these races. The fact that Kant conceived of the "fleshly enjoyment" of sex unsanctified by marriage as being "cannibalistic in principle, if not always in effect," because "in this reciprocal use of each other's sexual organs, each of [the parties] is a consumable thing *(res fungibilis)* to the other," is a further example of how the human body of his philosophy had to be continually reasserting and reenacting its limits against disorganizing possibilities within its own visceral nature.[37] As Susan Meld Shell puts it, Kant's writings show a "particularly acute sensitivity to the tenuousness (and uncanny reversibility) of his own bodily boundaries, a sensitivity that is bound up with his own avowed tendencies toward 'hypochondria' and consequently heightened awareness of the peculiarity of 'healthy' consciousness."[38]

The result is that the figurative movements in Kant's writings, like those in De Quincey's, show the gripping proliferation of mucous membranes, the kiss of viscous identity, through which soldiers become so sexy and guts so metaphysical that all of culture may appear to depend on a scene of one man kissing another, to the decided exclusion of women.[39] (In Sade's writings, a paradoxically related aesthetic of the sublime led to the argument that the anus is superior to the vagina, sodomy superior to hateful reproductive sexuality, and the pleasure of incest superior to any and all definitions of family relations.) Even as he besought his fellows not to let humanity so lose its sense of taste as recklessly to spill its guts, Kant established his own writing as a sublime sparagmos, or scattering, of highly civilized mucosae. In other words, in Kant's writings we learn that when it comes to slime, there is the right way of managing it, which is ceremoniously to take it up into the architectonics of the sublime body, and all sorts of other ways, which we must kiss off if we are to maintain this body.

Even as the "sublime sparagmos" of which I write is but a dutiful paraphrase of Kant's aesthetic rhetoric, "mucosae" is not just a figure of speech here. For in the late eighteenth and early nineteenth centuries it was a commonplace of physiological science to regard the mucous membranes of the human body as the internal equivalent to its skin. Like the outer surface, the inner allowed the body simultaneously to communicate with and to differentiate itself from all other matter with which it came into contact. As in some so-called primitive beliefs, then, spit was seen as closely related to spirit. So Xavier Bichat explained that in their capacity as organs "always in contact with bodies foreign to our own substance," the mucous membranes "are the seat of an internal sense of touch, analogous in all respects to the exterior touch of the skin on the bodies that surround us." Similarly, Théophile Bordeu had described mucous membranes within the body as "a sort of internal outer skin"; had noted that "the rectum is surrounded by a sheath that belongs as much to the cellular tissue of the interior as to that of the exterior"; and had further observed that in this regard the rectum was systematically related to the throat, mouth, and nose. "Thus the external and internal surfaces of the body are but two layers of cellular substance, more or less thick," which "contain within them, or in the space that separates them, all the other parts."[40] Thus it was that in these membranes the body was turned outside in (insofar as its interior was made imagistically and essentially exterior, as unassimilable aliment or slimy excrement) and inside out (insofar as its interior was made functionally and topologically exterior, as sealed and limitless flesh). As if the human body might be fundamentally identical to Abraham Trembley's polyps, its seeming exterior and interior were locked in a permanent kiss in which they were bound to lose their separate identities.

In fact, in the science of this era mucus came to be described as the most elemental substance of life. This was by no means a claim to which everyone subscribed, but it was a serious, influential, widely disseminated notion. Most notably, in contrast to the Renaissance theory of humors (which still obtruded itself, for instance, in Stahl's writings) and in deliberate opposition to the fibrillary theory of Boerhaave, Bordeu identified mucus as this primary and primordial substance. He argued that "the entire body is reducible, in the last analysis, to a mass of mucous, albuminous substance, the element nourishing every vegetable, every animal, and which is nothing but the extract of aliments digested in various ways." He compared this centerpiece of his theory with "the vortices of Descartes and the gravity of Newton." He saw this mucus, which owed something to Haller's theory of an elementary physiological "gluten," as perhaps "nourishing or forming . . . the epidermis and the skin" and in any case as "the nourishing essence" that "is the same throughout" the body.[41] As previously noted, this emphasis on mucous tissue was later to be taken up by Bichat, among others. Meanwhile, it enjoyed a popular currency in works such as La Mettrie's, as when he followed Bordeu in identifying semen as "a bit of mucus" that produces a creature "able to raise itself to sublimity in style, manners, and pleasure."[42]

In the body of this era, then, digestion was not simply noted to be an aspect of animal organisms crucially distinguishing them from vegetable life, as in John Abernethy's *Physiological Lectures*.[43] Because the mucous membranes involved in digestion might be seen as the elemental stuff of life and as partaking of both voluntary and involuntary movements, they could also be taken to incarnate the issues of human identity, free will, and supersensible reality. Long before Kant's third *Critique*, Stahl had described the vital nature of the human body as ruling over alimentary and excretory processes and as finding its exemplary representation in the experience of the sublime. Excretions and secretions, he wrote, "are in reality only the highest and most immediate *instrument* of which this nature avails itself in order to expel to the outside everything that is improper and foreign and to retain and assimilate within everything that is useful in terms of the conservation of the body." According to the logic of this vitalism, "as the ancients have already remarked, the soul recoils with a *true trembling before the infinite,* and . . . seeing the failure of the vain effort of all its energy, it flees before this infinity, as if stricken with impotence." He added that it was nonetheless necessary that the soul should "try to raise itself toward the ultimate limits and the sovereign, essential propriety of corporal things [in a] sublime effort toward that which cannot be reached."[44]

Given this context, it makes perfect sense that matters of digestion should have obtruded themselves upon Kant's attention in his third *Critique*—just as it makes perfect sense that Abernethy should have turned to the image of Nelson's glorious death in order to illustrate the intimate connection between one's feelings and "affections of the brain" arising "from disturbance of the nervous functions of the digestive organs."[45] By the same logic, it is only to be expected that an English physiologist in the early years of the nineteenth century, outraged by the scandal of Percy Bysshe Shelley's *The Necessity of Atheism* (1811), should have found support for the truth of Christianity within the limits of the digestive system alone.[46] It is curious, however—and then again, not—that aside from notable exceptions such as Lyotard and Shell, his commentators have shown so little interest in these passages in Kant's work.[47]

In Kant's work as in De Quincey's, we are led through table talk, jokes, scenes of nature, and moral judgments into twisting passages of transformations at once alimentary, reproductive, and excremental. As I hope has been made evident, these bowels of the text are not necessarily, and not even usually, those of a self-contained body. Instead they may appear, for example, as the sparagmos of the starry sky above us, which digests us and excretes us back into the earth from which we were kissed into life: "The . . . view of a countless multitude of worlds annihilates, as it were, my importance as an animal creature, which, after it has been for a short time provided with vital force (one knows not how), must give back to the planet (a mere speck in the universe) the matter from which it came."[48] Alternatively, these transformative bowels may appear, in De Quincey's writings, as the wave-tossed surface of a sea viewed under the influence of laudanum; as a pair of lips quivering with uncertainty on a deathbed; as the phantom image of woman.

In commenting on Jeremy Taylor's account of the death of Judas, which has him hanging himself in such wise that his guts burst forth, De Quincey sought to explicate this sealing of culture and philosophy within the bowels of humanity. He traced its logic to "the absurd physiology of our worshipful Pagan masters, Greek and Roman," for whom the viscera were "occupied by those functions of the moral sensibilities which *we* place in the central *viscus* of the heart." (In fact, De Quincey argued, "the *viscera* comprehended *all* the intestines" so that, "perhaps, in a very large acceptation, the brain might be regarded as co-viscus with the heart.")[49] Taylor's Judas, spilling his guts, could then be understood as an image of a broken heart. Even so can De Quincey's Kant, pursing his lips, be seen as ritually repairing the betrayal of Judas's kiss, courageously thrusting guts back into the human body (for "no guts, no glory," as our contemporary saying would have it), and so sealing the slippery, glistening, pulsing limits of experience, all the way to infinity, upon their own baffling necessity.

I have wondered what could have brought Kiki Smith to remark, "To me it's much more scary to be a girl in public than to talk about the digestive system. They both have as much meaning in your life, but I've been punished more for being a girl than I've been punished for having a digestive system."[50] Surely one need not be formally introduced to one of the Romeos limned by Jonathan Swift, say, in order to recognize that girls and guts have been so inextricably knotted together throughout history as to have rendered all but inevitable the negative pleasures to be found, for example, in the prose of Kathy Acker. The old adage, Inter urinas et faeces nascimur,[51] pretty much sums up the perceived problem for which Kant's last kiss, as represented by De Quincey, would be the solution. ("I hate the word *bowels*," Swift wrote to his beloved Stella, as no one will be surprised to learn who has read this wit's poem, "The Lady's Dressing Room," in which the true essence of woman is made to appear as the stinking waste in her chamber pot.) Smith's remark seems so artless in its dissociation of the punishing system of gender and the pulsing system of digestion, so much at odds with all the insight suggested by her art, that I am tempted to conclude she must have taken leave of her senses when she uttered it. Yet at the same time I must think that I am the senseless one and that her remark offhandedly recognizes what De Quincey could never come close to bringing within his consciousness, which is that "the phantom image of female tenderness" engendered by the kiss of philosophy is a gutless girl bound to be insulted in the streets. As Smith suggests, the digestive system must then be a different matter, an "other matter," indeed.

My lingering uncertainty over how I should take Smith's words must put me in a position like that of Wasianski with Kant's kiss. Philosophically speaking, for all the heartbreaking sincerity of its historian, that kiss ought not to have signified anything one way or another, being redundant if intentional and sheer nonsense if not. And strictly speaking, this sticky oscillation of positions in my writing here is entirely unnecessary, since I could easily have passed over this quotation in silence. If I hope to accomplish anything by leaving in this sign of uneasiness, by letting it still mess with me, I must be imagining that with words as with kisses, there is a limit, which it is sublime not to know.

As is too well (and so inadequately) known, in matters of beauty Kant thrust forth the bodies of his books to plug all repulsive breaches of decorum:

> Where fine art evidences its superiority is in the beautiful descriptions it gives of the things that in nature would be ugly or displeasing. The Furies, diseases, devastations of war, and the like, can (as evils) be very beautifully described, nay even represented in pictures. One kind of ug-

liness alone is incapable of being represented conformably to nature without destroying all aesthetic delight, and consequently artistic beauty, namely, that which excites *disgust*. For, as in this strange sensation, which depends purely on the imagination, the object is represented as insisting, as it were, upon our enjoying it, while we still set our face against it, the artificial representation of the object is no longer distinguishable from the nature of the object itself in our sensation, and so it cannot possibly be regarded as beautiful. (*Critique of Judgement*, 1:173–74)

I say that Kant's position in this regard is inadequately known, *because* of its familiarity, so as to point out that this matter of disgust is generally treated as if it were a mere byproduct of his aesthetics even though it generates central questions about the image of nature at the vital center of his work. For instance, the things Kant found aesthetically unrepresentable, because of the disgust presumed to attend upon them, included homosexuality and other *crimina carnis contra naturam*.[52] This disgust was also a generative organ and justification for racism, as Frantz Fanon recognized when he wrote, "My black skin is not the depository of specific values. It has been a long time since the starry sky that left Kant panting for breath has surrendered its secrets to us. And the moral law is suspicious of itself."[53] Here again Shell is an especially insightful critic of the philosopher: "For all its seeming insignificance, Kant's treatment of nausea and disgust reaches to the heart, as it were, of his concern with the boundaries of the individual, [with] an 'anxiety of influence' in the most literal sense. Aesthetic taste, one could say, is a rehabilitated version of the *Mittheilung* (or mutual imparting) whose primary, consumptive forms, be they alimentary, respiratory, or sexual, are 'dangerous to the animal.'"[54]

In De Quincey's writings, Kant's prescription against the aesthetic representation of disgust reappears, but with the unsettling movements in which it is implicated dramatically traced out to their tormentingly self-contradictory ends. Thus, in describing the last time he kissed a girl of the streets who had befriended him when he was down and out in London, De Quincey appears to follow Kant's prescription by taking pains to note that to him his Ann's lips "were not polluted" and so are not to be regarded as having been disgusting (*Confessions* [Lindop ed.], 76). Honi soit qui mal y pense; for as De Quincey envisioned himself, he had never been one to hold himself polluted by anyone's touch. "On the contrary," he wrote, "from my earliest youth it has been my pride to converse familiarly, *more Socratico,* with all human beings, man, woman, and child, that chance might fling in my way: a practice which is friendly to the knowledge of human nature, to good feelings, and to that frankness of address which becomes a man who would be thought a philosopher" (20). Obviously, this farewell scene would have been another matter if our historian had not been philosophical enough to wipe all the imaginable sliminess of its history from this child prostitute's mouth and thus, lovingly, to eviscerate her with a kiss.

Sublime antibodies notwithstanding, this slimily other matter does show up among De Quincey's visions. It appears, for instance, in the section of the *Confessions* titled "The Pains of Opium." Here De Quincey writes, "I was kissed, with cancerous kisses, by crocodiles; and laid, confounded with all unutterable slimy things, amongst reeds and Nilotic mud" (73). In this oft-quoted description, which is taken from what is arguably the most beautiful passage in either version of the *Confessions,* the crocodile is marked out as being loathsome above all other things and yet, *contra* Kant, aesthetically fascinating. Especially if one takes into account that the crocodile is a recurrent figure in De Quincey's writings, consistently associated with types of male authority, this kiss must seem a wracking discharge of the whole narcissistic, heterosexual, male, white, English, Christian, martial pleonasm that Kant's last kiss is elsewhere taken beatifically to incorporate.[55] In other words, Kant's kiss is turned into something closely resembling the one exchanged in *Vathek* (1786) by William Beckford's protagonist and the monstrous Giaour, whose curious merchandise has driven him crazy. The latter figure is soon to be revealed as an evil, supernatural, boy-devouring ogre, but at this moment he has just given Vathek a potion that has returned him to his senses: "In the transports of his joy, Vathek leaped upon the neck of the frightful Indian, and kissed his horrid mouth and hollow cheeks, as though they had been the coral lips and the lilies and roses of his most beautiful wives."[56]

It is no surprise that with his digestive tract giving passage to a drug that alters the limits of experience, De Quincey should find some alteration in his sense of personal identity. As with Kant, if one unplugs the holes in the philosophical body, what rushes forth is a flood of images of disgusting foreign cultures: "Chinese manners and modes of life and scenery"; "the wild, barbarous, and capricious superstitions of Africa"; "the ancient, monumental,

cruel, and elaborate religions of Indostan, &c" (*Confessions* [Lindop ed.], 72).
So much is sufficiently obvious, as is the way that De Quincey worked up the
matter of his opium visions as a calque drawn from orthodox images of the
sublime. This accounts for the correspondences, for example, among William
Wordsworth's vision of Mount Snowden in book 14 of *The Prelude* (1850),
Kant's analysis of sublime feelings in relation to storms at sea in *The Critique
of Judgement* (1:92), and De Quincey's image of the ocean as mind in "The
Pleasures of Opium" (*Confessions* [Lindop ed.], 49), which then is made terrible in "The Pains of Opium." In the latter episode, "the tyranny of the human face" begins to "unfold itself" by multiplying itself, tossing and surging
on the surface of the sea, even as Kant's philosophical body would be multiplied into all imaginable breaches in infinity. In this case, however, it multiplies itself as nothing but a scattering of decapitated faces, "innumerable
faces, upturned to the heavens: faces, imploring, wrathful, despairing" (72). It
is as if one were to see the smiling pavement in John Milton's paradise sud-
denly spitting and chomping at one's heels.[57]

More interesting than his stylings of sublime visions is De Quincey's admission of what Kant labored so hard not to recognize: that despite all the
differences the distinction may make, the negative pleasure of the sublime
must remain kissing cousins with primitive fear. Yet even this admission remains a generally predictable trope of psychological, aesthetic, and cultural
regression from within the confining terms of a sublime faith in progress.
More interesting still is the suggestion in "The Pains of Opium" (73–74) that
even if it should bear no sign of metaphysics and culture, a kiss is still a kiss.
Though it be from the "cancerous" mouth of the metastatically "multiplied"
body of a phantasmic reptile, whose slimy grin unsexes a man in a perfectly
disgusting manner, the kiss is still felt as such. If a meeting can take place and
a sign be thus exchanged, *more crocodilo,* then loving necessity compels us to
face down the body of culture: to face the sublime *as* slime, philosophy *as* kissing.[58] This is precisely the task with which De Quincey wrestled.

In his account of Kant's last kiss, when he indulged himself in a typically
scornful reference to France, De Quincey recognized that all of history must
be on one's lips for the kiss, as such, to be possible. As he was aware, in medieval and earlier times it had been common for men to kiss each other; the
custom had declined, as had the casual frequency of kisses between men and
women; lips had become more personal and specifically erotic things.[59]

Moreover, long before the climate created by Freud, one could scarcely have avoided noticing that to kiss in the civilized manner is markedly to turn away from speaking, biting, licking, and sucking, not to mention (as with the logical extremes of Kant's logical disgust) vomiting and defecating. It is for this reason that the English Opium-Eater opened his essay "Conversation" by adverting in the opening paragraph to eating and, at some length, to spitting—those other activities conjoined in the membranes of the mouth.[60] Furthermore, as long recognized in jests of the sort in which Chaucer and Rabelais took delight, as well as in the folklore (which Sade adored) that had the devil preferring to receive his kisses *in ano,* to offer a kiss is implicitly to articulate the entire body, as one articulates a statement, into a series of parts and relationships systematized with a view to social and metaphysical orders.[61] An educated man would be aware as well that some peoples, such as those in New Zealand and other South Sea islands, were said not to practice the kiss as it was known to "civilization." Historically speaking, then, after the Kantian exposition of taste as a transcendent trope of tropes, a word at once literally and figuratively triumphing over slimy origins, it could seem that no one was better situated than this philosopher to appreciate the sublime sacrifice of his lips in a kiss. Moreover, it could seem that no one was better situated than De Quincey to feel how that monstrous old German crocodile, who even before his death had admitted that he should long have been confined to the grave, still was in need of a kiss, and of *his* kiss.[62]

Three years after the initial publication in *Blackwood's* of "The Last Days of Kant" (1827), there appeared in the same journal De Quincey's essay "Kant in His Miscellaneous Writings." In this piece he lauded Kant for standing against "an age which, if any ever *did,* idolatrizes the tangible and the material." He praised him as well for opposing the "vassalage to the eye" represented by "the empire of sense absolutely systematized by education" and thus upholding "the shadowy (but not therefore unreal or baseless) texture of metaphysics."[63] In the course of his praise, however, he did note that for Kant, literature was another matter. His taste had failed him in relation to literature, and especially in terms of the question of style that was so markedly De Quincey's personal concern throughout his career. "It is very evident that Kant's original determination was to a coarse, masculine pursuit of science," wrote De Quincey, "and that literature in its finer departments, whose essence is power and not knowledge, was to him, at all parts of his life, an object of

secret contempt. Out of regard for what he considered the prejudices of society, it is true he concealed his contempt, and perhaps, in its whole extent,
he did not even avow it to himself; but it is clear that it lurked in his inner
nature" (91).[64]

In other words, De Quincey found in Kant an opening to be repaired. By
offering himself as Kant's translator and interpreter—his mouthpiece—he
would soften the coarseness of his masculine sensibility. Like the phantom
image of woman at a deathbed, or like the abused prostitute who brought De
Quincey a saving glass of wine when he was falling into a deathly faint, he
would bring Kant to his senses. He would be that spiced wine, that Keatsian
kiss, that phantom female blissfully lubricating Kant's dessicated philosophical body. He would share with Kant the knowledge he bore within him, in
his very bowels, and so offer him life.

To do so meant offering him opium, since it was this that so defined De
Quincey's visceral identity and literary fame. In fact, De Quincey had represented opium as providing just such a harmony of the mental faculties as Kant
had urged through his philosophy. Opium, he wrote, "communicates seren-
ity and equipoise to all the faculties, active or passive: and with respect to the
temper and moral feelings in general, it gives simply that sort of vital warmth
which is approved by the judgment, and which would probably always accompany a bodily constitution of primeval or antediluvian health" (*Confessions* [Lindop ed.], 40–41). Following this logic, the English Opium-Eater
claimed to be quite certain that a judicious dosage of the drug "would have
been the best remedy, perhaps a perfect remedy," for the "morbid affection of
the stomach" that was said to have caused Kant nightmares toward the end
of his life ("Last Days of Kant," 359n, 359). As he made clear in offering himself as a translator of Kant, however, the full significance of this opium would
not be comprehensible apart from the entire digestive system of his own writing. To comprehend this, we need to return to that other figure co-viscous
with Kant, Lord Nelson.

In one of the additions in the 1856 version of the *Confessions*, De Quincey
noted, "It is recorded of Lord Nelson that, even after the Nile and Copenhagen, he still paid the penalty, on the first day of resuming his naval life,
which is generally exacted by nature from the youngest little middy or the
rawest griffin—*viz.* sea-sickness. . . . The very same thing happens to
opium-eaters" (*Confessions* [Masson ed.], 420). As he could hope to repair the

breach in Kant's taste because he had so thoroughly digested the philosopher's writings, so could De Quincey find repair for faults in himself through his recollection of the breaching of Nelson's digestive system. The logic is exceedingly slippery in its texture, but no less significant for that. In the first place, the sea is to Nelson as opium is to De Quincey. Moreover, both men are identified with the Nile, a locale associated with slime and kisses, whether from crocodiles or from Lady Hamilton, the quondam goddess in James Graham's erotic Temple of Health. (Nelson had met Emma Hamilton in Naples immediately after his defeat of Napoleon's forces in the Battle of the Nile.) Finally, it seems that for both men a feeling of disgust, to the point of visceral revulsion, is necessarily comprehended within their humanity.

De Quincey was liable to seem a subject confessing shame, "a crazy enthusiast or visionary" (*Confessions* [Lindop ed.], 44). In his own view, he was one who might at best call forth the "playful reproach" of the neologism *hedonist* (*Confessions*, [Masson ed.], 428n), and one, moreover, identified with the vices of unmanly alien races. Yet his association with the officially consecrated heroism of Nelson might make him seem a man, and an Englishman, for all that. Nelson would then be a more attractive version of Bishop Edmund Bonner, the figure who appears in De Quincey's characterization as a "fiery disciplinarian to weak, relapsing *perverts* (such is the modern slang): sneaking perverts like myself and my ever-honoured reader."[65] De Quincey, in fact, not only named his second son after Nelson but also admired his hero's notorious paramour and appeared to share his attraction to large-bodied women.[66]

So it only makes sense that De Quincey should have turned to Nelson in the 1856 revision of the scene in which he tells how, as a youth, he fled his school in Manchester. For as he tells of it, this was an act with which he was often to reproach himself even though he felt it to be a categorically "sublime" decision, which, in his erotic description, "swallowed up all capacities of rankling care and heart-corroding doubt" and seemed "passively received" as a command "from some dark oracular legislation external" to himself (*Confessions* [Masson ed.], 278–79). Imagistically, this is a scene authorized by Kant's system of reason, and yet it still has something indigestible about it. In this regard it recalls to De Quincey's mind a visit to the Whispering Gallery in St. Paul's Cathedral, which found him standing "nearly on the very spot where rather more than five years subsequently Lord Nelson was buried." Through these associations this transformative passage in the text suggests that De Quincey might confess to the reverberations of this event, to the unfathomable oscillations of matter that would totally disperse the future forged in sublime decision into "tempestuous uproars" of dreadful loss, uncertainty, and dissipation (*Confessions* [Masson ed.], 296), while still finding support within it for a sense of masculine identity.

It is fitting, then, that in both versions of the *Confessions* this scene is sealed with De Quincey's kissing of a phantom image of woman: a portrait hanging on his wall that depicts a lady of moving loveliness, "radiant with benignity, and divine tranquility" (*Confessions* [Lindop ed.], 10). At once receiving, suffering himself to be swallowed, kissing, and being generally "transfigured," all under the ominous sign of a "nervous recoil" from the convulsive effects his act would have (*Confessions* [Masson ed.], 278, 296), De Quincey himself appears as that moving thing, that viscous system, imaged in the farewell kiss: "I went up to the picture, kissed it, and then gently walked out, and closed the door for ever!" (*Confessions* [Lindop ed.], 10).[67] Again—to let this point vibrate a bit more—it only makes sense that Nelson's public image, for all its iconic masculinity, might occasionally appear in feminine guise, as in Robert Southey's account of the love his men had for him: "'Our Nel,' they used to say, 'is as brave as a lion, and as gentle as a lamb.' Severe discipline he detested, though he had been bred in a severe school: he never inflicted corporal punishment, if it were possible to avoid it, and when compelled to enforce it, he, who was familiar with wounds and death, suffered like a woman."[68]

As anyone who has ever been carried away by a kiss must (in some sense) know, to refer to a kiss that has really taken place at some point in time is yet to refer to a fully imaginary, weirdly prescribed, as yet unfinished occurrence. For we never kiss simply as historical individuals: the kiss as an act of individuals is simultaneously a cultural and transcendental proposition. The materiality of the kiss is the paradoxical "other matter" of mucous membranes through which aesthetic values come to be historically assigned as a destiny of anatomy. In accord with this sense of things, the body in Kiki Smith's works is always a slippery, unfinished business. In all its aspects and parts it is a digestive system designed to chew on transcendent notions of beauty, sublimity, pathos, and heroism—without, however, proving offensive.[69] There is a propriety here still, which seems designed to elicit the contemplation of its own regrettable sense of necessity.

To judge by the forms played with in her works, Smith would be willing to agree with Kant at least so far as to maintain that the body is a crazy "other matter" forever throwing itself into the holes it pokes in itself, thus engendering upsetting paradoxes of definition. Furthermore, her art, like his philosophy, might be said to work at eliminating the sense of disgust that Burke saw as disturbing any attempt to shift back and forth between scientific and imaginative perspectives.[70] Her work pursues this end differently from Kant's, of course, in its insistence that culture's kiss dissects, eviscerates, divides, and multiplies that which it unctuously professes to enjoy. In other words, hers is still a Romantic art, not only gnawing at the structures of neoclassical propriety but also spitting out those of Romantic pathos. In this respect Smith's work proves to be co-viscous with Goya's witches and De Quincey's crocodiles (not to mention William Butler Yeats's Crazy Jane). It may serve to remind us that while the sleep of reason may breed monsters, monstrous slime breeds reason. Nonetheless, in its mournful attitude, her work does appear still to share something of Kant's stoic sadness.

Yet this art may still offer us sufficient reason, in the face of despair, nightmare, loss of power—and (heaven help us) in the face of militant Christian morality and stoic courage—to imagine Smith, Kant, and all of us together sharing in De Quincey's conception of happiness. "I (it will be admitted) must surely know what happiness is, if any body does" (*Confessions* [Lindop ed.], 58): thus De Quincey, who found Kant's writing obnoxious and yet an absolutely vital part of himself. Similarly, Kiki Smith's works might just have the power to surprise us into swallowing the otherwise hallucinatory notion that happiness has never been, will never be, a finer thing than what De Quincey, in all the disgusting pathologies of his senses, was capable of feeling. For what else is this transformative "other matter," this visceral matter of the kiss, which Kant's theory of the sublime shudders to enjoy even, and especially, in its sadness, if not the very substance of happiness, which answers to no one; solves nothing; is endless?

Notes

Chapter 1
In the Bowels of Enlightenment

Translations not otherwise credited are my own.

1. Voltaire, quoted in Peter Gay, *The Enlightenment: An Interpretation*, 2 vols. (New York: Alfred A. Knopf, 1969), 2:131.

2. Joseph Glanvill, *Plus Ultra, or The Progress and Advancement of Knowledge since the Days of Aristotle* (1668) (Gainesville, Fla.: Scholars' Facsimiles and Reprints, 1958), 12.

3. [Pierre Louis Moreau de] Maupertuis, *Venus physique*, in vol. 2 of *Oeuvres de Mr. de Maupertuis*, rev. ed., 4 vols. (Lyons: Jean-Marie Bruyset, 1756), 3, 5.

4. On this topic see Barbara Maria Stafford, "Dissecting," chap. 1 in *Body Criticism: Imaging the Unseen in Enlightenment Art and Medicine* (Cambridge: MIT Press, 1991).

5. See Jean-François Lyotard, *The Postmodern Condition: A Report on Knowledge*, trans. Geoff Bennington and Brian Massumi (Minneapolis: University of Minnesota Press, 1984).

6. See Jean-François Lyotard, "Judicieux dans le différend," in *La faculté de juger*, by Jacques Derrida, Jean-Luc Nancy, Vincent Descombs, Garbis Kortian, Phillipe Lacoue-Labarthe, and Jean-François Lyotard (Paris: Éditions de Minuit, 1985).

7. Cf. the argument about the body as a basic trope, through which various concepts of power are articulated, presented by Rebecca Haidt in *Embodying Enlightenment: Knowing the Body in Eighteenth-Century Spanish Literature and Culture* (New York: St. Martin's Press, 1998). For an analysis of some of the most important complexities of this trope in the period immediately preceding the one I study, see Jonathan Gil Harris, *Foreign Bodies and the Body Politic: Discourses of*

Social Pathology in Early Modern England (Cambridge: Cambridge University Press, 1998).

8. Denis Diderot, *Suite de l'apologie de l'Abbé de Prades* (1752), in vol. 4 of *Oeuvres complètes*, ed. Jean Varloot, 25 vols. (Paris: Hermann, 1980), 328.

9. Voltaire (François-Marie Arouet de Voltaire), "Lettre XIII—Sur M. Locke," *Lettres philosophiques*, in vol. 22 of *Oeuvres complètes de Voltaire*, ed. Louis Moland, 52 vols. (Paris: Garnier Frères, 1877–85), 122–23.

10. Laurence Sterne, *The Life and Opinions of Tristram Shandy, Gentleman* (1759–67) (New York: Modern Library, 1950), 86.

11. Ralph Cudworth, *The True Intellectual System of the Universe* (1678), 2 vols. (Andover, Mass.: Gould and Newman, 1837), 1:223.

12. See Robert Hooke, preface to *Micrographia* (1665) (New York: Dover, 1961): "Thus all the uncertainty, and mistakes of humane actions, proceed either from the narrowness and wandring of our *Senses,* from the slipperiness or delusion of our Memory, from the confinement or rashness of our *Understanding.*"

13. Sterne, *Tristram Shandy,* 374.

14. Johann Friedrich Blumenbach, "On the Natural Variety of Mankind" (1795), in *Anthropological Treatises of Johann Friedrich Blumenbach,* ed. and trans. Thomas Bendysh (London: Longman, Green, Longman, Roberts, and Green, 1865), 91.

15. Isaac Newton, *The Mathematical Principles of Natural Philosophy,* 2d ed. (New York: Citadel Press, 1964), 19.

16. Hilary Putnam, "Sense, Nonsense, and the Senses: An Inquiry into the Powers of the Human Mind" (Dewey Lectures, 1994), *Journal of Philosophy* 91 (September 1994): 488.

17. See Claude-Adrien Helvétius, *De l'esprit* (1758), ed. Jacques Montaux (Paris: Arthème Fayard, 1988), 486.

18. Newton, *Mathematical Principles,* 445. This passage was among those added to the second edition of the *Principia,* apparently in response to criticism from Berkeley and Leibniz.

19. On this point, and with specific reference to the speculations on angels discussed below, see Simon Schaffer, "Regeneration: The Body of Natural Philosophers in Restoration England," in *Science Incarnate: Historical Embodiments of Natural Knowledge,* ed. Christopher Lawrence and Steven Shapin (Chicago: University of Chicago Press, 1998), 83–120.

20. Thomas Hobbes, *Leviathan* (1651), ed. Richard Tuck (Cambridge: Cambridge University Press, 1991), 13; Gottfried Wilhelm von Leibniz, "Reflections on the Doctrine of a Single Universal Spirit," in vol. 2 of *Philosophical Papers and*

Letters, ed. and trans. Leroy E. Loemker, 2 vols. (Chicago: University of Chicago Press, 1956), 903. For some other examples of the dissemination of this maxim, see those cited in John W. Yolton, *Locke and French Materialism* (Oxford: Oxford University Press, 1991), 68, 105. See also Peter Alexander's explanation of how this maxim, if understood simplistically, may be misleading in terms of Locke's philosophy, in *Ideas, Qualities, and Corpuscles: Locke and Boyle on the External World* (Cambridge: Cambridge University Press, 1985), 130. Ernst Cassirer also noted the problematic nature of this saying in *The Philosophy of the Enlightenment*, trans. Fritz C. A. Koelln and James P. Pettegrove (Princeton: Princeton University Press, 1951), 99.

21. Quoted in Kenneth Dewhurst, *John Locke (1632–1704): Physician and Philosopher* (London: Wellcome Historical Medical Library, 1963), 285.

22. See G[eorge]-E[rnst] Stahl, *Theoria Medica Vera*, in vol. 3 of *Oeuvres médico-philosophiques et pratiques de G.-E. Stahl*, trans. T. Blondin, 6 vols. (Paris: J.-B. Baillière et fils, 1863), 392n.

23. Georg Wilhelm Friedrich Hegel, *Encyclopedia of the Philosophical Sciences in Outline* (1817), ed. Ernst Behler, trans. Steven A. Taubeneck (New York: Continuum, 1990), 228 (translation slightly altered).

24. Anne C. Vila, *Enlightenment and Pathology: Sensibility in the Literature and Medicine of Eighteenth-Century France* (Baltimore: Johns Hopkins University Press, 1998), 7.

25. [Louis] Bourguet, *Lettres philosophiques sur la formation des sels et des crystaux et sur la génération & le mechanisme organique des plantes et des animaux* (Amsterdam: François L'Honore, 1729), 73.

26. M. Mirabaud [Paul Henry Thiry, Baron d'Holbach], *Système de la nature, ou des loix du monde physique & du monde moral*, 2 vols. (London: n. p., 1781), 1:214.

27. W. V. Quine, *Pursuit of Truth* (Cambridge: Harvard University Press, 1990), 19.

28. D. A. F. de Sade, *L'histoire de Juliette, ou, Les prospérités du vice* (1797), in vols. 8 and 9 of *Oeuvres complètes*, 16 vols. (Paris: Cercle du Livre Précieux, 1966), 8:307. On this topic of sensibility, see John Mullan, *Sentiment and Sociability: The Language of Feeling in the Eighteenth Century* (Oxford: Oxford University Press, 1988), esp. chap. 5, "Hypochondria and Hysteria: Sensibility and the Physicians."

29. Friedrich Nietzsche, *The Will to Power*, ed. Walter Kaufmann, trans. Walter Kaufmann and R. J. Hollingdale (New York: Vintage, 1968), 47.

30. [Julien Offroy de] La Mettrie, *L'homme machine*, ed. Paul-Laurent Assoun (Paris: Éditions Denoël/Gouthier, 1981), 98.

31. Denis Diderot, *Le rêve de D'Alembert*, in vol. 17 of *Oeuvres complètes*, 140–

42. See the editor's note to *Le neveau de Rameau,* in vol. 12 of *Oeuvres complètes,* 130–31n, for an explanation of the *entraille* idiom.

32. David Hillman, "Visceral Knowledge: Shakespeare, Skepticism, and the Interiority of the Early Modern Body," in *The Body in Parts: Fantasies of Corporeality in Early Modern Europe,* ed. David Hillman and Carla Mazzio (New York: Routledge, 1997), 86. This essay in its entirety (81–105) is relevant to my argument here.

33. Gottfried Wilhelm von Leibniz, "On What Is Independent of Sense and of Matter," in vol. 2 of *Philosophical Papers and Letters,* 884.

34. Immanuel Kant, *Critique of Pure Reason,* trans. Werner S. Pluhar (Indianapolis: Hackett Publishing, 1996), 149–50.

35. Thomas Sprat, *History of the Royal Society* (1667), ed. Jackson S. Cope and Harold Whitmore Jones (Saint Louis: Washington University Studies, 1958), 92, 348–49. See also the parallel contradiction in Glanvill's *Plus Ultra,* in which we are told that the Royal Society's *"Aims* are to free *Philosophy* from the vain *Images* and *Compositions* of *Phansie,* by making it *palpable,* and bringing it down to the *plain objects* of the *Senses"* (89) even as we are also told that "our *Senses* must be *aided* [with instruments]; for of themselves they are too narrow for the *vastness* of things, and too *short* for *deep Researches"* (52–53). The markedly Protestant rhetoric here is relevant to my claims in this chapter about cultural politics; the fact that the rhetoric in question is also markedly catechrestic, in its rhetorical opposition to rhetoric, is also relevant to my comments on this subject. It might be worth noting as well that through various tropes, the works of these writers characterize science as a definitively masculine pursuit (as does the poem by Abraham Cowley that prefaces Sprat's *History*), thus marking another aspect of the cultural politics with which I am concerned in this study. On this topic see Evelyn Fox Keller, *Reflections on Gender and Science* (New Haven: Yale University Press, 1985), esp. chap. 3, "Spirit and Reason at the Birth of Modern Science."

36. John Locke, *An Essay Concerning Human Understanding* (1690), ed. Peter H. Nidditch (Oxford: Oxford University Press, 1975), 312.

37. Alexander Pope, *An Essay on Man,* ed. Maynard Mack, in vol. 3 of *The Twickenham Edition of the Poems of Alexander Pope,* ed. John Butt, 6 vols. (London: Methuen, 1950), 1.7.

38. David Hume, *An Enquiry Concerning Human Understanding* (1748), in *Enquiries Concerning Human Understanding and Concerning the Principles of Morals,* ed. L. A. Selby-Bigge and P. H. Nidditch, 3d ed. (Oxford: Oxford University Press, 1975), 131.

39. Jonathan Swift, *A Tale of a Tub* (1710), in vol. 1 of *The Prose Works of Jonathan Swift,* ed. Herbert Davis, 14 vols. (Oxford: Basil Blackwell, 1939), 109.

40. Andrew Cunningham, *The Anatomical Renaissance: The Resurrection of the Anatomical Projects of the Ancients* (Hants, England: Scolar Press, 1997), 54. See also the comments on this engraving by Hogarth in Carol Houlihan Flynn, *The Body in Swift and Defoe* (Cambridge: Cambridge University Press, 1990), 26–28. Jacques Attali writes of the generalization of the autopsy in the eighteenth century in *L'ordre cannibale: Vie et mort de la médecine* (Paris: Bernard Grasset, 1979), 164; John McManners notes the symptomatic spread of anxiety over the possibility of being autopsied alive in *Death and the Enlightenment: Changing Attitudes to Death among Christians and Unbelievers in Eighteenth-Century France* (Oxford: Oxford University Press, 1981), 48.

41. William Wordsworth, "A Poet's Epitaph" (1800) and "The Tables Turned" (1798), in *Selected Poems and Prefaces*, ed. Jack Stillinger (Boston: Houghton Mifflin, 1965), 119, 107.

42. See Bourguet, *Lettres philosophiques sur la formation des sels*, 158–59; and [Claude-Nicolas] Le Cat, *Traité des sensations et des passions en général, et des sens en particulier* (1739), in vols. 1 and 2 of *Oeuvres physiologiques*, 3 vols. (Paris: Vallat-La-Chapelle, 1767–68), 2:202, 522. See also Jacques Roger's discussion of the Abbé Mariotte's speculations on other orders of sense perception (in his *Essay de logique contenant les principes des sciences et la manière de s'en servir pour faire les bons raissonemens* [1678]) in *Les sciences de la vie dans la pensée française du dix-huitième siècle* ([Paris]: Armand Colin, 1963), 200–202.

43. Pope, *Essay on Man*, 1.201–4.

44. Cf. the similar arguments as to the providential formation of the human senses in George Berkeley, *A New Theory of Vision* (1709), in vol. 1 of *The Works of George Berkeley, Bishop of Cloyne*, ed. A. A. Luce and T. E. Jessop, 9 vols. (London: Thomas Nelson and Sons, 1948), 206, 231.

45. George Eliot, *Middlemarch*, ed. W. J. Harvey (New York: Viking Penguin, 1985), 226.

46. W. V. Quine, "Ontological Relativity," in *Ontological Relativity and Other Essays* (New York: Columbia University Press, 1969), 35. See also Maurice Mandlebaum's comment—"Locke's attack on the independent reality of species was in many places couched in terms of biological facts, and must have been of at least indirect influence in undermining the biological theory of the invariance of species"—in *Philosophy, Science, and Sense Perception: Historical and Critical Studies* (Baltimore: Johns Hopkins University Press, 1964), 43n.

47. Thomas Willis, "The Preface to the Reader," in *Two Discourses Concerning the Soul of Brutes* (1683), trans. Samuel Pordage (Gainesville, Fla.: Scholars' Facsimiles and Reprints, 1971).

48. See Benedict de Spinoza, *The Ethics* (1677), in *A Spinoza Reader,* ed. and trans. Edwin Curley (Princeton: Princeton University Press, 1994), 114, 122; and Pierre-Jean-Georges Cabanis, quoted in Martin S. Staum, *Cabanis: Enlightenment and Medical Philosophy in the French Revolution* (Princeton: Princeton University Press, 1980), 202: "We see food, with its own characteristic qualities fall into this organ [of the stomach] and leave it with new qualities, and we conclude that the stomach, in fact, altered the food. We also see isolated and incoherent impressions arrive at the brain by means of the nerves; the organ begins acting, acts upon them, and soon transmits them metamorphosed into ideas."

49. [John] Turbervill[e] Needham, *Observations upon the Generation, Composition, and Decomposition of Animal and Vegetable Substances* (London: n.p., 1749), 40; and see Jonathan Swift, *Gulliver's Travels* (1726) (New York: Modern Library, 1931), 218.

50. Hooke, preface to *Micrographia.*

51. Isaac Newton, *Opticks* (1704) (New York: Dover, 1952; reprint, based on the 4th ed. [1730]), 403, 370, 374–75.

52. Margaret Cavendish, Duchess of Newcastle, *The Description of a New World, Called the Blazing World* (1666), in *The Blazing World and Other Writings,* ed. Kate Lilley (London: Penguin, 1994), 152–53, 133–34.

53. Robert Boyle, "Free Considerations about Subordinate Forms," in vol. 2 of *The Works of the Honourable Robert Boyle,* 5 vols. (London: A. Millar, 1744), 536.

54. Jean-Jacques Rousseau, "Seconde préface," *La nouvelle Héloïse,* in vol. 2 of *Oeuvres complètes,* ed. Bernard Gagnebin and Marcel Raymond, 5 vols. (Paris: Éditions Gallimard, 1961), 12.

55. See David-Renaud Bouillier, *Essai philosophique sur l'âme des bêtes* (1728) (reprint of 2d ed. [1737], [Paris]: Fayard, 1985), 295; also see Kant's effort, through "the transcendental power of imagination," to dismiss such possibilities as that a human being might be "changed now into this and then into that animal shape," in *Critique of Pure Reason,* 154–55.

56. J. B. Robinet, *Considérations philosophiques de la gradation naturelle des forms de l'être, ou les essais de la nature qui apprend a faire l'homme* (Paris: Charles Saillant, 1768), 198.

57. Diderot, *Le rêve de D'Alembert,* 138, 126.

58. Maupertuis, *Venus physique,* 6; and *Système de la nature,* in vol. 2 of *Oeuvres,* 154.

59. [Bernard de] Fontenelle, *De l'origine des fables* (1724), ed. J.-R. Carré (Paris: Librarie Félix Alcan, 1932), 26. See also the considerably more sophisticated theory of images of metamorphosis as early acts of cognition in Giambattista Vico,

The New Science of Giambattista Vico (1725), trans. Thomas Goddard Bergin and Max Harold Fisch (Ithaca: Cornell University Press, 1968), 131–32.

60. Bouillier, *Essai philosophique*, 417. On this topic see also the section titled "The Metamorphic Language of Reason" (73–77), in vol. 1 of Paul Ilie, *The Age of Minerva*, 2 vols. (Philadelphia: University of Pennsylvania Press, 1995).

61. Pierre Bayle, "Spinoza (Benoît)," in vol. 3 of *Dictionaire historique et critique* (1696), 3d ed., rev., 4 vols. (Rotterdam: Michel Bohm, 1720), 2639, 2645; and "Epicure," in vol. 2 of *Dictionaire historique*, 1083.

62. Bayle, "Ovide Nason (Publius)," in vol. 3 of *Dictionaire historique*, 2142.

63. Nietzsche, *Will to Power*, 548.

64. See Wayne Glausser's argument that Locke and Blake should be seen not simply as "spiritual enemies" but also as parallel figures, in "Locke and Blake as Physicians: Delivering the Eighteenth-Century Body," in *Reading the Social Body*, ed. Catherine B. Burroughs and Jeffrey David Ehrenreich (Iowa City: University of Iowa Press, 1993), 218–43.

65. William Blake, *Milton* (ca. 1809–10), in *The Complete Poetry and Prose of William Blake*, ed. David V. Erdman, rev. ed. (New York: Doubleday, 1988), sec. 1, plate 28, ll. 34–35. P

66. Newton, quoted in Gay, *The Enlightenment*, 2:134.

67. William Blake, *Jerusalem*, in *Complete Poetry and Prose*, sec. 1, plate 15, ll. 11–20.

68. Sprat, *History of the Royal Society*, 341.

69. William Blake, "To the Public," in *Complete Poetry and Prose*, 95.

70. A[braham] Trembley, *Mémoires, pour servir à l'histoire d'un genre de polypes d'eau douce, à bras en forme de cornes* (Leyden: Jean and Herman Verbeek, 1744), 52, 266–68.

71. C[harles] Bonnet, *Considerations sur les corps organisés*, 2 vols. (Amsterdam: Marc-Michel Rey, 1762), 2:164; on this point in Cudworth, see John W. Yolton, *Thinking Matter: Materialism in Eighteenth-Century Britain* (Minneapolis: University of Minnesota Press, 1983), 7. 2:See also Virginia P. Dawson, *Nature's Enigma: The Problem of the Polyp in the Letters of Bonnet, Trembley, and Reaumur* (Philadelphia: American Philosophical Society, 1987).

72. William Blake, *The Book of Urizen*, in *Complete Poetry and Prose*, sec. 9, plate 25, ll. 30–42.

73. William Blake, "To the Deists," in *Complete Poetry and Prose*, 200–201.

74. James Joyce, *Ulysses* (New York: Random House, 1961), 743, 720, 418.

75. Cf. Ruth Salvaggio's suggestion, in writing of Pope and Newton, that "there was a good deal of the 'woman' in these Enlightenment men," in *Enlight-*

ened Absence: Neoclassical Configurations of the Feminine (Urbana: University of Illinois Press, 1988), 66. (Salvaggio's entire study is relevant to this point.) The way female bodies were imaged within the generalized body of a markedly masculine science is also relevant to my contention here; see Ludmilla Jordanova, *Sexual Visions: Images of Science and Medicine between the Eighteenth and Twentieth Century* (Madison: University of Wisconsin Press, 1989). See also the commentary, which responds in part to Salvaggio's study, in William Walker, *Locke, Literary Criticism, and Philosophy* (Cambridge: Cambridge University Press, 1994), 56–72; and George Rousseau, "Cultural History in a New Key: Towards a Semiotics of the Nerve," in *Interpretation and Cultural History*, ed. Joan H. Pittock and Andrew Wear (New York: St. Martin's Press, 1991), 25–81.

76. William Blake, *The Marriage of Heaven and Hell*, in *Complete Poetry and Prose*, plate 3, l. 6.

CHAPTER 2
Orifices Extended in Space

1. Quoted in Theodore Reff, "Painting and Theory in the Final Decade," in *Cézanne: The Late Work*, ed. William Rubin (New York: Museum of Modern Art, 1977), 46. The quotation is taken from a 1904 letter to Emile Bernard; Reff argues that the fame of this statement, especially among the popularizers of Cubism, rests upon a misunderstanding of its original context.

2. Michael Baxandall, *Shadows and Enlightenment* (New Haven: Yale University Press, 1995), 141.

3. *La Raie* (also referred to in English as *The Ray-Fish* and *The Skate*) now hangs in the Louvre; contemporary accounts suggest that it was painted some years before 1728, while Chardin was still an unmarried young man in his twenties. About four months before his acceptance into the Royal Academy, Chardin had publicly exhibited this work at the annual open-air Exhibition de Jeunesse, held on the feast of Corpus Christi.

4. Pierre Rosenberg, *Chardin*, trans. Helga Harrison (Lausanne: Éditions d'Art Albert Skira, 1963), 30.

5. Of course, some critics have disagreed with the general praise of this work—in the nineteenth century, Pierre Hédouin called it one of Chardin's "less remarkable productions" (*Mosaique* [Paris: Heugel, 1856], 176)—but such opinions have been the exception.

6. "This is realism of a kind Chardin did not repeat, at least in such an aggressive manner. It is arresting certainly, and is doubtless intended to be so—per-

haps something of a youthful riposte to the highly ornamental, tasteful, and polished still lifes of Desportes and Oudry" (Michael Levey, *Painting and Sculpture in France 1700–1789* [New Haven: Yale University Press, 1993], 205).

7. Ronald Paulson, *Emblem and Expression: Meaning in English Art of the Eighteenth Century* (Cambridge: Harvard University Press, 1975), 107.

8. On this point, see Norman Bryson's critique in "The Gaze in the Expanded Field," in *Vision and Visuality*, ed. Hal Foster (Seattle: Bay Press, 1988), 87–108.

9. Claude Lévi-Strauss, *Totemism*, trans. Rodney Needham (Boston: Beacon Press, 1963), 89.

10. Jonathan Crary, *Techniques of the Observer: On Vision and Modernity in the Nineteenth Century* (Cambridge: MIT Press, 1990), 62.

11. See Michel Foucault, *Les mots et les choses: Une archéologie des sciences humaines* (Paris: Gallimard, 1977).

12. Paul Ilie, *The Age of Minerva*, 2 vols. (Philadelphia: University of Pennsylvania Press, 1995), 2:68. The entire chapter, "Metamorphoses of the Bat" (51–69), is relevant to my concerns here.

13. René Descartes, *Meditations on First Philosophy*, in vol. 2 of *The Philosophical Writings of Descartes*, trans. John Cottingham, Robert Stoothoff, Dugald Murdoch, and Anthony Kenny, 3 vols. (Cambridge: Cambridge University Press, 1991), 5.

14. For an analysis of the popularization of Blaise Pascal's phrase "the geometric spirit," and for the changes undergone by "geometry" as an idiom for philosophical inquiry, see Isabel F. Knight, *The Geometric Spirit: The Abbé de Condillac and the French Enlightenment* (New Haven: Yale University Press, 1968), 18–20. In *Leviathan and the Air-Pump: Hobbes, Boyle, and the Experimental Life* (Princeton: Princeton University Press, 1985), 328, Steven Shapin and Simon Schaffer note the differing conceptions that Hobbes and Boyle had of geometry: the former identified it as a model of philosophy, while the latter, the experimentalist, did not. See also the description of the "shift of mathematical emphasis from geometry to analysis" in Thomas L. Hankins, *Science and the Enlightenment* (Cambridge: Cambridge University Press, 1985), 17–22. Also, for an overview of this identification of Descartes, geometry, and perspectivism and for a discussion of some of the problems with this identification in regard to the understanding of art, see Martin Jay, "Scopic Regimes of Modernity," in Foster, *Vision and Visuality*.

15. Immanuel Kant, *Critique of Pure Reason*, trans. Werner S. Pluhar (Indianapolis: Hackett Publishing, 1996), 678. Kant, of course, had other examples in

mind beyond Descartes—perhaps most notably, Benedict de Spinoza, who had famously declared, "I shall consider human actions and appetites just as if it were a question of lines, planes, and bodies," in *The Ethics* (1677), in *A Spinoza Reader,* ed. and trans. Edwin Curley (Princeton: Princeton University Press, 1994), 153.

16. Descartes, *Meditations on First Philosophy,* 14.

17. For a discussion of Descartes's dissections in relation to his metaphysics, his medical concerns, and modern medicine in general, see Drew Leder, "A Tale of Two Bodies: The Cartesian Corpse and the Lived Body," in *Body and Flesh: A Philosophical Reader,* ed. Donn Welton (Malden, Mass.: Blackwell Publishers, 1998), 117–30.

18. Reported in Charles-Nicolas Cochin, "Essai sur la vie de Chardin" (1780), in *Précis analytique des travaux de l'Académie des Sciences, Belles-lettres et Arts de Rouen pendant l'année 1875–1876* (Rouen: H. Boissel, 1876), 434.

19. George Berkeley, *A New Theory of Vision,* in vol. 1 of *The Works of George Berkeley, Bishop of Cloyne,* ed. A. A. Luce and T. E. Jessop, 9 vols. (London: Thomas Nelson and Sons, 1948), 190–91. Other passages in this work make it clear that Berkeley had Descartes in mind in his critique of this geometric approach; see, for example, 186. Although he was no empiricist, Berkeley's sensationist idealism still brought him close to figures such as Haller on this point.

20. "Chardin . . . recognized that an object does not have its own color, but that its color depends on the lighting and the proximity of the things surrounding it. In his work, forms are never subjected to a closed and hermetic world. He establishes a continual exchange among them, each feeling the influence of the others near it. The atmosphere is filled with secret messages" (Michel Faré, *La nature morte en France: Son historie et son évolution du XVII e au XX e siècle,* 2 vols. [Geneva: Pierre Cailler, 1962], 1:162).

21. Marcel Proust, "Chardin," in *Contre Sainte-Beuve suivi de nouveaux mélanges* (Paris: Gallimard, 1954), 368. On this topic of revelation, and for the relation between Proust and Chardin, see Mieke Bal, *The Mottled Screen: Reading Proust Visually,* trans. Anna-Louise Milne (Stanford: Stanford University Press, 1997), esp. 31–68.

22. Albrecht von Haller, *Elementa physiologiæ corporis humani* (1747), 8 vols., 2d ed. (Lausanne: Marci-Michael Bousquet, 1757–58), 1:2.

23. Denis Diderot, *Éléments de physiologie* (ca. 1774–84), in vol. 17 of *Oeuvres complètes,* ed. Jean Varloot, 25 vols. (Paris: Hermann, 1980), 63, 64.

24. Diderot, *Le rêve de D'Alembert,* in vol. 17 of *Oeuvres complètes,* 116, 148.

25. Diderot, *Lettre sur les aveugles* (1749), in vol. 4 of *Oeuvres complètes,* 33.

26. Denis Diderot, *Pensées détachées sur la peinture* (1776), in *Salons IV: Héros et*

martyrs, ed. Else Marie Bukdahl et al. (Paris: Hermann, 1995), 408. Also, on this point and others related to this chapter, see the important essay by Jean Starobinski, "Le philosophe, le géomètre, l'hybride," *Poétique* 21 (1975): 8–23.

27. Denis Diderot, *Salon de 1769,* in *Salons IV,* 43. Cf. his statement that matters of precision in geometry "are but approximations in nature" (Denis Diderot, *Suite de l'apologie de l'Abbé de Prades* [1752], in vol. 4 of *Oeuvres complètes,* ed. Jean Varloot, 25 vols. [Paris: Hermann, 1980], 328).

28. See Jean Mayer, *Diderot: Homme de science* (Rennes: Brettone, 1959), 99–104; see also the discussion of Diderot's conception of geometric truth as a matter of human convention rather than eternal order, in Daniel Brewer, *The Discourse of Enlightenment in Eighteenth-Century France: Diderot and the Art of Philosophizing* (Cambridge: Cambridge University Press, 1993), 85.

29. On this point see Michael Fried's analysis of Chardin's work in *Absorption and Theatricality: Painting and Beholder in the Age of Diderot* (Berkeley: University of California Press, 1980), esp. 44–53.

30. Yve-Alain Bois, Jean-Claude Bonne, Christian Bonnefoi, Hubert Damisch, and Jean-Claude Lebensztejn, "La Raie," *Critique* no. 315–16 (August–September 1973): 685. The authors of this essay draw extensively on the writings of Georges Bataille.

31. Camille Mauclair, "Psychologie de la nature-morte," *Revue politique et littéraire (Revue bleue)* (1 July 1905): 21.

32. Edmund de Goncourt and Jules de Goncourt, *L'art du dix-huitième siècle* (1873), 3 vols. (Paris: Flammarion, 1906), 1:115.

33. L.-G. Baillet de Saint Julien, "Lettre a mr. [sic] Ch[ardin] sur les caractères en peinture" (1753), in *Réflexions et lettres* (Geneva: Minkoff Reprint, 1972), 17–18.

34. In the case of things other than food, these processes are the cultural mechanisms that incorporate and transfigure various matters, whether one is speaking of something like the clay used in pottery or of the human clay raised to be cook, woman, or artist. Diderot offered just such an analogy between digestive and cultural processes, in the course of tracing the connections between human beings and statues, at the beginning of "La suite d'un entretien entre M. D'Alembert et M. Diderot," in *Le rêve de D'Alembert* (1769), 92–96.

35. Robert Boyle, "The Origins of Forms and Qualities, According to the Corpuscular Philosophy," in vol. 2 of *The Works of the Honourable Robert Boyle,* 5 vols. (London: A. Millar, 1744), 474.

36. [Jean-Baptiste-René Robinet], *De la nature,* rev. ed., 4 vols. (Amsterdam: E. Van Harrevelt, 1763–66), 1:45.

37. Jean-Baptiste-René Robinet, *Considerations philosophiques de la gradation naturelle des formes de l'être, ou les essais de la nature qui apprend a faire l'homme* (Paris: Charles Saillant, 1768), 2, 174.

38. Robinet, *De la nature*, 4:114–15. For the historical context to Robinet's reference to the Hottentot, see Alexander Butchart, *The Anatomy of Power: European Constructions of the African Body* (London: Zed Books, 1998).

39. C[harles] Bonnet, *Considerations sur les corps organisés*, 2 vols. (Amsterdam: Marc-Michel Rey, 1762), 1:41, 60; 2:55; 1:228.

40. René Descartes, *Discourse on the Method*, in vol. 1 of *Philosophical Writings*, 112.

41. For an analysis related to this point, of how Descartes's social life and self-conception were implicated in his conception of automata, see Peter Dear, "A Mechanical Microcosm: Bodily Passions, Good Manners, and Cartesian Mechanism," in *Science Incarnate: Historical Embodiments of Natural Knowledge*, ed. Christopher Lawrence and Steven Shapin (Chicago: University of Chicago Press, 1998), 51–82.

42. Descartes, *Discourse on the Method*, 112.

43. See Michael Baxandall, "Pictures and Ideas: Chardin's *A Lady Taking Tea*," in *Patterns of Intention: On the Historical Explanation of Pictures* (New Haven: Yale University Press, 1985), 83. Baxandall points out that the Academy in Chardin's time included the post of professor of geometry and persuasively argues, on the basis of contemporary conceptions of geometry as well as on the basis of a sensationism diffused through optics, physiology, physics, and Lockean philosophy, that in this time "the old Renaissance simplicity of depicting 'Nature' was gone" (97). See also the analysis by René Demoris of how the "finesse" of Chardin's style represents a defiance of geometry, in *Chardin, la chair et l'objet* (Paris: Éditions Adam Biro, 1991), 46.

44. André Gide, "The Lesson of Poussin," trans. Dorothy Bussy, *Arts* 2 (October 1946): 64.

45. Denis Diderot, *Salon de 1765*, in vol. 14 of *Oeuvres complètes*, 117.

46. Denis Diderot, *Salon of 1763*, in vol. 13 of *Oeuvres complètes*, 379.

47. L.-G. Baillet de Saint Julien, "Caractères des peintres françois, actuellement vivans" (1755), in *Réflexions et lettres*, 5.

48. From the Academy's proceedings, quoted in André Pascal and Roger Gaucheron, *Documents sur la vie et l'oeuvre de Chardin* (Paris: Éditions de la Galerie Pigalle, 1931), 60.

49. Abbé Raynal (Guillaume-Thomas-François Raynal), quoted in Pierre Rosenberg, *Chardin: 1699–1779* (Cleveland: Cleveland Museum of Art, 1979), 289. See also Barbara Stafford's comment in *Body Criticism: Imaging the Unseen in En-*

lightenment Art and Medicine (Cambridge: MIT Press, 1991), 79: "The artist's *morceau de reception* vicariously offered a suffering animal substitute for the epic modes his lowly academic ranking would preclude him from officially exhibiting." Symptomatic of this situation was Chardin's desire that his son might become a history painter and his efforts to help him in this career, which then might have been of the highest rank; proving only moderately accomplished at best, the son ended up a suicide.

50. André Malraux, *The Voices of Silence*, trans. Stuart Gilbert (Princeton: Princeton University Press, 1978), 295.

51. Marianne Roland Michel, *Chardin* (Paris: Éditions Hazan, 1994), 213.

52. On the relation of Chardin's work to domesticity, see Ella Snoep-Reitsma, "Chardin and the Bourgeois Ideals of His Time," *Nederlands Kunsthistorisch Jaarboek* 24 (1973): 147- 243; and Norman Bryson, "Still Life and 'Feminine' Space," in *Looking at the Overlooked: Four Essays on Still-Life Painting* (Cambridge: Harvard University Press, 1990), 136–78. Bryson's entire study is a valuable work in relation to my concerns here.

53. Bruce Thomas Boehrer, *The Fury of Men's Gullets: Ben Jonson and the Digestive Canal* (Philadelphia: University of Pennsylvania Press, 1997), 120. See, for instance, how Jan Baptista (or Jean-Baptiste) van Helmont, the seventeenth-century physiologist, described digestion as taking place in "particular Kitchins of the Members" of the body, as quoted (from a contemporary English translation) in Elizabeth Haigh, *Xavier Bichat and the Medical Theory of the Eighteenth Century* (London: Wellcome Institute for the History of Medicine, 1989), 19n. Haigh's work in its entirety is also relevant here.

54. Voltaire (François-Marie Arouet de Voltaire), *Éléments de la philosophie de Newton* (1738), in vol. 22 of *Oeuvres complètes de Voltaire*, ed. Louis Moland, 52 vols. (Paris: Garnier Frères, 1877–85), 430.

55. L.-G. Baillet de Saint Julien, "Lettre sur la peinture, la sculpture, et l'architecture" (1749), in *Réflexions et lettres*, 108, 109.

56. See the 1753 letter by a M. Estève (but also the response to it) included among the documents in Georges Wildenstein, *Chardin* (Paris: Les Beaux-Arts, 1933), 88.

57. Abbé Raynal, quoted in Rosenberg, *Chardin: 1699–1779*, 289. See also the gloss on this remark in Thomas E. Crow, *Painters and Public Life in Eighteenth-Century Paris* (New Haven: Yale University Press, 1985), 137.

58. Mathon de la Cour, quoted in Wildenstein, *Chardin*, 109.

59. Diderot, *Salon de 1763*, 380. Diderot was given to occasional sniping at Pierre, even though he sometimes also quoted him approvingly.

60. Ibid.

61. De Goncourt and de Goncourt, *L'art du dix-huitième siècle*, 1:84, 106, 93–94.

62. Ibid., 1:84.

63. Francis Ponge, "De la nature morte et de Chardin" (1963), in *Nouveau recueil* (Paris: Éditions Gallimard, 1967), 174.

64. Proust, "Chardin," 365.

65. Michel Faré and Fabrice Faré, *La vie silencieuse en France: La nature morte au dix-huitième siècle* (Fribourg, Switzerland: Office du Livre, 1976), 152.

66. Michel, *Chardin*, 147.

67. Cf. Proust's reference to the common complaint among artists that *littérateurs* see in paintings what their makers never meant to put there: "But it is sufficient for me that they *have* put it there" ("Chardin," 376).

68. Especially valuable is the early essay by René Demoris, "La nature morte chez Chardin," *Revue d'esthétique* 22 (1969): 363–85. Also of interest is his previously cited book, *Chardin, la chair et l'objet*. My allusion to Bal's work is to the text cited above, *Mottled Screen*, esp. 31–68.

69. Jacques Derrida, "'Eating Well,' or the Calculation of the Subject," trans. Peter Connor and Avital Ronell, in *Points . . . : Interviews, 1974–1994*, ed. Elisabeth Weber (Stanford: Stanford University Press, 1995), 282.

70. Sir Thomas Browne, *Religio Medici*, in *Religio Medici and Other Works*, ed. L. C. Martin (Oxford: Oxford University Press, 1964), 36.

Chapter 3
The Work of Art in the Age of Mechanical Digestion

1. J[acques] de Vaucanson, *Le mécanisme du fluteur automate* (1738) (Buren, The Netherlands: Frits Knuf, 1979), 20.

2. [Marie-Jean Antoine Nicolas Caritat] Condorcet, "Éloge de M. de Vaucanson," in vol. 3 of *Éloges des académiciens de l'académie royale des sciences, morts depuis l'an 1666 jusqu'en 1790*, 5 vols. (Paris: Didot, 1799), 210–11.

3. Laurence Sterne, *The Life and Opinions of Tristram Shandy, Gentleman* (1759–67) (New York: Modern Library, 1950), 551.

4. See the *Encyclopédie, ou dictionnaire raisonné des sciences, des arts, et des métiers*, ed. Denis Diderot, 17 vols. (Paris: Briasson, 1751–65), 1:448–51.

5. For my information about Vaucanson and his works, I am indebted especially to André Doyon and Lucien Liaigre, *Jacques Vaucanson: Mécanicien de génie* (Paris: Presses Universitaires de France, 1966). I have also drawn upon David

Lasocki's preface to Vaucanson, *Le mécanisme du fluteur automate;* Alfred Chapuis and Edouard Gélis, *Le monde des automates: Étude historique et technique,* 2 vols. (Geneva: Éditions Slatkine, 1984); Alfred Chapuis and Edmond Droz, *Les automates: Figures artificielles d'hommes et d'animaux* (Neuchatel: Éditions du Griffon, [1949]); Alfred Chapuis, *Les automates dans les oeuvres d'imagination* (Neuchatel: Éditions du Griffon, 1947); and Condorcet, "Éloge de M. de Vaucanson," 203–32.

6. See, e. g., the imaginary gathering of "all the marvelous things that the Vaucansons of all ages have invented" in [Claude-Nicolas] Le Cat, *Traité des sensations et des passions en général, et des sens en particulier* (1739), in vols. 1 and 2 of *Oeuvres physiologiques,* 3 vols. (Paris: Vallat-La-Chapelle, 1767–68), 1:xix.

7. See the references to Vaucanson's duck in Christopher G. Langton, "Artificial Life," in *The Philosophy of Artificial Life,* ed. Margaret A. Boden (Oxford: Oxford University Press, 1996), 42–43; and in Richard Powers, *Galatea 2.2* (New York: Farrar, Straus and Giroux, 1995), 245. See also the appearance made by this duck in Thomas Pynchon's *Mason & Dixon* (New York: Henry Holt, 1997).

8. C[harles] Bonnet, *Considerations sur les corps organisés* (Amsterdam: Marc-Michel Rey, 1762), 2:23. See also the reference by Margaret C. Jacobs, in "Scientific Culture in the Early English Enlightenment: Mechanisms, Industry, and Gentlemanly Facts," to "an itinerant lecturer, avid Freemason, and progressive schoolmaster named Martin Clare," who, in the 1730s, "lectured on the history of automata . . . on the circulation of the blood . . . [and] on magnetism," in *Anticipations of the Enlightenment in England, France, and Germany,* ed. Alan Charles Kors and Paul J. Korshin (Philadelphia: University of Pennsylvania Press, 1987), 139.

9. On this point, see Betsy Rosasco, *The Sculptures of the Chateau of Marly during the Reign of Louis XIV* (New York: Garland Publishing, 1986), 76–77. It should be noted that technology was already being articulated in, through, and as mythological figuration in the era of Louis XIV, in gardens and elsewhere, as the following discussion of Descartes indicates; on this topic see Kenneth J. Knoespel, "Gazing on Technology: *Theatrum Mechanorum* and the Assimilation of Renaissance Machinery," in *Literature and Technology,* ed. Mark L. Greenberg and Lance Schachterle (London: Associated University Presses, 1992), 99–124. For the relationship of machinery to Versailles, see Jean-Marie Apostolidès, *Le roi-machine: Spectacle et politique au temps de Louis XIV* (Paris: Éditions de Minuit, 1981), esp. 107 and 151.

10. Quoted from the prospectus reproduced in Chapuis and Gélis, *Le monde des automates,* 2:185.

11. Barbara Maria Stafford, *Artful Science: Enlightenment Entertainment and the Eclipse of Visual Education* (Cambridge: MIT Press, 1994), 197. On this and other points related to this chapter, see also Michael Cardy, "Technology as Play: The Case of Vaucanson," *Studies on Voltaire and the Eighteenth Century* 241 (1986): 109–24; and Reed Benhamou, "From *Curiosité* to *Utilité:* The Automaton in Eighteenth-Century France," *Studies in Eighteenth-Century Culture* 17 (1987): 91–105.

12. See [John Turberville] Needham, *Nouvelles observations microscopiques, avec des découvertes intéressantes sur la composition & la décomposition des corps organisés* (Paris: Louis-Étienne Ganeau, 1750), 164n. (This reference does not appear in the English version of this work.)

13. Condorcet, "Éloge de M. de Vaucanson," 221. For the context of this incident, see Jacques Proust, *Diderot et l'Encyclopédie*, 3d ed. (Paris: Albin Michel, 1995), 171.

14. See Voltaire (François-Marie Arouet de Voltaire), "Discours en vers sur l'homme," in vol. 9 of *Oeuvres complètes de Voltaire*, ed. Louis Moland, 52 vols. (Paris: Garnier Frères, 1877–85), 420; and [Julien Offroy de] La Mettrie, *L'homme machine*, ed. Paul-Laurent Assoun (Paris: Éditions Denoël/Gonthier, 1981), 143.

15. René Descartes, *Discourse on the Method*, in vol. 1 of *The Philosophical Writings of Descartes*, trans. John Cottingham, Robert Stoothoff, Dugald Murdoch, and Anthony Kenny, 3 vols. (Cambridge: Cambridge University Press, 1991), 139.

16. René Descartes, *Treatise on Man*, in vol. 1 of *Philosophical Writings*, 100.

17. Henry Fielding, *Tom Jones* (1744), ed. Sheridan Baker (New York: W. W. Norton, 1973), 503.

18. [Charles] Bonnet, *Essai analytique sur les facultés de l'ame* (1760), 2d ed. (Copenhagen: Philibert, 1769), viii; Denis Diderot, *Le rêve de D'Alembert*, in vol. 17 of *Oeuvres complètes*, ed. Jean Varloot, 25 vols. (Paris: Hermann, 1980), 122. For analyses of the relation between the work of physicians and metaphysicians in this era, see especially Anne C. Vila, *Enlightenment and Pathology: Sensibility in the Literature and Medicine of Eighteenth-Century France* (Baltimore: Johns Hopkins University Press, 1998). See also Peter Gay, "The Enlightenment as Medicine and as Cure," in *The Age of the Enlightenment: Studies Presented to Theodore Besterman*, ed. W. H. Barber (Edinburgh: Oliver and Boyd, 1967), 375–86; Kathleen Wellman, *La Mettrie: Medicine, Philosophy, and Enlightenment* (Durham: Duke University Press, 1992); and François Duchesneau, *La physiologie des lumières: Empirisme, modèles, et théories* (The Hague: Martinus Nijhoff, 1982).

19. Théophile Bordeu, *Recherches sur l'histoire de la médecine*, in vol. 2 of *Oeuvres complètes*, 2 vols. (Paris: Caille et Ravier, 1818), 667. On this topic of the pro-

liferating metaphor of the machine, see Aram Vartanian, *Diderot and Descartes: A Study of Scientific Naturalism in the Enlightenment* (Princeton: Princeton University Press, 1953), esp. 203–90.

20. "Machine," in vol. 9 of Diderot, *Encyclopédie*, 798.

21. John Locke, *An Essay Concerning Human Understanding* (1690), ed. Peter H. Nidditch (Oxford: Oxford University Press, 1975), 77.

22. Thomas Hobbes, *Leviathan* (1651), ed. Richard Tuck (Cambridge: Cambridge University Press, 1991), 9.

23. "Ame des bêtes," in vol. 1 of Diderot, *Encyclopédie*, 345–46. For La Mettrie's comment on Descartes as the first who "perfectly demonstrated that animals were pure machines," see *L'homme machine*, 144. For the passages the Abbé (Claude) Yvon borrowed, see David Renaud Bouillier, *Essai philosophique sur l'âme des bêtes* (1728) (reprint of 2d ed. [1737], [Paris]: Fayard, 1985), esp. 209–10 and 224.

24. See "Ame des bêtes," 346; and Charles-Georges Leroy, *Lettres philosophiques sur l'intelligence et la perfectibilité des animaux* (1781) (Paris: De Valade, 1802), 99–102. With this argument Leroy and Yvon were again echoing Bouillier; see his *Essai philosophique*, 222.

25. Frances Burney, *Evelina: Or the History of a Young Lady's Entrance into the World* (1778), ed. Edward A. Bloom (London: Oxford University Press, 1968), 76–77; and Joseph Berington, quoted in John W. Yolton, *Thinking Matter: Materialism in Eighteenth-Century Britain* (Minneapolis: University of Minnesota Press, 1983), 199. For the context of his reference to Priestley, see, e.g., Richard Price, *A Free Discussion of the Doctrines of Materialism and Philosophical Necessity in Correspondence with Joseph Priestley* (London: J. Johnson and T. Cadell, 1778; reprint, New York: Garland Publishing, 1978), esp. 49, 86, and 355–56, where relationships among the senses, scientific instruments, and mechanism in general are at issue. For an account of Cox's Museum, see Richard D. Altick, *The Shows of London* (Cambridge: Harvard University Press, 1978), 69–73.

26. Immanuel Kant, "What Is Enlightenment?" in *Practical Philosophy*, ed. and trans. Mary J. Gregor (Cambridge: Cambridge University Press, 1996), 22.

27. G[eorge]-E[rnst] Stahl, *Recherches sur la différence qui existe entre le mécanisme et l'organisme* (1706), in vol. 2 of *Oeuvres médico-philosophiques et pratiques de G.-E. Stahl*, trans. T. Blondin, 6 vols. (Paris: J.-B. Baillière et fils, 1863), 223.

28. La Mettrie, *L'homme machine*, 109. The wishful nature of this dismissal of automatons is also indicated by the aggressively hostile reception accorded La Mettrie's works; see the account of this reception in Aram Vartanian, *La Mettrie's "L'homme machine": A Study in the Origins of an Idea* (Princeton: Princeton University Press, 1960), 95–136.

29. See Pierre Bayle's argument that if the soul of an animal were put into "a well-chosen human body, it would be the soul of a clever man and no longer that of an animal," in "Rorarius (Jerôme)," in vol. 3 of *Dictionaire historique et critique* (1696), 3d ed., rev., 4 vols. (Rotterdam: Michel Bohm, 1720), 2476. For contemporary debates about humans in relation to apes, see Londa Schiebinger, *Nature's Body: Gender in the Making of Modern Science* (Boston: Beacon Press, 1993), 78–87.

30. Cf. the theory of "desiring machines" in Gilles Deleuze and Félix Guattari, *Anti-Oedipus: Capitalism and Schizophrenia,* trans. Robert Hurley, Mark Seem, and Helen R. Lane (Minneapolis: University of Minnesota Press, 1983), esp. 44 and 284–86, where the eighteenth-century distinction between *mechanism* and *vitalism* is challenged.

31. Voltaire (François-Marie Arouet de Voltaire), "Lettre XIII—Sur M. Locke," *Lettres philosophiques,* in vol. 22 of *Oeuvres complètes,* 125 (this passage dates from 1739); and Denis Diderot, *Éléments de physiologie* (ca. 1774–84), in vol. 17 of *Oeuvres complètes,* 335. Diderot's editor notes that while this passage might seem to indicate an antipathy to the Stahlians and an allegiance to iatromechanical theory, statements elsewhere in his writings establish that this impression is misleading. I would argue that rather than being all of a piece on this point, Diderot's writings are traversed by a number of inconsistencies and problems in the contemporary theorization of bodies. (See, for instance, the complex account of the "human automaton" as an "ambulatory clock" in "Lettre sur les sourds et muets," in vol. 4 of *Oeuvres complètes,* 159–60.) It should also be noted that this satirical image of the clockwork with a soul had already been established in the first half of the century, as in Voltaire's works.

32. [Gabrielle Emilie, Marquise Du Chatelet], *Institutions de physique* (Paris: Prault Fils, 1740), 156, 176; David Hume, *An Enquiry Concerning Human Understanding* (1748), in *Enquiries Concerning Human Understanding and Concerning the Principles of Morals,* ed. L. A. Selby-Bigge and P. H. Nidditch, 3d ed. (Oxford: Oxford University Press, 1975), 87. It should be added that even where the mechanical model was dismissed in favor of vitalism, clinical practice "remained almost identical under the new theory," as Christopher Lawrence observes in "The Nervous System and Society in the Scottish Enlightenment," in *Natural Order: Historical Studies of Scientific Culture,* ed. Barry Barnes and Steven Shapin (Beverly Hills: Sage Publications, 1979), 34. For a discussion of the varying interpretations that could be wrought from the "convergence of vitalism and mechanism" among the physicians of the renowned school of Montpellier (of whom one of the most notable was Théophile Bordeu), see Martin S. Staum, *Cabanis: En-*

lightenment and Medical Philosophy in the French Revolution (Princeton: Princeton University Press, 1980), 89–90.

33. Bouillier, *Essai philosophique,* 353. (Despite his reference here to "pure mechanism," Bouillier was arguing, against Descartes, that animals do have souls, albeit of an inferior sort.) On the attitudes of Condorcet and other philosophes toward workers and the common people, see Harry C. Payne, *The Philosophes and the People* (New Haven: Yale University Press, 1976). On this topic of docile machines, see the suggestive comments on the relation between automatons and eighteenth-century conceptions of the body in Michel de Certeau, "Des outils pour écrire le corps," *Traverses* 14–15 (April 1979): 6.

34. Jean Paul, "Personalien vom Bedienten-und Maschinenmann," in vol. 4 of *Werke,* ed. Norbert Miller, 6 vols. (Munich: Carl Hauser Verlag, 1962), 901–7.

35. See Paul Ilie's suggestion that the "paradoxical concept of an automaton . . . is conducive to those deformations, inversions, inverisimilitudes, and grotesqueries that Reason seeks to annihilate," in *The Age of Minerva,* 2 vols. (Philadelphia: University of Pennsylvania Press, 1995), 1:171.

36. Gottfried Wilhelm von Leibniz, "Reply to the Thoughts on the System of Preestablished Harmony Contained in the Second Edition of Mr. Bayle's Critical Dictionary, Article Rorarius," in vol. 2 of *Philosophical Papers and Letters,* ed. and trans. Leroy E. Loemker, 2 vols. (Chicago: University of Chicago Press, 1956), 939; *The Monadology,* in vol. 2 of *Philosophical Papers and Letters,* 1055.

37. See Denis Diderot, *Les bijoux indiscrets,* in vol. 3 of *Oeuvres complètes,* 127–28; Nicolas Réstif de la Bretonne, *La paysanne pervertie ou les dangers de la ville* (1787) (Paris: Garnier-Flammarion, 1972), 152; and D. A. F. de Sade, *Les cent vingt journées de Sodom* (ca. 1785), in vol. 13 of *Oeuvres complètes,* 16 vols. (Paris: Cercle du Livre Précieux, 1966), 9.

38. Herbert Dieckmann, ed., *Le Philosophe: Texts and Interpretation* (Saint Louis: Washington University Studies—New Series, 1948), 30. The text has been attributed to Diderot and César Chesnau Dumarsais; see Dieckmann's introduction for a discussion.

39. See Chapuis and Gélis, *Le monde des automates,* 2:204.

40. Quoted in Jacques Roger, *Les sciences de la vie dans la pensée française du dix-huitième siècle* ([Paris]: Armand Colin, 1963), 208.

41. For the history of avian automatons, see Chapuis and Gélis, *Le monde des automates,* vol. 1, chaps. 1–3, and vol. 2, chap. 18; and Chapuis and Droz, *Les automates,* chap. 10. For an account of the eighteenth-century "passion for birds, and for canaries in particular," discussed below, see Chapuis and Gélis, *Le monde des automates,* vol. 1, chaps. 12–14, and vol. 2, chaps. 15–19 and 21. For a philosophical

analysis of the history of such manufactures, see Otto Mayr, *Authority, Liberty, and Automatic Machinery in Early Modern Europe* (Baltimore: Johns Hopkins University Press, 1986).

42. Vaucanson, "Lettre de M. Vaucanson à M. l'Abbé D[e] F[ontaine]," in *Le mécanisme du fluteur automate*, 19. ("Trituration" refers to an iatromechanical process of abrasion as distinct from the iatrochemical process of dissolution, which represented the more modern theory.)

43. See the reference to this invention (given here as by "General de Genes") in Carl von Heister, *Nachrichten über Gottfried Christoph Beireis* (Berlin: Nicolai, 1860), 208; and in Chapuis and Gélis, *Le monde des automates*, 2:149. (The authors of the latter volume attribute their account to P. Labat's *Récit de voyages* [1688]; I have not been able to track down the original reference.) See also the reference to the same invention, here attributed to a "Gen. Degennes," in Sir David Brewster, *Letters on Natural Magic, Addressed to Sir Walter Scott, Bart.* (London: John Murry, 1834), 268.

44. Bertrand Gille, preface to Doyon and Liaigre, *Jacques Vaucanson*, ix.

45. Quoted in Doyon and Liaigre, *Jacques Vaucanson*, 18.

46. Bouillier, *Essai philosophique*, 195. Bouillier's examples were familiar ones; Ralph Cudworth, for example, represented habit in terms of the actions of the musician and the dancer in *The True Intellectual System of the Universe* (1678), 2 vols. (Andover, Mass.: Gould and Newman, 1837), 1:224–29; and as part of his critique of Leibniz, Bayle used the example of an "animal musician," one "created by God and destined to sing incessantly" according to the fixed order of a "tablature," in "Rorarius (Jerôme)," 2484.

47. William Blake, *Jerusalem*, in *The Complete Poetry and Prose of William Blake*, ed. David V. Erdman, rev. ed. (New York: Doubleday, 1988), sec. 2, plate 39, l. 25.

48. See Thomas Laqueur, "Orgasm, Generation, and the Politics of Reproductive Biology," in *The Making of the Modern Body: Sexuality and Society in the Nineteenth Century*, ed. Catherine Gallagher and Thomas Laqueur (Berkeley: University of California Press, 1987), 1–41. For a valuable study relevant to this point about the potential of technologies "to disrupt given symbolic systems that construct the maternal and the paternal as stable positions," which focuses on works from *L'Eve future* to *Blade Runner*, see Mary Ann Doane, "Technophilia: Technology, Representation, and the Feminine," in *Body/Politics: Women and the Discourses of Science*, ed. Mary Jacobus, Evelyn Fox Keller, and Sally Shuttleworth (New York: Routledge, 1990), 163–76.

49. See the excerpt from J.-B. Fermel'huis, *Éloge funèbre de M. Coysevox* (1721),

quoted in Geneviève Bresc-Bautier and Anne Pingeot, *Sculptures des jardins du Louvre, du Carrousel, et des Tuileries*, 2 vols. (Paris: Éditions de la Réunion des Musées Nationaux, 1986), 2:127–28.

50. On this subject of the political implications of the way the body was imaged in the early modern period, see Moira Gatens, *Imaginary Bodies: Ethics, Power, and Corporeality* (London: Routledge, 1996), esp. chap. 2, "Corporeal Representation in/and the Body Politic," 21–28. On the case of Shelley's *Frankenstein* in particular, see Ludmilla Jordanova, *Nature Displayed: Gender, Science and Medicine, 1760–1820* (London: Longman, 1999), chap. 4, "Melancholy Reflection: Constructing an Identity for Unveilers of Nature," 69–85. (Jordanova's entire work is relevant to my concerns here, as is Schiebinger's *Nature's Body*, cited above.) For a brief sketch of the vacillations, differences, and contradictions on the question of the female body among the philosophes, see Elizabeth J. Gardner, "The Philosophes and Women: Sensationalism and Sentiment," and also Robert Niklaus, "Diderot and Women," in *Women and Society in Eighteenth-Century France: Essays in Honour of John Stephenson Spink*, ed. Eva Jacobs (London: Athlone Press, 1979). A more extended treatment, with a valuable focus on theories of "sexual incommensurability," is provided in Vila, "Moral Anthropologies: Sensibility and the New Biology of Enlightenment," chap. 7 in *Enlightenment Pathology*. It is important to note here how a general reference to "the body" in the Enlightenment may be misleading in the light of comments such as the following, from Voltaire, *Éléments de la philosophie de Newton*, in vol. 22 of *Oeuvres complètes*, 406: "It seems evident that the Americans and the peoples of the world of old, the Negroes and the Laplanders, are not descended from the first man. The inferior constitution of the organs of the Negroes is a palpable demonstration of this." Cf. G. S. Rousseau's comment—"Nowhere in that world lying on the edge of the Industrial Revolution was there either our broad concept of sustained health as something natural, given, indigenous, or our belief that whatever health is in the abstract, it cuts across the social classes"—in "Medicine and the Muses: An Approach to Literature and Medicine," in *Literature and Medicine during the Eighteenth Century*, ed. Marie Mulvey Roberts and Roy Porter (London: Routledge, 1993), 26–27.

51. Robert Boyle, "A Free Inquiry into the Vulgarly Conceived Notion of Nature" (1682), in vol. 4 of *The Works of the Honourable Robert Boyle*, 5 vols. (London: A. Millar, 1744), 373.

52. David Hume, *Dialogues Concerning Natural Religion*, ed. Norman Kemp Smith (Indianapolis: Bobbs-Merrill, 1964), 180–81.

53. See, e. g., Locke's reference to the Strasbourg clock, and his use of it to re-

flect upon plant and animal life, in his *Essay Concerning Human Understanding*, 440; the comparable passage in George Berkeley, *Siris: A Chain of Philosophical Reflexions and Inquiries Concerning the Virtues of Tar-Water, and divers other Subjects connected together and arising One from Another* (1744), in vol. 5 of *The Works of George Berkeley, Bishop of Cloyne*, ed. A. A. Luce and T. E. Jessop, 9 vols. (London: Thomas Nelson and Sons, 1953), 42–43; and Juliette's characterization of herself as a machine of vegetation, like all men and animals, in D. A. F. de Sade, *L'histoire de Juliette, ou, Les prospérités du vice* (1797), in vols. 8 and 9 of *Oeuvres complètes*, 9:147. But see also Berkeley's mockery of this conflation of animal, plant, and man, through the figure of the materialist and atheist Lysicles, in *Alciphron, or The Minute Philosopher* (1732), in vol. 3 of *The Works of George Berkeley, Bishop of Cloyne*, ed. A. A. Luce and T. E. Jessop, 9 vols. (London: Thomas Nelson and Sons, 1948), 244–46. On this point, Wellman's analysis of La Mettrie's sense that mechanistic theory might be taken too far or conceived too broadly (*La Mettrie*, 118–20, 202) becomes important.

54. [Louis] Bourguet, *Lettres philosophiques sur la formation des sels et des crystaux et sur la génération & le mechanisme organique des plantes et des animaux* (Amsterdam: François L'Honore, 1729), 153; Nehemiah Grew, "The Epistle Dedicatory," in *The Anatomy of Plants* ([London?]: W. Rawlins, 1682); and [John Turberville] Needham, *An Account of Some New Microscopical Discoveries* ([London]: F. Needham, 1745), 82.

55. Cf. Hilary Putnam's warning that "a certain metaphysical picture" derived from modern physics and "well captured by the claim of La Mettrie that man is a machine" has come to be "confused with physics itself," in *Renewing Philosophy* (Cambridge: Harvard University Press, 1992), 19.

56. On this point see the perceptive analysis by Kathleen Wellman, "Dilemma and Opportunity: The Physiology of the Soul," *Studies in Eighteenth-Century Culture* 22 (1992): 301–16. See also Pierre Naville's attempt to redress an overly simplified, mechanical image of eighteenth-century materialism, in *D'Holbach et la philosophie scientifique au dix-huitième siècle* (Paris: Éditions Gallimard, 1967). Also relevant to this point is the distinction between "the body as a machine" and "the body imbued with the mechanics of life," in Michel Foucault, *The History of Sexuality*, vol. 1, *An Introduction*, trans. Robert Hurley (New York: Vintage, 1990), 139; and in terms of this issue of biotechnology see also Aram Vartanian, "Diderot and the Technology of Life," *Studies in Eighteenth-Century Culture* 15 (1986): 11–31. Of more direct importance to my argument is Donna Haraway, "A Cyborg Manifesto: Science, Technology, and Socialist-Feminism in the Late Twentieth Century," in *Simians, Cyborgs, and Women: The Reinvention of Nature* (New York:

Routledge, 1991), 149–82—although the monstrosity in Diderot's *Rêve de D'Alembert* may indicate the effective limits to Haraway's political mobilization of this image.

57. Jonathan Swift, "A Discourse Concerning the Mechanical Operation of the Spirit" (1704), in vol. 1 of *The Prose Works of Jonathan Swift*, ed. Herbert Davis, 14 vols. (Oxford: Basil Blackwell, 1939). See Susan Meld Shell, *The Embodiment of Reason: Kant on Spirit, Generation, and Community* (Chicago: University of Chicago Press, 1996), 116. The joke in question here is Kant's invocation of *Hudibras* to satirize inspiration as an intestinal, rather than divine, flatus.

58. Quoted in L. J. Rather, *Mind and Body in Eighteenth-Century Medicine: A Study Based on Jerome Gaub's "De regimine mentis"* (Berkeley: University of California Press, 1965), 115–16.

59. On this point, cf. Jacques Lacan's elaboration of the relation between *automaton* ("the network of signifiers") and *tuché* ("the encounter of the Real") in "Tuché et automaton," in *Le séminaire de Jacques Lacan, livre XI: Les quatre fondamentaux de la psychanalyse*, ed. Jacques-Alain Miller (Paris: Éditions du Seuil, 1973), 53–62. See also the analysis of the Lacanian notion of the automaton in relation to Max Ernst and dada in Rosalind E. Krauss, *The Optical Unconscious* (Cambridge: MIT Press, 1993), 71–76.

60. Diderot, *Élements de physiologie*, 330.

61. E. T. A. Hoffmann, "Die Jesuiterkirche in G.," in vol. 3 of *Sämtliche Werke*, ed. Harmut Steinecke with Gerhard Allroggen, 6 vols. (Frankfurt am Main: Deutscher Klassiker Verlag, 1985), 118.

62. Ibid., 123. The reference in this passage to the mating of fibers in the brain may be an allusion to the influential physiological theory of Albrecht von Haller, which was based on a fibrillary theory of anatomy that was taken up, for instance, in Diderot's *Élements de physiologie*. Haller was associated with the crassest materialism by way of La Mettrie's malicious dedication of *L'homme machine* to him—despite, or because of, Haller's well-known piety. (Haller denied any acquaintance or sympathy with La Mettrie in a disavowal of this dedication published in the *Journal des savants* in May 1749.) However, this sort of fibrillary imagery was commonplace in materialist conjecture and in parodies of the same; see, for instance, Swift, "Discourse Concerning the Mechanical Operation of the Spirit," 18: "For, it is the Opinion of Choice *Virtuosi*, that the Brain is only a Crowd of little Animals, but with Teeth and Claws extremely sharp, and therefore, cling together in the Contexture we behold . . . that all Invention is formed by the Morsure of two or more of these Animals, upon certain capillary Nerves." See also the summary of a 1720 work on physiology by Jean Astruc in Ephraim

Chambers's popular 1728 *Cyclopædia* (an inspiration for the *Encylopédie*), quoted in John W. Yolton, *Perceptual Acquaintance from Descartes to Reid* (Minneapolis: University of Minnesota Press, 1984), 183: "From the texture, Disposition, and tone of the Fibres of the *Brain*, Philosophers ordinarily account for the Phænomena of *Sensation* and *Imagination*. . . . Dr. *Astruc* goes further and . . . lays it down as an Axiom, that every simple idea is produc'd by the Oscillation of one determinate Fibre; that the greater or less degree of Evidence follows the greater or less Force wherewith the Fibre oscillates. He hence proceeds to show that the Affirmation or Negation of any Proposition, consists in the equal or unequal Number of Vibrations, which the moving Fibres, representing the two Parts of the Proposition, *viz.* the Subject, make in the same time."

63. E. T. A. Hoffmann, "Der Sandmann," in vol. 3 of *Sämtliche Werke*, 24, 27.

64. See Sigmund Freud, "The 'Uncanny,'" in vol. 17 of *The Standard Edition of the Complete Psychological Works of Sigmund Freud*, ed. James Strachey, 24 vols. (London: Hogarth Press and the Institute of Psycho-Analysis, 1955), 217–53.

65. Diderot, *Élements de physiologie*, 500–501. Diderot drew this notion of the bodily organs as diverse animals from Bordeu, who himself attributed it to a tradition extending back to antiquity but more recently represented by Jean-Baptiste van Helmont and the Stahlians. On this point see Jean Mayer, *Diderot: Homme de science* (Rennes: Brettone, 1959), 294–95.

66. Aileen Douglas, *Uneasy Sensations: Smollett and the Body* (Chicago: University of Chicago Press, 1995), 6.

67. Robert Hooke, preface to *Micrographia* (1665) (New York: Dover, 1961).

68. Le Cat, *Traité des sensations et des passions*, 1:13, 2:201–2.

69. Maurice Mandelbaum, *Philosophy, Science, and Sense Perception: Historical and Critical Studies* (Baltimore: Johns Hopkins University Press, 1964), 240, 210.

70. See Abraham Wolf, *A History of Science, Technology, and Philosophy in the Eighteenth Century*, 2d ed., rev. D. McKie (London: George Allen and Unwin, 1952), 469.

71. Immanuel Kant, *Critique of Pure Reason* (1781), trans. Werner S. Pluhar (Indianapolis: Hackett Publishing, 1996), 566n. More recently, the hallucinatory potential of this fusion of senses and instruments was nicely captured in a photo caption in "Doors of Perception: The Hubble Space Telescope," *New York Times*, October 2, 1997, sec. 4, p. 5.

72. Georg Wilhelm Friedrich Hegel, *Encyclopedia of the Philosophical Sciences in Outline* (1817), ed. Ernst Behler, trans. Steven A. Taubeneck (New York: Continuum, 1990), 49–50.

73. As a further illustration of this point, see also the use made of Vaucanson's

flute player and duck in Achim von Arnim's quasi-allegorical, moralistic, sentimental Christian narrative, *Gräfin Dolores,* in vol. 1 of *Werke,* ed. Roswitha Burwick, 7 vols. (Frankfurt am Main: Deutscher Klassiker Verlag, 1989), esp. 401–25. Von Arnim based this episode on Gottfried Christoph Bereis, a professor and mystic healer at Helmstadt who came into possession of Vaucanson's automatons in 1785; in *Gräfin Dolores* their mechanisms come to be associated with the devices of adultery and self-deception. When Goethe visited Bereis in 1805, he saw the flute player and the duck, both somewhat the worse for wear; see Johann Wolfgang Goethe, *Tag- und Jahreshefte,* in vol. 17 of *Sämtliche Werke,* 40 vols. (Frankfurt am Main: Deutscher Klassiker Verlag, 1994), 156.

74. Perhaps it is relevant to recall, as Hoffmann may have, that a contemporary French idiom for engaging in a terrific argument was *s'arracher les yeux* ("to tear out the eyes").

75. On this point see Arjun Appadurai, *Modernity at Large: Cultural Dimensions of Globalization* (Minneapolis: University of Minnesota Press, 1995), esp. chap. 2, "Disjuncture and Difference in the Global Cultural Economy."

76. Stafford, *Artful Science,* 76. See also her discussion of Vaucanson in particular, 190–95; and on the relationship between science and chicanery, see Simon Schaffer, "The Consuming Flame: Electrical Showmen and Tory Mystics in the World of Goods," in *Consumption and the World of Goods,* ed. John Brewer and Roy Porter (London: Routledge, 1993), 489–526.

77. See Doyon and Liaigre, *Jacques Vaucanson,* 125–27.

78. Walter Benjamin, "The Work of Art in the Age of Mechanical Reproduction," in *Illuminations,* ed. Hannah Arendt, trans. Harry Zohn (New York: Schocken Books, 1969), 233.

79. See Donald Davidson's argument, based on a hermeneutics of belief and meaning, as to why the creation of an *homme machine* (which he joshingly dubs "Art") could not yield a reduction of psychology to physics, in "The Material Mind," in *Mind Design: Philosophy, Psychology, Artificial Intelligence,* ed. John Haugeland (Montgomery, Vt.: Bradford Books, 1981), 339–54.

80. Immanuel Kant, *The Critique of Judgement,* trans. James Creed Meredith (2 vols. in 1) (Oxford: Oxford University Press, 1952), 1:89.

81. Bonnet, *Considérations sur les corps organisés,* 1:61.

82. See Immanuel Kant, *Critique of Practical Reason* (1788), trans. Mary Gregor (Cambridge: Cambridge University Press, 1997), 85.

83. Stahl, *Recherches sur la différence,* 179.

84. Cf. the example of a speaking goldfinch, which serves to elucidate epistemology as distinct from any determinate aesthetic response, in Stanley Cavell,

The Claim of Reason: Wittgenstein, Skepticism, Morality, and Tragedy (Oxford: Oxford University Press, 1979), 61–62. In this example Cavell is concerned, inter alia, with a critique of Kant's notion of the thing in itself.

85. Max Horkheimer and Theodor Adorno, *Dialectic of Enlightenment*, trans. John Cumming (New York: Seabury Press, 1972), 86.

86. Claude Lévi-Strauss, *The Raw and the Cooked: Introduction to a Science of Mythology: 1*, trans. John and Doreen Weightman (New York: Harper and Row, 1969), 11, 19n.

CHAPTER 4
The Exchange of Fluids in the Beau Monde

1. [John Feltham], *A Guide to All the Watering and Sea-Bathing Places* (London: Richard Phillips, [1803]), 14–15, 17.

Here and throughout this chapter, for the history of Bath and related watering places, I am especially indebted to Phyllis Hembry, *The English Spa, 1560–1815: A Social History* (London: Athlone Press, 1990). See also Barry Cunliffe, *The City of Bath* (New Haven: Yale University Press, 1986); Barbara Brandon Schnorrenberg, "Medical Men of Bath," *Studies in Eighteenth-Century Culture* 13 (1984): 189–203; Sylvia McIntyre, "Bath: The Rise of a Resort Town, 1660–1800," in *Country Towns in Pre-Industrial England*, ed. Peter Clark (New York: St. Martin's Press, 1981); R. S. Neale, *Bath, 1680–1850: A Social History* (London: Routledge and Kegan Paul, 1981); A. J. Turner, *Science and Music in Eighteenth-Century Bath* (Bath: University of Bath, 1977); David Gadd, *Georgian Summer: Bath in the Eighteenth Century* (Park Ridge, N.J.: Noyes Press, 1972); Lewis Melville, *Bath under Beau Nash—and After* (London: Eveleigh Nash and Grayson, 1926); [John Meade Falker], *Bath: Its History and Social Tradition* (London: John Murray, 1918); and Alfred Barbeau, *Life and Letters at Bath in the Eighteenth Century* (London: William Heinemann, 1904).

2. Théophile Bordeu, *Recherches sur les maladies chroniques, leurs rapports avec les maladies aiguës, leur périodes, leur nature, et sur la manière dont on les traite aux eaux minérales de Barèges, et des autres sources de l'Aquitaine* (1775), in vol. 2 of *Oeuvres complètes*, 2 vols. (Paris: Caille et Ravier, 1818), 827.

3. Sir Walter Scott, *St. Ronan's Well* (1832), in vol. 3 of *The Waverley Novels*, ed. Andrew Lang, 48 vols. (Boston: Estes and Lauriat, 1894), 33, 13–14.

4. Quoted in Melville, *Bath under Beau Nash*, 168. These lines were first published in the *Gentleman's Magazine* in 1741; Melville notes that although Oliver Goldsmith, in his biography of Nash, attributed these lines to Lord Chester-

field—an attribution repeated elsewhere—they are more likely by Jane Brereton.

5. Quoted in Cunliffe, *City of Bath*, 72; Edmund Spenser, *The Faerie Queene*, ed. A. C. Hamilton (London: Longman, 1977), 263 (bk. 2, canto 10).

6. Doctor [David] Kinneir, *A New Essay on the Nerves, and the Doctrine of Animal Spirits Rationally Considered*, 2d ed. (London: W. Innys and R. Mauby, 1739), 61; Tobias Smollett, *An Essay on the External Use of Water* (1752), ed. Claude E. Jones (Baltimore: Johns Hopkins University Press, 1935), 69; also see Rev. John Penrose, *Letters from Bath: 1766–1767*, ed. Brigitte Mitchell and Hubert Penrose (Gloucester: Alan Sutton, 1983), 94.

7. See the marvelously credulous recounting of this legend in John Wood [the Elder], *An Essay Towards a Description of Bath*, 2d ed., 2 vols. (London: James Bettenham, 1749), 1:40, 71–77, 117–59. A statue of Bladud, with an inscription telling of this legend, was erected in the King's Bath in 1699.

8. Christopher Smart, "Jubilate Agno" (fragment B), in vol. 1 of *The Poetical Works of Christopher Smart*, ed. Karina Williamson, 6 vols. (Oxford: Oxford University Press, 1980), 51.

9. James Schofield, *A Historical and Descriptive Guide to Scarbrough and Its Environs* (York: W. Blanchard, [1787]), 2.

10. William Oliver, *A Practical Essay on Fevers . . . To Which is Annex'd, A Dissertation on the Bath-Waters* (London: T. Goodwin, 1704), 288. See also the work of the younger William Oliver, the most famous Bath physician in his day, *A Practical Essay on the Use and Abuse of Warm Bathing in Gouty Cases* (Bath: T. Boddeley, 1753).

11. William Falconer, *An Essay on the Bath Waters* (London: T. Lowndes, 1772), 1. See the commendation of Falconer's work in Richard Warner, *The History of Bath* (Bath: R. Cruttwell, 1801), 377n.

12. Smollett, *Essay on the External Use of Water*, 53; Penrose, *Letters from Bath*, 94.

13. [Philip Thicknesse], *The New Prose Bath Guide, for the Year 1778*, 2d ed. ([London]: n.p., [1780?]), 113–14. For analyses of the issues of professionalism, commercialism, and social status involved in the accusation of quackery at this time, see Irvine London, "'The Vile Race of Quacks with Which This Country Is Infested,'" in *Medical Fringe and Medical Orthodoxy, 1750–1850*, ed. W. F. Bynum and Roy Porter (London: Croom Helm, 1987), esp. 106–7; Peter Wagner, "The Satire on Doctors in Hogarth's Graphic Works," in *Literature and Medicine during the Eighteenth Century*, ed. Marie Mulvey Roberts and Roy Porter (London: Routledge, 1993), 200–225; and Anita Guerrini, "'A Club of Little Villains':

Rhetoric, Professional Identity, and Medical Pamphlet Wars," in Roberts and Porter, *Literature and Medicine during the Eighteenth Century*, 226–44.

14. William Blake, *Jerusalem* (1804), in *The Complete Poetry and Prose of William Blake*, ed. David V. Erdman, rev. ed. (New York: Doubleday, 1988), sec. 2, plate 37, ll. 1–2.

15. Anders Sparrman, *A Voyage Round the World with Captain James Cook in H. M. S. Resolution* (ca. 1783–1818), ed. Owen Rutter, trans. Averil MacKenzie-Grieve (Great Britain: Golden Cockerell Press, 1944), 58; *The Diseases of Bath: A Satire* (London: J. Roberts, 1737), 5.

16. *Diseases of Bath*, 6.

17. Schofield, *Historical and Descriptive Guide*, 2.

18. Richard Graves, *The Spiritual Quixote: Or the Summer's Ramble of Mr. Geoffrey Wildgoose*, ed. Clarence Tracy (London: Oxford University Press, 1967), 179.

19. See Geo[rge] Cheyne, *An Essay of the True Nature and Due Method of Treating the Gout . . . Together with an Account of the Nature and Quality of Bath-Waters* (London: G. Strahan, 1722), 45–46; and Rice Charleton, *A Treatise on the Bath Waters* (Bath: T. Boddely, 1754), 63–74.

20. Daniel Defoe, *A Tour through England and Wales* (1724–26), 2 vols. (London: J. M. Dent and Sons, 1928), 2:35.

21. Kinneir, *New Essay on the Nerves*, 70.

22. Feltham, *Guide to All the Watering and Sea-Bathing Places*, 27.

23. John Elliot, *An Account of the Nature and Medicinal Virtues of the Principal Mineral Waters of Great Britain and Ireland; and Those Most in Repute on the Continent*, 2d ed. (London: J. Johnson, 1789), 138. It has been argued that the eighteenth century was characterized by an attention to the bowels, specifically in the training of young children, markedly different from that in previous centuries: see Harmut Böhme and Gernot Böhme, *Das Andere der Vernunft: Zur Entwicklung von Rationalitätsstrukturen am Beispiel Kants* (Frankfurt am Main: Suhrkamp, 1983), 64. See also the emphasis on the importance of disciplining children in regular bowel movements in John Locke, *Some Thoughts Concerning Education*, ed. John W. and Jean S. Yolton (Oxford: Oxford University Press, 1989), 99–107; and see Porter's description of how "popular physiology" in the eighteenth century "attended to evacuations no less than to appetites," in "Consumption: Disease of the Consumer Society?" in *Consumption and the World of Goods*, ed. John Brewer and Roy Porter (London: Routledge, 1993), 60.

24. Friedrich Hoffmann, *New Experiments and Observations upon Mineral*

Waters, ed. Peter Shaw, 2d ed. (London: T. Longman, 1743), 6. (This is an abridged contemporary translation of Hoffmann's work.)

25. See the description of the return from the springs of Geronstere to Spa, attended as it was by "some little inconveniences, or embarrassments, especially to the ladies," when the reluctant company is finally obliged to stop so that "one, perhaps, finds out a commodious place behind some large stone, and another screens himself behind a bush," in J. P. De Limbourg, *New Amusements of the German Spa,* 2 vols. (London: L. Davis and C. Reymers, 1764), 2:71–72.

26. [Christopher Anstey], *The New Bath Guide: Or, Memoirs of the B——R——D Family* (1766), 7th ed. (London: J. Dodsley, 1770), 12–13. "Hypochondria" was traditionally conceived to be an abdominal disorder associated with digestive problems. On this topic, see Aileen Douglas's pertinent discussion of how hypochondria and gout were regarded "as marks of moral and social standing" in *Uneasy Sensations: Smollett and the Body* (Chicago: University of Chicago Press, 1995), 168–80.

27. Frances Burney, *Evelina: Or the History of a Young Lady's Entrance into the World* (1778), ed. Edward A. Bloom (London: Oxford University Press, 1968), 8, 296.

28. [Anstey], *New Bath Guide,* 47, 49.

29. Feltham, *Guide to All the Watering and Sea-Bathing Places,* 29; P[ierce] Egan, *Walks through Bath* (Bath: Meyler and Son, 1819), 91n.

30. [Anstey], *New Bath Guide,* 158–59.

31. William Conner Sydney, *England and the English in the Eighteenth Century,* 2 vols. (London: Ward and Downey, 1892), 2:59.

32. Samuel Pepys, *The Diary of Samuel Pepys,* ed. Robert Latham and William Matthews, 11 vols. (Berkeley: University of California Press, 1976), 9:23.

33. *Diseases of Bath,* 14–15.

34. Walter Pater, "Leonardo da Vinci," in *The Renaissance: Studies in Art and Poetry,* ed. Donald C. Hill (Berkeley: University of California Press, 1980; based on the 4th ed. [1893]), 81; Oliver Goldsmith, *The Life of Richard Nash,* in vol. 3 of *Collected Works of Oliver Goldsmith,* ed. Arthur Friedman, 5 vols. (Oxford: Oxford University Press, 1966), 307.

35. Tobias Smollett, *The Expedition of Humphry Clinker* (1771), ed. O. M. Brack Jr. (Athens: University of Georgia Press, 1990), 152. On this issue of the status of signifiers in the novel, especially in terms of its gender politics, see Aileen Douglas, "'The Frolick May Go Round': Bodies as Signs in *Humphry Clinker,*" in *Uneasy Sensations,* 162–84.

36. W. H. Auden, "In Memory of Sigmund Freud," in *Selected Poetry of W. H. Auden* (New York: Modern Library, 1958), 57.

37. Jane Austen, *Northanger Abbey,* in vol. 5 of *The Novels of Jane Austen,* ed. R. W. Chapman, 5 vols. (London: Oxford University Press, 1954), 38.

38. See Smollett, *Expedition of Humphry Clinker,* 344n.

39. Jonathan Swift, *A Tale of a Tub* (1710), in vol. 1 of *The Prose Works of Jonathan Swift,* ed. Herbert Davis, 14 vols. (Oxford: Basil Blackwell, 1939), 104n.

40. See Kenneth Dewhurst, *Thomas Willis's Oxford Lectures* (Oxford: Sandford Publications, 1980), 24; and Kenneth Dewhurst, *John Locke (1632–1704): Physician and Philosopher* (London: Wellcome Historical Medical Library, 1963), 207. In *Death and the Enlightenment: Changing Attitudes to Death among Christians and Unbelievers in Eighteenth-Century France* (Oxford: Oxford University Press, 1981), 35, John McManners notes that human excrement was listed as a remedy in Nicolas Lemery's *Pharmacopée universelle simples* (1738) and *Dictionnaire universel des drogues simples* (1759).

41. See Roy Porter, "Consumption: Disease of the Consumer Society?" in *Consumption and the World of Goods,* 69–70.

42. Robert Boyle, "The Origins of Forms and Qualities, According to the Corpuscular Philosophy," in vol. 2 of *The Works of the Honourable Robert Boyle,* 5 vols. (London: A. Millar, 1744), 473–74. See also Boyle's pioneering analysis of mineral waters, "Short Memoirs for the Natural Experimental History of Mineral Waters," in vol. 4 of *Works,* 231–50.

43. See my discussion of Boyle's writing on this topic in the next chapter.

44. David Hume, *An Enquiry Concerning the Principles of Morals* (1751), in *Enquiries Concerning Human Understanding and Concerning the Principles of Morals,* ed. L. A. Selby-Bigge and P. H. Nidditch, 3d ed. (Oxford: Oxford University Press, 1975), 198.

45. D. A. F. de Sade, *L'histoire de Juliette, ou, Les prospérités du vice,* in vols. 8 and 9 of *Oeuvres complètes,* 16 vols. (Paris: Cercle du Livre Précieux, 1966), 8:161. In relation to this point, see Marcel Hénaff, *Sade: The Invention of the Libertine Body,* trans. Xavier Callahan (Minneapolis: University of Minnesota Press, 1999), esp. chap. 7, "The Expenditures of the Body."

46. Quoted in G. S. Rousseau, "Rationalism and Empiricism in Enlightenment Medicine," in *Enlightenment Borders: Pre- and Post-Modern Discourse* (Manchester: Manchester University Press, 1991), 120.

47. See, e. g., John Rutty, *A Methodical Synopsis of Mineral Waters, Comprehending the Most Celebrated Medicinal Waters, Both Hot and Cold, of Great-Britain,*

Ireland, France, Germany, and Italy, and Several Other Parts of the World (London: William Johnston, 1757), 603–4. Rutty also speaks of the waters as a specific for gonnorhea.

48. See John Wilmot, "Tunbridge Wells" (1674), in *The Complete Poems of John Wilmot, Earl of Rochester*, ed. David M. Vieth (New Haven: Yale University Press, 1968), 79: "For here walk Cuff and Kick, / With brawny back and legs and potent prick, / Who more substantially will cure thy wife, / And on her half-dead womb bestow new life. / From these the waters get the reputation / Of good assistants unto generation"; and Tobias Smollett, *The Adventures of Peregrine Pickle*, ed. James L. Clifford (London: Oxford University Press, 1964), 371. On this point see also Reginald Lennard, "The Watering-Places," in *Englishmen at Rest and Play: Some Phases of English Leisure, 1558–1714*, ed. Reginald Lennard (Oxford: Oxford University Press, 1931), 56–58.

49. [Thomas] D'Urfey, *The Bath: Or, The Western Lass: A Comedy* (London: Peter Buck, 1701), 1.

50. Quoted in Trevor Fawcett, ed., *Voices of Eighteenth-Century Bath* (Bath: Ruton, 1995), 90.

51. Burney, *Evelina*, 393.

52. Austen, *Northanger Abbey*, 21–22.

53. Sade, *Juliette*, 9:380.

54. The figure of the Hottentot was closely related to that of the cannibal in European discourse of this era, serving to represent the presumptively outrageous identifications of the philosopher; in addition to the way this figure crops up in the work of Jean-Baptiste-René Robinet, quoted in chapter 2, see the statement by Lysicles, portrayed as being a typical materialist and atheistic philosopher, in George Berkeley, *Alciphron, or The Minute Philosopher* (1732), in vol. 3 of *The Works of George Berkeley, Bishop of Cloyne*, ed. A. A. Luce and T. E. Jessop, 9 vols. (London: Thomas Nelson and Sons, 1948), 102: "The Hottentots we think well of, believing them to be an unprejudiced people: but it is to be feared their diet and customs would not agree with our philosophers." See Alexander Butchart, *The Anatomy of Power: European Constructions of the African Body* (London: Zed Books, 1998).

55. Immanuel Kant, *The Critique of Judgement*, trans. James Creed Meredith (2 vols. in 1) (Oxford: Oxford University Press, 1952), 1:195.

56. See G. S. Rousseau, "Medicine and the Muses: An Approach to Literature and Medicine," in Roberts and Porter, *Literature and Medicine during the Eighteenth Century*, 37–38.

57. Kant, *Critique of Judgement*, 1:196.

58. Immanuel Kant, *Critique of Pure Reason* (1781), trans. Werner S. Pluhar (Indianapolis: Hackett Publishing, 1996), 502.

59. Mary Wortley Montagu, "To Lady—1 April [1717]," in vol. 1 of *The Complete Letters of Lady Mary Wortley Montagu,* ed. Robert Halsbaud, 3 vols. (Oxford: Oxford University Press, 1965), 312.

60. Jane Austen, *Persuasion,* in vol. 5 of *The Novels of Jane Austen,* 146.

61. De Limbourg, *New Amusements of the German Spa,* 1:iii.

62. [Anstey], *New Bath Guide,* 26. On this topic of the interrelation of fashion and science, see Christopher Hamlin, "Chemistry, Medicine, and the Legitimization of English Spas, 1740–1840," in *The Medical History of Waters and Spas,* ed. Roy Porter (London: Wellcome Institute for the History of Medicine, 1990), 67–81.

63. "Fashion determined many aspects of the spas, but it was often medical fashion, as we can see in the eighteenth-century change from the inland spas to the seaside resorts" (McIntyre, "Bath: Rise of a Resort Town," 199).

64. See Terry Castle, *Masquerade and Civilization: The Carnivalesque in Eighteenth-Century English Culture and Fiction* (Stanford: Stanford University Press, 1986).

65. See J. H. Plumb's article, "The Commercialization of Leisure," in which he compares Bath to these other resorts and argues that assembly rooms such as those at Bath "mark the transitional stage between private and fully public entertainment," in *The Birth of a Consumer Society: The Commercialization of Eighteenth-Century England,* by Neil McKendrick, John Brewer, and J. H. Plumb (Bloomington: Indiana University Press, 1982), 283.

66. "The titles of rank, birth, and fortune, are received at a watering-place without any very strict investigation, as adequate to the purpose for which they are preferred; and as the situation infers a certain degree of intimacy and sociability for the time, so to whatever heights it may have been carried, it is not understood to imply any duration beyond the length of the season. No intimacy can be supposed more close for the time, and more transitory in its endurance, than that which is attached to a watering-place acquaintance" (Scott, introduction to *St. Ronan's Well,* xviii).

67. Francis Coventry, *The History of Pompey the Little: Or the Life and Adventures of a Lap-Dog* (1751), ed. Robert Adams Day (London: Oxford University Press, 1974), 87–88.

68. Austen, *Persuasion,*178; *Northanger Abbey,* 35.

69. [Anstey], *New Bath Guide,* 28.

70. [Thicknesse], *New Prose Guide,* 85n. The speciousness of this explanation

for the exclusion of the local poor becomes especially apparent if one notes that in 1714, pressure from some Bathonians had moved Parliament to repeal the 1597 act that had given the "diseased and impotent poor of England" free use of the baths. See Audrey Heywood, "A Trial of the Bath Waters: The Treatment of Lead Poisoning," in Porter, *Medical History of Waters and Spas*, 87– 92.

71. Quoted in Feltham, *Guide to All the Watering and Sea-Bathing Places*, 17–18.

72. Charlotte Lennox, *The Female Quixote, or The Adventures of Arabella*, ed. Margaret Dalziel (London: Oxford University Press, 1970), 262.

73. Peter Paul Pallet [Richard Warner], *Bath Characters: Or Sketches from Life* (London: G. Wilkie and J. Robinson, 1807), 40.

74. Goldsmith, *Life of Richard Nash*, 3:295.

75. See the characterization of Nash as "'play' personified" in Peter M. Briggs, "The Importance of Beau Nash," *Studies in Eighteenth-Century Culture* 22 (1992): 226.

76. A counterpart to Berkeley was John Wesley, who admired the bishop's work and whose extremely popular *Primitive Physick* (1747) sought to substitute cheap natural remedies for the professional pharmacopoeia; and it is worth noting in this respect that the Methodists made considerable inroads among the population at Bath, their most famous convert being Selina, Countess of Huntingdon. For an account of Wesley's book, and of Berkeley, see Lester S. King, *The Medical World of the Eighteenth Century* (Chicago: University of Chicago Press, 1958), 34–44. The arguably conjoined role of Methodism and medicine in disciplining bodies in the service of modern society is discussed by Bryan S. Turner, "The Government of the Body: Medical Regimens and the Rationalization of Diet," in *Regulating Bodies: Essays in Medical Sociology* (London: Routledge, 1992), esp. 190.

77. See G. S. Rousseau, "Praxis I: Bishop Berkeley and Tar-Water," in *Enlightenment Borders*, 161, 166.

78. See Charles F. Mullett, "Public Baths and Health in England, Sixteenth-Eighteenth Century," in *Supplements to the Bulletin of the History of Medicine*, no. 5 (Baltimore: Johns Hopkins University Press, 1946), 33. Whytt was by no means the only person to experiment with artificial waters; in 1676, for example, Claude Bouchier had recommended one such water to Locke (Dewhurst, *John Locke*, 68). On this topic see Noel G. Coley, "Physicians, Chemists, and the Analysis of Mineral Waters: 'The Most Difficult Part of Chemistry,'" in Porter, *Medical History of Waters and Spas*, 63.

79. George Berkeley, "Letter to Thomas Prior, Esq.," in vol. 5 of *The Works of*

George Berkeley, Bishop of Cloyne, ed. A. A. Luce and T. E. Jessop, 9 vols. (London: Thomas Nelson and Sons, 1953), 173.

80. George Berkeley, *Siris: A Chain of Philosophical Reflexions and Inquiries Concerning the Virtues of Tar-Water, and divers other Subjects connected together and arising One from Another* (1744), in vol. 5 of *Works,* 52.

81. Hoffmann, *New Experiments and Observations,* 5; A[lexander] Hunter, *The Buxton Manual: Or, A Treatise on the Nature and Virtues of the Waters of Buxton* (1765), 4th ed. (London: J. Dodsley and T. Cadell, 1787), 5. See also, e. g., Charles Lucas's agreement with Hoffmann's claim of water as a "universal medicine" in *An Essay on Waters* (3 vols. in 1) (London: A. Millar, 1756), 1:159; and Rutty's similar statement, *Methodical Synopsis of Mineral Waters,* 20.

82. George Berkeley, "A Second Letter to Thomas Prior," in vol. 5 of *Works,* 186.

83. See Fawcett, *Voices of Eighteenth-Century Bath,* 180, 49–50.

84. Richard Sheridan, *The School for Scandal,* in vol. 1 of *The Dramatic Works of Richard Brinsley Sheridan,* ed. Cecil Price, 2 vols. (Oxford: Oxford University Press, 1993), 255.

85. Austen, *Northanger Abbey,* 133.

CHAPTER 5

Cannibalism, Trade, Whatnot

1. James Cook, *The Voyage of the "Resolution" and "Adventure," 1772–1775,* vol. 2 of *The Journals of Captain James Cook on His Voyages of Discovery,* ed. J. C. Beaglehole (Cambridge: Cambridge University Press, 1961), 255.

2. Johann Friedrich Blumenbach, "On the Natural Variety of Mankind" (1795), in *Anthropological Treatises of Johann Friedrich Blumenbach,* ed. and trans. Thomas Bendysh (London: Longman, Green, Longman, Roberts, and Green, 1865), 160. On the topic of Cook's seeming apotheosis, see Marshall Sahlins, *Islands of History* (Chicago: University of Chicago Press, 1987), and *How "Natives" Think: About Captain Cook, for Example* (Chicago: University of Chicago Press, 1995). This second book is largely a reply to the critique of his earlier work by Gananath Obeyesekere, *The Apotheosis of Captain Cook: European Mythmaking in the Pacific* (Princeton: Princeton University Press, 1992). For a valuable overview of Cook's posthumous image and of this debate between Obeyesekere and Sahlins, see Rod Edmund, "Killing the God: The Afterlife of Cook's Death," chap. 2 in *Representing the South Pacific: Colonial Discourse from Cook to Gaugin* (Cambridge: Cambridge University Press, 1997).

3. Bartolomé de Las Casas, *In Defense of the Indians: The Defense of the Most Reverend Lord, Don Fray Bartolomé de Las Casas, of the Order of Preachers, Late Bishop of Chiapa, Against the Persecuters and Slanderers of the Peoples of the New World Discovered Across the Seas* (ca. 1552), ed. and trans. Stafford Poole (DeKalb: Northern Illinois University Press, 1992), 165–66.

4. On this topic of the paradigmatic relation between cannibalism and the consumption of excrement, see also, for example, the description of the Hurons driven to cannibalism by war and starvation in "Letter of Father Paul Ragueneau to the Very Reverend Father General, Vincent Caraffa" (1650), in vol. 35 of *The Jesuit Relations and Allied Documents*, ed. Reuben Gold Thwaites, trans. Finlow Alexander, John Cutler Covert, William Frederic Giese, John Dorsey Wolcott, and Mary Sifton Pepper, 73 vols. (Cleveland: Burrow Brothers, 1899), 21: "Doubtless the teeth of the starving man make no distinction in food, and do not recognize in the dead body him who a little before was called, until he died, father, son, or brother. Nay, more, even the dung of man or beast is not spared." See also the similar account in Ragueneau's "Relation," in vol. 35 of Thwaites, *Jesuit Relations,* 89–93.

5. See John Locke, *An Essay Concerning Human Understanding* (1690), ed. Peter H. Nidditch (Oxford: Oxford University Press, 1975), 70–74, 87–94. On this topic of the recognition of cultural diversity in the Enlightenment, see Peter Hulme, "The Spontaneous Hand of Nature: Savagery, Colonialism, and the Enlightenment," in *The Enlightenment and Its Shadows*, ed. Peter Hulme and Ludmilla Jordanova (London: Routledge, 1990); 16–34.

6. William Shakespeare, *The Tempest*, in *The Riverside Shakespeare*, ed. G. Blakemore Evans (Boston: Houghton Mifflin, 1974), 1.2.363–64.

7. Louis-Ange Pitou, *Voyage forcé à Cayenne, dans les deux Amériques et chez les anthropophages*, ed. Elisabeth Hausser (Paris: Club Français du Livre, 1962), 75.

8. John Atkins, *A Voyage to Guinea, Brasil, and the West-Indies* (London: Caesar Ward and Richard Chandler, 1735), xxiii.

9. Bartolomé de Las Casas, *Historia de las Indias* (ca. 1559), ed. Agustín Millares Carlo, 3 vols. (México: Fonda de Cultura Económica, 1951), 3:231.

10. For his comments on translation, see Atkins, *Voyage to Guinea, Brasil, and the West-Indies,* 127. For the arguments of one of the most well-known contemporary doubters of cannibalism, see W[illiam] Arens, *The Man-Eating Myth: Anthropology and Anthropophagy* (New York: Oxford University Press, 1979). A much more important work in this vein, based upon a literary-critical form of discourse analysis, is that of Peter Hulme, *Colonial Encounters: Europe and the Native Caribbean, 1492–1797* (London: Methuen, 1986); and see also Annerose Men-

ninger, "Die Kannibalen Amerikas und die Phantasien der Eroberer: Zur Problem der Wirklichkeitswahrnehmung außereuropäischer Kulturen durch europäische Reisende in der frühen Neuzeit," in *Kannibalismus und Europäische Kultur,* ed. Hedwig Röckelein (Tübingen: Edition Diskord, 1996), 115–41. In addition to the other works cited below, notable anthropological writings on this topic include Garry Hogg, *Cannibalism and Human Sacrifice* (New York: Citadel Press, 1966); Blanco Villalta, *Ritos caníbales en América* (Buenos Aires: Casa Pardo, 1970); Eli Sagan, *Cannibalism: Human Aggression and Cultural Form* (New York: Harper and Row, 1974); Peggy Reeves Sanday, *Divine Hunger: Cannibalism as a Cultural System* (Cambridge: Cambridge University Press, 1986); Isabelle Combès, *La Tragédie cannibale chez les anciens Tupi-Guarani* (Paris: Presses Universitaires de France, 1992); and Philip P. Boucher, *Cannibal Encounters: Europeans and Island Caribs, 1492–1763* (Baltimore: Johns Hopkins University Press, 1992). The most valuable literary-historical study is that of Frank Lestringant, *Cannibals: The Discovery and Representation of the Cannibal from Columbus to Jules Verne,* trans. Rosemary Morris (Berkeley: University of California Press, 1997). Other works of interest are those of Christian W. Thomsen, *Menschenfresser in der Kunst und Literatur* (Vienna: Christian Brandstätter, 1983); and Pierre-Antoine Bernheim and Guy Stavridès, *Cannibales!* (Paris: Plon, 1992). See also C. J. Rawson, "Cannibalism and Fiction: Reflections on Narrative Form and 'Extreme' Situations," *Genre* 10 (Winter 1977): 667–711, and 11 (Summer 1978): 227–313; and the scattered comments relevant to this topic in Obeyesekere, *Apotheosis of Captain Cook.*

11. Atkins, *Voyage to Guinea, Brasil, and the West-Indies,* xxiii.

12. Cook, *Voyage,* 294; William Wales, "Journal of William Wales," appendix 5 in Cook, *Journals,* 2:790–91.

13. Francis Coventry, *The History of Pompey the Little: Or the Life and Adventures of a Lap-Dog* (1751), ed. Robert Adams Day (London: Oxford University Press, 1974), 93. One might compare this sort of popular suspicion to the more scholarly view, in the early nineteenth century, of William Sheldon in his "Brief Acount of the Caraibs Who Inhabited the Antilles," *Transactions and Collections of the American Antiquarian Society* 1 (1820): 417: "On touching at Montserrat, Columbus was informed, that *the Caraibs had eaten up all the inhabitants of that island.* If that had been true, it would have been strange that any person should remain to give Columbus the information. These facts ought, probably, to be classed with a great many stories and wonderful events related by voyagers. The Caraibs were a warlike people, and gave the Spaniards some trouble; they were a terror to the other islanders, beating them in war, and on that account, were prob-

ably unjustly stigmatized as the most ferocious of cannibals . . . . I pretend not to deny that the Caraibs, like the Mohegans or Narrangansets, sometimes took a slice of a dead enemy." This account is also of interest here because of the contrast between its studied worldliness and the contemporaneous writings of Hegel (discussed below), in which all reports of cannibalism are accepted with a pornographic eagerness. For a much earlier account of the Caribs similar to Sheldon's, see [Jean Baptiste] Labat, *Voyages aux isles de l'Amérique* (1722), 2 vols. (Paris: Éditions Duchartre, 1931), 2:117. For an analysis of this issue of the believability of cannibalism in relation to the composition, marketing, and reception of travelers' tales in the early modern period, see Annerose Menninger, *Die Macht der Augenzeugen: Neue Welt und Kannibalen-Mythos, 1492–1600* (Stuttgart: Franz Steiner, 1995).

14. An exception to this opinion was that of [Joseph-François] Lafitau, *Moeurs des sauvages Ameriquains, comparées aux moeurs des premiers temps*, 2 vols. (Paris: Saugrain l'aîné et Charles Estienne Hochereau, 1724), 2:307: "Almost all the barbarous nations of America are anthropophagi." Other examples could be found, of course; in this case as in my account of the other contemporary generalizations about cannibalism, I describe the dominant climate of opinion.

15. See John Martin [with William Mariner], *An Account of the Natives of the Tonga Islands*, 2d ed., 2 vols. (London: John Murray, 1818), 1:194: "This was the second instance of cannibalism that Mr. Mariner witnessed, but the natives of these islands are not to be called cannibals on this account: so far from its being a general practice, it is on the contrary generally held in abhorrence, and where it is occasionally done, it is only by young warriors, who do it in imitation of the Fiji islanders, attaching to it an idea that there is something in it designating a fierce, warlike, and manly spirit. When they returned to Neafoo after their inhuman repast, most persons who knew it, particularly women, avoided them, saying, 'Iá-whé moe ky-tangata,' away! you are a man-eater."

16. In *From Communion to Cannibalism: An Anatomy of Metaphors of Incorporation* (Princeton: Princeton University Press, 1990), 96, Maggie Kilgow points out that the association of the legal system with cannibalism was already long established by this era; her analyses throughout this book are relevant to my concerns here. See also Ludmilla Jordonova's reference to the cannibalistic imagery used by Chateaubriand for an antirevolutionary motif akin to Gillray's in "The Authoritarian Response," in Hulme and Jordanova, *The Enlightenment and its Shadows*, 211–12; and for a study of other matters of the body related to this chapter, see Carol Houlihan Flynn, *The Body in Swift and Defoe* (Cambridge: Cambridge University Press, 1990).

17. See Jacques Attali, *L'ordre cannibale: Vie et mort de la médecine* (Paris: Bernard Grasset, 1979).

18. Michel de Montaigne, "Of Cannibals," in *Essays and Selected Writings*, ed. and trans. Donald M. Frame ([New York]: St. Martin's Press, 1963), 155.

19. Jean de Léry, *History of a Voyage to the Land of Brazil, Otherwise Called America* (1578), trans. Janet Whatley (Berkeley: University of California Press, 1990), 133.

20. Montaigne, "Of Cannibals," 99–103, 115–17. Although, as Lestringant points out (*Cannibals*, 72–73), this ironic representation of cannibalism had been established before Montaigne's essay was written, this work arguably became its most celebrated instance—later to be referred to, for instance, in Voltaire's famous comments on this subject, cited below.

21. [Julien Marie] Crozet, *Nouveau voyage à la mer du sud*, [ed. A. M. de Rochon] (Paris: Barrois l'aîné, 1783), 126–29.

22. Editor's note, in Crozet, *Nouveau voyage*, 141–46n.

23. Anders Sparrman, *A Voyage Round the World with Captain James Cook in H. M. S. Resolution* (ca. 1783–1818), ed. Owen Rutter, trans. Averil MacKenzie-Grieve (Great Britain: Golden Cockerel Press, 1944), 186–87.

24. See Montaigne, "Of Cannibals," 111: "I have a song composed by a prisoner which contains this challenge, that they should all come boldly and gather to dine off him, for they will be eating at the same time their own fathers and grandfathers, who have served to feed and nourish his body. 'These muscles,' he says, 'this flesh and these veins are your own, poor fools that you are. You do not recognize that the substance of your ancestors' limbs is still contained in them. Savor them well; you will find in them the taste of your own flesh.' An idea that certainly does not smack of barbarity." For the politics of this apparent opposition between the noble and the barbarous savage, characterized in this case as "the gentle Taino / ferocious Carib division," see the analysis throughout Hulme, *Colonial Encounters*.

25. John Liddiard Nicholas, *Narrative of a Voyage to New Zealand*, 2 vols. (London: James Black and Son, 1817), 2:69.

26. See Claude Lévi-Strauss, *La pensée sauvage* (Paris: Plon, 1962), esp. 139–41; and Denis Diderot, *Supplément à la voyage de Bougainville*, in vol. 12 of *Oeuvres complètes*, ed. Jean Varloot, 25 vols. (Paris: Hermann, 1980), 583. The interrelationship of incest and cannibalism is dramatized and discussed in many places in Sade's oeuvre. On this topic see also Jean Pouillon, "Manières de table, manières de lit, manières de langage," *Nouvelle revue de psychanalyse* [Special Issue, *Destins de cannibalisme*] 6 (Autumn 1972): 9–25.

27. Alexander Pope, *An Essay on Man*, ed. Maynard Mack, in vol. 3 of *The Twickenham Edition of the Poems of Alexander Pope*, ed. John Butt, 6 vols. (London: Methuen, 1950), 1.113.

28. Guillaume-Thomas-François Raynal, *Histoire philosophique et politique des établissemens et du commerce des Européens dans les deux Indes*, 4 vols. (Geneva: Jean-Leonard Pellet, 1780), 2:124, 298.

29. Claude-Adrien Helvétius, *De l'esprit* (1758), ed. Jacques Montaux (Paris: Arthème Fayard, 1988), 37n.

30. Nicholas, *Narrative of a Voyage to New Zealand*, 1:403–4.

31. Marshall Sahlins, "Raw Women, Cooked Men, and Other 'Great Things' of the Fiji Islands," in *The Ethnography of Cannibalism*, ed. Paula Brown and Donald Tuzin (Washington, D. C.: Society for Psychological Anthropology, 1983), 88. For the way Freud drew out the relationship between cannibalism and the Christian communion, see *Moses and Monotheism*, in vol. 23 of *The Standard Edition of the Complete Psychological Works of Sigmund Freud*, ed. James Strachey, 24 vols. (London: Hogarth Press and the Institute of Psycho-Analysis, 1955), 84; and in vol. 13 of the same edition, *Totem and Taboo*, 154–55.

32. "Letter from Father [Pierre Roubaud], Missionary to the Abnakis" (1757), in vol. 70 of Thwaites, *Jesuit Relations*, 131. As Lestringant comments (*Cannibals*, 63), "In fact, the first missionaries of the New World were sometimes confusedly aware, by analogy with the Christian mysteries, of the similarity between this ritual anthropophagy and the sacrament of the Eucharist." In terms of my argument below, it is notable that although Hegel does not directly mark the comparison between his views on cannibals and on the Eucharist, there is a strict logic binding his racist conception of those alleged to be the former and his spiritual (as against the Catholic or the merely figurative) conception of the latter. For his views on cannibalism in the context of religion (in addition to the passages cited below), see Georg Wilhelm Friedrich Hegel, *Lectures on the Philosophy of Religion*, ed. Peter C. Hodgson, trans. R. F. Brown, P. C. Hodgson, and J. M. Stewart, 3 vols. (Berkeley: University of California Press, 1987), 2:276–77, 544–45, 725. For a contemporary observation of the relation between Christian ritual and cannibalism (although discussed here as an error of interpretation), see the Abbé Mallet's entry on "Anthropophages," in vol. 1 of *Encyclopédie, ou dictionnaire raisonné des sciences, des arts, et des métiers*, ed. Denis Diderot, 17 vols. (Paris: Briasson, 1751–65), 498.

33. Donald Tuzin, "Cannibalism and Arapesh Cosmology: A Wartime Incident with the Japanese," in Brown and Tuzin, *Ethnography of Cannibalism*, 62.

34. Claude Lévi-Strauss, *The Raw and the Cooked: Introduction to a Science of*

Mythology: 1, trans. John and Doreen Weightman (New York: Harper and Row, 1969), 151.

35. Sahlins, "Raw Women, Cooked Men," 88.

36. Lévi-Strauss, *La pensée sauvage*, 341, 341n.

37. Here the most relevant critique remains that of Jacques Derrida, "The Violence of the Letter: From Lévi-Strauss to Rousseau," in *Of Grammatology*, trans. Gayatri Chakravorty Spivak (Baltimore: Johns Hopkins University Press, 1976), 101–40.

38. Voltaire (François-Marie Arouet de Voltaire), *Candide, ou l'optimisme*, in vol. 21 of *Oeuvres complètes de Voltaire*, ed. Louis Moland, 52 vols. (Paris: Garnier Frères, 1877–85), 162.

39. See Bernal Diaz del Castillo, *Historia Verdadera de la Conquista de la Neuva España* (1632; written ca. 1568) (Argentina: Editoria Porrúa, 1994); Fray Bernadino de Sahagún, *General History of the Things of New Spain* (ca. 1547-?), (Santa Fe, N.M.: School of American Research, 1953–82).

40. Hernán Cortés, "The Third Letter of Cortés" (1523), trans. Francis A. MacNutt, in *The Conquistadors: First-Person Accounts of the Conquest of Mexico*, ed. and trans. Patricia de Fuentes (Norman: University of Oklahoma Press, 1993), 112.

41. See also Cook, *Voyage*, 292–93; and John Marra, *Journal of the Resolution's Voyage in 1771–1775* (1775) (Amsterdam: N. Israel, 1967), 102–3.

42. Sparrman, *Voyage Round the World*, 115.

43. Johann Reinhold Forster, *The "Resolution" Journal of Johann Reinhold Forster*, ed. Michael E. Hoare, 4 vols. (London: Hakluyt Society, 1982), 3:426–27. On the Forsters' recognition of the European incitement to cannibalism, see Barry Brailsford, "Maori Life in Queen Charlotte Sound (Totaranui): The Forster Perspective," in *Enlightenment and New Zealand, 1773–1774* (Wellington: National Art Gallery, [ca. 1979]), 19–20.

44. On this point see Hedwig Röckelein, "Einleitung: Kannibalismus und europäische Kultur," in *Kannibalismus und Europäische Kultur*, esp. 14.

45. Raynal, *Histoire philosophique et politique*, 2:3.

46. See Sparrman, *Voyage Round the World*, 115. This incident of the head was popularly disseminated in the following century by G. L. Craik in *The New Zealanders* (London: Charles Knight, 1830), 103.

47. Sparrman, *Voyage Round the World*, 115–17. Sparrman also draws an analogy to his bloodthirsty Viking ancestors; Robert Southey made this same identification in his *History of Brazil* (1810), 2d ed., 3 vols. (London: Longman, Hurst, Rees, Orme, and Brown, 1822), 1:231.

48. Sydney Parkinson, *A Journal of a Voyage to the South Seas* (1784) (London: Caliban Books, 1984), 115–16. See also the account of how some Tonga islanders teased a hungry William Mariner with what appeared to be cooked human flesh, in a scene that reverses the one described above that was witnessed by William Wales, in Martin, *Account of the Natives of the Tonga Islands*, 1:108–10.

49. John Hawkesworth, *An Account of the Voyages Undertaken by the Order of His Present Majesty for Making Discoveries in the Southern Hemisphere, and Successively Performed by Commodore Byron, Captain Wallis, Captain Carteret, and Captain Cook, in the* DOLPHIN, *the* SWALLOW, *and the* ENDEAVOUR, 2d ed., 3 vols. (London: W. Strahan and T. Cadell, 1773), 2:395. See also the references to this trade in the same volume, 390, and in Joseph Banks, *The "Endeavour" Journal of Joseph Banks: 1768–1771*, ed. J. C. Beaglehole, 2 vols. (Sydney: Angus and Robertson, 1962), esp. 1:455 and 2:30–31. (This is one of the journals on which Hawkesworth drew for his account.)

50. Bartolomé de Las Casas, *A Short Account of the Destruction of the Indies* (1552), ed. and trans. Nigel Griffin (London: Penguin Books, 1991), 63. See Southey's similar claim that the Europeans in Brazil had manipulated feuds for their ends, *History of Brazil*, 1:226.

51. Raynal, *Histoire philosophique et politique*, 2:251.

52. Anthony Pagden, *The Fall of Natural Man: The American Indian and the Origins of Comparative Ethnology* (Cambridge: Cambridge University Press, 1982), 83.

53. See Olaudah Equiano, *The Interesting Narrative of the Life of Olaudah Equiano or Gustavus Vassa, the African*, in *The Classic Slave Narratives*, ed. Henry Louis Gates Jr. (New York: New American Library, 1987), 33; and Mungo Park, *Travels in the Interior Districts of Africa* (1799) (London: Folio Society, 1984), 54, 116, 171.

54. Daniel Defoe, *Robinson Crusoe* (1719), ed. Michael Shinagel (New York: W. W. Norton, 1975), 123.

55. [James Mario Matra?], *A Journal of a Voyage Round the World in His Majesty's Ship Endeavour* (1771) (Adelaide: Antonio Giordano, 1975), 100.

56. See Woodes Rogers, *A Cruising Voyage Round the World* (1712) (New York: Dover, 1970), 92.

57. [Abbé Mallet], "Anthropophagie," 498; and see [Cornelius] de Pauw, *Recherches philosophiques sur les Américains*, in vol. 1 of *Oeuvres philosophiques* (1768–69), 7 vols. (Paris: Jean-François Bastien, 1794), 270. On this subject of "the cannibal within," see Jean Biou, "Lumières et anthropophagie," *Revue des sciences humaines* 46 (April–June 1972): 223–33.

58. [Jean-Baptiste-René Robinet], *De la nature,* rev. ed., 4 vols. (Amsterdam: E. Van Harrevelt, 1763–66), 1:88–89.

59. Johann Reinhold Forster, *Observations Made During a Voyage Round the World* (1778), ed. Nicholas Thomas, Harriet Guest, and Michael Dettelbach (Honolulu: University of Hawai'i Press, 1996), 343. (Johann Reinhold Forster, the naturalist, is to be distinguished from his son, Georg Forster, who accompanied him on this voyage and also wrote about it.)

60. Edward Gibbon, *The Decline and Fall of the Roman Empire,* 3 vols. (New York: Modern Library, [1932]), 1:879. In terms of the discussion of Sade below, it is worth noting that Sade has Noirceuil refer to this same account of cannibalism among the ancient Scots in *L'histoire de Juliette, ou, Les prospérités du vice* (1797), in vols. 8 and 9 of *Oeuvres complètes,* 16 vols. (Paris: Cercle du Livre Précieux, 1966), 8:185, and *Aline et Valcour, ou, Le roman philosophique,* in vols. 4 and 5 of *Oeuvres complètes,* 4:197n.

61. Historical accidents that led some to see *canis* (dog) in *cannibal* further complicated this association; on this point, see Lestringant, *Cannibals,* 18–22.

62. Martin, *Account of the Natives of the Tonga Islands,* 1:187–88n.

63. Robert Boyle, "Upon the Eating of Oysters," *Occasional Reflections upon Several Subjects,* in vol. 2 of *The Works of the Honourable Robert Boyle,* 5 vols. (London: A. Millar, 1744), 220. See also Boyle's recommendation of the spirit of human blood as "a good remedy in no small number of internal affections of the human body," as in "many distempers, especially wherein either spirit of urine, or the urinous spirit of sal-ammoniac, have been found successful medicines," in "The Natural History of Human Blood," in vol. 4 of *Works,* 193.

64. Tobias Smollett, *The Adventures of Peregrine Pickle,* ed. James L. Clifford (London: Oxford University Press, 1964), 262.

65. See Miguel de Cervantes Saavedra, *Don Quixote,* trans. Walter Starkie (New York: New American Library, 1979), 175 (pt. 1, chap. 19).

66. Atkins, *Voyage to Guinea, Brasil, and the West-Indies,* xxiv–xxv. For the historical background to such rivalry among Europeans for the distinction of being the more edible, see Lestringant, *Cannibals,* 27–31.

67. Heinrich von Kleist, *Penthesilea,* in *Five Plays,* trans. Martin Greenberg (New Haven: Yale University Press, 1988), 266.

68. See Joseph Conrad, *Heart of Darkness,* ed. Robert Kimbrough, 3d ed. (New York: W. W. Norton, 1988), 43.

69. See Pagden's remark (*Fall of Natural Man,* 82) about this privileging of human flesh as a cross-cultural element in cannibal mythology.

70. Susan Meld Shell, *The Embodiment of Reason: Kant on Spirit, Generation,*

and Community (Chicago: University of Chicago Press, 1996), 111. See also Shell's mention of "Kant's peculiar (and notorious) comparison of sexual intercourse to cannibalism," 153.

71. See also *Juliette*, 8:363n, where Sade describes the theological doctrine of hell as an image of the divinity eating his children. The figure of the vampire is, of course, not simply to be assimilated to the figure of the cannibal; but see the intriguing argument about the relationship between vampirism and the Enlightenment's "recognition of an autonomous body, a mechanical body," in Charles Porset, "Vampires et Lumières," *Studies on Voltaire and the Eighteenth Century* 266 (1989): 125–50.

72. See, for instance, the references to La Mettrie in Sade, *Juliette*, 8:500 and 9:115; and Juliette's identification of her thinking with that of Hobbes and Montesquieu (*Juliette*, 9:336). On the relationship of Sade's conception of cannibalism to that of Enlightenment philosophes, see Beatrice Fink, "Lecture alimentaire de l'utopie sadienne," in *Sade: Écrire la crise*, ed. Michel Camus and Phillipe Roger (Paris: Pierre Belfond, 1983), 184–85.

73. Stanley Cavell, "*Coriolanus* and Interpretations of Politics ('Who Does the Wolf Love?')," in *Themes Out of School: Effects and Causes* (San Francisco: North Point Press, 1984), 96. This essay in its entirety is very evocative in relation to the topics addressed in this chapter.

74. Raynal, *Histoire philosophique et politique*, 2:372.

75. Nicolas Réstif de la Bretonne, *La paysanne pervertie ou les dangers de la ville* (1787) (Paris: Garnier-Flammarion, 1972), 169.

76. [Matra?], *Journal of a Voyage Round the World*, 95–96. For the relevant passages from Voltaire, see *Essai sur les moeurs* (1753–78), in vol. 12 of *Oeuvres complètes*, 388; "Anthropophages," in *Dictionnaire philosophique* (1764–69), in vol. 17 of *Oeuvres complètes*, 263; and the speech by Cacambo in *Candide* (1759), in vol. 21 of *Oeuvres complètes*, 171: "Certainly it is better to eat one's enemies than to abandon the fruit of one's victory to the ravens and crows." Cacambo is explaining to the Oreillons, an imaginary people in South America, that because he and Candide are not Jesuits, as they have appeared to be, the feedings on their flesh that would otherwise be justified ought not to be carried out.

This emphasis on bodies as carrion in relation to bodies as cannibal victuals antedated Voltaire's work, however; see, for instance, the description of Brazilians in Father Jerom [*sic*] Merolla da Sorrento, *A Voyage to the Congo and Several Other Countries Chiefly in Southern Africk* (1682), in *A Collection of Voyages and Travels*, ed. Awnsham Churchill, 3d ed. (London: H. Lintot, 1744–46), 530: "Sometimes they feed upon man's flesh, and that upon the following occasion:

when any one of their relations or friends falls desperately sick, before he grows worse they knock him on the head, and cutting his body to pieces, distributing it amongst the rest to eat; alleging, *that it is much more honourable for him to be devoured by them, than to be preyed upon by worms and insects."*

77. Hawkesworth, *An Account of the Voyages*, 3:44. It should be noted, though, that what I characterize here as Hawkesworth's "unexceptional" mind was not necessarily perceived as such in his day, in which his work found many critics; see Jonathan Lamb's argument related to this point in "Minute Particulars and Representation of South Pacific Discovery," *Eighteenth-Century Studies* 28 (Spring 1995): 281–94.

78. De Pauw, *Recherches philosophiques sur les Américains*, 266.

79. D. A. F. de Sade, *Les cent vingt journées de Sodom* (ca. 1785), in vol. 13 of *Oeuvres complètes*, 141–42.

80. See Sade, *Juliette*, 8:572n and 9:190; see also the references to Cook in Sade, *Aline et Valcour*, 4:197n, 201n, 219n, 249–50, 305, and 5:220.

81. For an example of the connections Sade drew between colonialism and cannibalism, see *Aline et Valcour*, 4:206: "It is no more surprising to see Europe enchain Africa than to see a butcher fell the ox that serves to nourish you."

82. For an analysis of Sade's work relevant to this and other points in my discussion, see Marcel Hénaff, *Sade: The Invention of the Libertine Body*, trans. Xavier Callahan (Minneapolis: University of Minnesota Press, 1999).

83. Cf. the scene a few pages later, in *Les cent vingt journées de Sodom*, 424: "A fellow seeks out two good friends, binds them together mouth to mouth, an excellent repast facing them, but they cannot reach it, he watches them devour each other when their hunger becomes pressing."

84. Georg Wilhelm Friedrich Hegel, *Phenomenology of Spirit* (1807), trans. A. V. Miller (Oxford: Oxford University Press, 1977), 65;

85. Georg Wilhelm Friedrich Hegel, *Encyclopedia of the Philosophical Sciences in Outline* (1817), ed. Ernst Behler, trans. Steven A. Taubeneck (New York: Continuum, 1990), 187.

86. Georg Wilhelm Friedrich Hegel, "Reason in History," introduction to *Lectures on the Philosophy of World History*, trans. H. B. Nisbet (Cambridge: Cambridge University Press, 1975), 182–83.

87. Georg Wilhelm Friedrich Hegel, *The Philosophy of Nature*, trans. A. V. Miller (Oxford: Oxford University Press, 1970), 404.

88. William Blake, *Jerusalem* (1804), in *The Complete Poetry and Prose of William Blake*, ed. David V. Erdman, rev. ed. (New York: Doubleday, 1988), sec. 1, plate 11, ll. 5–7.

89. See Immanuel Kant, *Critique of Pure Reason* (1781), trans. Werner S. Pluhar (Indianapolis: Hackett Publishing, 1996), 696–97.

CHAPTER 6
Kant Comes to His Senses

1. See the quotation from Augustine's *Joannis Evangelium* in Nicolas James Perella, *The Kiss Sacred and Profane: An Interpretative History of Kiss Symbolism and Related Religio-Erotic Themes* (Berkeley: University of California Press, 1969), 276–77n. Perella's wide-ranging work is valuable in relation to all the issues of kissing that I address here; also of interest is Christopher Nyrop, *The Kiss and Its History*, trans. William Frederick Harvey (New York: E. P. Dutton, 1902). For an example of the classical precedent to which I allude, see the description of the views of Archelaus in Diogenes Laertius, *Lives of Eminent Philosophers* (A.D. 200–250), trans. R. D. Hicks, 2 vols. (London: William Heinemann), 1:147.

2. Sigmund Freud, *Three Essays on a Theory of Sexuality*, in vol. 7 of *The Standard Edition of the Complete Psychological Works of Sigmund Freud*, ed. James Strachey, 24 vols. (London: Hogarth Press and the Institute of Psycho-Analysis, 1955), 150.

3. See Pierre J. Payer, *The Bridling of Desire: Views of Sex in the Later Middle Ages* (Toronto: University of Toronto Press, 1993), 29.

4. Cf. Bruce Thomas Boehrer's analysis of how "the various terms of the anatomy become promiscuously interchangeable" in Ben Jonson's writing, and the related analysis of the body as conceived of in early modern medicine, in *The Fury of Men's Gullets: Ben Jonson and the Digestive Canal* (Philadelphia: University of Pennsylvania Press, 1997), 150, 188. Cf. also Paul Ilie's description of the "anastomotic derangement" potentially implicated in Denis Diderot's image of "the spider brain," in *The Age of Minerva*, 2 vols. (Philadelphia: University of Pennsylvania Press, 1995), 2:145.

5. On this topic see Evelyn Fox Keller's argument about the relationship between the development of modern science and the demonization of women as witches, in *Reflections on Gender and Science* (New Haven: Yale University Press, 1985), 56–65; see also Charles Zika, "Kannibalismus und Hexerei: Die Rolle der Bilder im frühneuzeitlichen Europa," in *Kannibalismus und Europäische Kultur*, ed. Hedwig Röckelein (Tübingen: Edition Diskord, 1996), 75–114.

6. Kiki Smith, quoted in *Kiki Smith* (exhibition catalogue) (London: Whitechapel Art Gallery, 1995), 32.

7. On this topic see the highly suggestive essay by John P. Leavey, "French

Kissing: Whose Tongue Is It Anyway?" in *French Connections: Exploring the Literary and National Contexts of Derridean Discourse,* ed. Julian Wolfreys (Albany: State University of New York Press, 1999), 149–63.

8. Immanuel Kant, *The Conflict of the Faculties* (1798), trans. Mary J. Gregor (Lincoln: University of Nebraska Press, 1992), 209. Although Kant is describing a general case at this point in this work, which was written near the end of his life, he identifies himself with this case ("in this respect I myself am guilty") and continues with further remarks about himself.

9. Thomas De Quincey, *Confessions of an English Opium-Eater,* in vol. 3 of *Collected Writings of Thomas De Quincey,* ed. David Masson, 14 vols. (London: Adam and Charles Black, 1897), 467.

10. Thomas De Quincey, "The Last Days of Kant," in vol. 4 of *Collected Writings,* 375n.

11. I have elided the third example in De Quincey's footnote, of the death of General Ludlow's nephew, which would extend but not materially alter the present argument.

12. See De Quincey's description of Kant's "masculine taste" and consequent antipathy to "sentimental pathos," in "Last Days of Kant," 361n: "In this, as in many other things, the taste of Kant was entirely English and Roman." For a discussion of "the sexed subject" of the eighteenth-century sublime, see Peter De Bolla, *The Discourse of the Sublime: Readings in History, Aesthetics, and the Subject* (Oxford: Basil Blackwell, 1989), 56–58.

13. Thomas De Quincey, "Coleridge and Opium-Eating," in vol. 5 of *Collected Writings,* 190n.

14. Thomas De Quincey, "A Brief Appraisal of the Greek Literature in Its Foremost Pretensions," in vol. 10 of *Collected Writings,* 300–301n.

15. De Quincey's offer bears reference to the long-standing practice of "penal anatomy," in which the bodies of condemned malefactors were subjected to the further punishment of dissection; the practice had been codified in the "Murder Act" of 1752. See Jonathan Sawday, *The Body Emblazoned: Dissection and the Human Body in Renaissance Culture* (London: Routledge, 1995), 54–57. De Quincey's rhetorical gesture may also have alluded to the encouragment of such voluntary donations as a patriotic gesture in late eighteenth-century France; John Mc-Manners describes this in *Death and the Enlightenment: Changing Attitudes to Death among Christians and Unbelievers in Eighteenth-Century France* (Oxford: Oxford University Press, 1981), 41–42.

16. A[ndreas] Ch[ristoph] Wasianski, *Immanuel Kant in seinem letzten lebens-*

jahren, in *Immanuel Kant: Sein leben in darstellungen von zeitgenossen* (Darmstadt: Wissenschaftliche Buchgesellschaft, 1968), 301–2.

17. William Beatty, *The Death of Lord Nelson: 21 October 1805* (1807) (Westminster: Archibald Constable, 1895), 47–48.

18. Quoted in Helmut von Erffa and Allen Staley, *The Paintings of Benjamin West* (New Haven: Yale University Press, 1986), 222. However, West followed his *Death of Lord Nelson* (1806) with another rendering, *The Death of Lord Nelson in the Cockpit of the Victory* (1808), which was more accurate as to place and Nelson's (undressed) condition, though no less heroic and spiritual in design. It may be noted that West was among those who testified to Nelson's habit of prolepsis in regard to his own death; in fact, he said that Nelson had admired the painting of Wolfe and had offered his own future fall in battle as an apt subject for West. It may further be noted that the kiss on which De Quincey lingers is, in effect, a translation of the touch of the masculine hand established in this genre of artwork.

19. Thomas De Quincey, *Confessions of an English Opium-Eater,* ed. Grevel Lindop (1821; Oxford: Oxford University Press, 1985), 78.

20. Cf. the argument that "the stomach occupies a central site of ethical discrimination and devotional interiority in early modern culture," in Michal Schoenfeldt, "Fables of the Belly in Early Modern England," in *The Body in Parts: Fantasies of Corporeality in Early Modern Europe,* ed. David Hillman and Carla Mazzio (New York: Routledge, 1997), 244.

21. For an analysis of Sterne's binding of character to physiology, see James Rodgers, "Sensibility, Sympathy, Benevolence: Physiology and Moral Philosophy in *Tristram Shandy,*" in *Languages of Nature: Critical Essays on Science and Literature,* ed. L. J. Jordanova (London: Free Association Books, 1986), 117–58.

22. For an argument relevant to this point and others in this essay, see Paul Youngquist, "De Quincey's Crazy Body," *PMLA* 114 (May 1999): 346–58.

23. See Immanuel Kant, *Critique of Pure Reason* (1781), trans. Werner Pluhar (Indianapolis: Hackett Publishing, 1996), 19. On the relation between Kant's work and contemporary theories of tonic movement, such as those of John Brown, Thomas Willis, Thomas Sydenham, William Cullen, and Robert Whytt, among others, see Harmut Böhme and Gernot Böhme, *Das Andere der Vernunft: Zur Entwicklung von Rationalitätsstrukturen am Beispiel Kants* (Frankfurt am Main: Suhrkamp, 1983), 117–20. See also François Duchesneau's analysis of the significance of peristaltic movement in the work of Friedrich Hoffmann, *La physiologie des lumières: Empirisme, modèles, et théories* (The Hague: Martinus Nijhoff, 1982), 52–53.

24. See Susan Meld Shell, *The Embodiment of Reason: Kant on Spirit, Generation, and Community* (Chicago: University of Chicago Press, 1996), 396n.

25. See Jean-François Lyotard, "Judicieux dans le différend," in *La faculté de juger*, by Jacques Derrida, Jean-Luc Nancy, Vincent Descombs, Garbis Kortian, Phillipe Lacoue-Labarthe, and Jean-François Lyotard (Paris: Éditions de Minuit, 1985), 198. This entire essay (195–236) is relevant to my concerns here.

26. Théophile Bordeu, *Recherches sur les maladies chroniques, leurs rapports avec les maladies aiguës, leur périodes, leur nature, et sur la manière dont on les traite aux eaux minérales de Barèges, et des autres sources de l'Aquitaine* (1775), in vol. 2 of *Oeuvres complètes*, 2 vols. (Paris: Caille et Ravier, 1818), 802; [Julien Offroy de] La Mettrie, *L'homme machine*, ed. Paul-Laurent Assoun (Paris: Éditions Denoël/Gonthier, 1981), 138.

27. By 1778 it was possible for Paul-Joseph Barthez to disparage the two main contemporary theories, the oscillationist and the fluidist, as being of a kind in reaching beyond the available evidence; see *Nouveau éléments de la science de l'homme*, 2 vols. (Montpellier: Jean Martel Aîné, 1778), 1:207–8. Nonetheless, they continued to be influential; see, for instance, [Johann Friederich] Blumenbach, *The Institutions of Physiology*, [trans. John Elliotson] (London: E. Cox and Son, 1815), 88: "Most opinions on this subject may be divided into two classes. The one class regards the action of the nervous system as consisting in an oscillatory motion. The other ascribes it to the motion of a certain fluid, whose nature is a matter of dispute." The author goes on to offer the compromise hypothesis of "a nervous fluid thrown in oscillatory vibrations by the action of stimulants." Blumenbach's work was widely influential and admired by Kant, Coleridge (who studied with Blumenbach), and others. In this regard, see Ilie's discussion of the "opposing paradigms of sensibility" in this age, "the vibrationist" and "the fluidist" models, in *The Age of Minerva*, 2:11–12, 151–58, 188–90, 229, and 282–85. See also Aram Vartanian's discussion of "the precious ambiguity of meaning" conveyed by Denis Diderot's usage of the term *sensibilité*, in "Intertextures of Science and Humanism in the French Enlightenment," *Studies in Eighteenth-Century Culture* 1 (1971): 118. For an indication of how widely disseminated this image of things was, see, for instance, the following passage describing the "communication [to the brain] of the impressions made on the senses by external objects," from the popular novel by Charles Johnstone, *Chrysal: Or, The Adventures of a Guinea* (1760–65), ed. E. A. Baker (London: George Routledge and Sons, [1932]), 4–5: "How this communication is made, I cannot, however, so well inform you; whether it is by the oscillations of the nervous fibres, or by the operation of a certain invisible fluid, called animal spirits, on the nerves." In this regard, cf. the dis-

cussion of De Quincey's "perpetual 'oscillation' between highs and lows" and of his "convulsions," in Alina Clej, *A Genealogy of the Modern Self: Thomas De Quincey and the Intoxication of Writing* (Stanford: Stanford University Press, 1995), 73–75, 86–88, 184–94.

28. Isaac Newton, *The Mathematical Principles of Natural Philosophy* (New York: Citadel Press, 1964), 447.

29. See David Hartley, *Observations on Man, His Frame, His Duty, and His Expectations* (1749) (2 vols. in 1) (Gainesville, Fla.: Scholars' Facsimiles and Reprints, 1966).

30. Laurence Sterne, *The Life and Opinions of Tristram Shandy, Gentleman* (New York: Modern Library, 1950), 311; George Berkeley, *Siris: A Chain of Philosophical Reflexions and Inquiries Concerning the Virtues of Tar-Water, and divers other Subjects connected together and arising One from Another* (1744), in vol. 5 of *The Works of George Berkeley, Bishop of Cloyne*, ed. A. A. Luce and T. E. Jessop, 9 vols. (London: Thomas Nelson and Sons, 1953), 77; and Georg Wilhelm Friedrich Hegel, *Phenomenology of Spirit*, trans. A. V. Miller (Oxford: Oxford University Press, 1977), 36.

31. Immanuel Kant, *The Critique of Judgement*, trans. James Creed Meredith (2 vols. in 1) (Oxford: Oxford University Press, 1952), 1:199, 201.

32. See Maine de Biran, *Nouvelles considérations sur les rapports du physique et du moral de l'homme* (1821), in vol. 9 of *Oeuvres*, ed. François Azouri, 13 vols. (Paris: J. Vrin, 1990), 35–37.

33. In addition to the foregoing quotation, see, e. g., Kant, *Critique of Judgement*, 2:27: "We see, then, that the grass is required as a means of existence by cattle, and cattle, similarly, by man. But we do not see why after all it should be necessary that men should in fact exist (a question that might not be easy to answer if the specimens of humanity that we had in mind were, say, the New Hollanders or Fuegians)."

34. Denis Diderot, À Sophie Volland" (14 October 1762), in vol. 4 of *Correspondance*, ed. Georges Roth, 16 vols. (Paris: Éditions de Minuit, 1958), 196.

35. Cf. Shell's analysis of the significance of Kant's statement, in one of his writings on race and generation: "The bounds [*Schranken*] of reason once penetrated [*durch brochen*], delusion presses through the same gap [*Lücke*] by the thousands" (*Embodiment of Reason*, 195).

36. Immanuel Kant, "Über den Gebrauch teleologischer Principien in der Philosophie" (1788), in vol. 8 of *Gesammelte Schriften*, 29 vols. (Berlin: George Reimer, 1914), 179.

37. Immanuel Kant, *Die Metaphysik der Sitten* (1797), in vol. 6 of *Gesammelte Schriften*, 359–60.

38. Shell, *Embodiment of Reason*, 3.

39. See Shell's discussion of a passage in Kant's writings (*Embodiment of Reason*, 232–33) in which he "compares—in a tone that combines a literally visceral sympathy with woman's lot with an equally visceral abhorrence—the trials of inspired genius with the noisy birth pangs of a pregnant housewife"; and her discussion (224) of female beauty as "the missing centerpiece of Kant's critique of taste," in which "disinterested pleasure and disgust cannot, in woman's case, be long kept apart." See also the analysis of the relation between female and destructive forces in Kant's philosophy in Böhme and Böhme, *Das Andere der Vernunft*, 367–68.

40. Xav[ier] Bichat, *Recherches physiologiques sur la vie et la mort*, 3d ed. (Paris: Brosson et Gabon, 1805), 45–46; Théophile Bordeu, *Recherches sur le tissu muqueux, ou l'organe cellulaire, et sur quelques maladies de la poitrine* (1767), in vol. 2 of *Oeuvres complètes*, 744, 748–51. It may be worth remembering that Bichat is the figure who inspires Dr. Lydgate in George Eliot's *Middlemarch*—in which De Quincey is also mentioned, in passing, as an influence on the literary career of Will Ladislaw (George Eliot, *Middlemarch*, ed. W. J. Harvey [New York: Viking Press, 1985] 177, 109.

41. Bordeu, *Recherches sur les maladies chroniques*, 802; *Recherches sur le tissu muqueux*, 739–40, 786, 741.

42. Julien Offroy de La Mettrie, *Système d'Epicure*, in *Oeuvres philosophiques* (2 vols. in 1) (Hildesheim: Georg Olms, 1970), 1:239.

43. See John Abernethy, "Lecture IV" (1817), in *Physiological Lectures Addressed to the College of Surgeons* (London: Longman, Hurst, Rees, Orme, and Brown, 1821), 158.

44. G[eorge]-E[rnst] Stahl, *Paroenesis ou exhortation sur la nécessité d'éloigner de la doctrine médicale tout ce qui lui est étranger* (1706), in vol. 2 of *Oeuvres médico-philosophiques et pratiques de G.-E. Stahl*, trans. T. Blondin, 6 vols. (Paris: J.-B. Baillière et fils, 1863), 169; G[eorge]-E[rnst] Stahl, *Recherches sur la différence qui existe entre le mécanisme et l'organisme* (1706), in vol. 2 of *Oeuvres médico-philosophiques et pratiques*, 212. In addition to the aforementioned reference to Stahl in the preface to the second edition of the *Critique of Pure Reason*, see Kant's reference to Albrecht von Haller's conception of the sublime (*Critique of Pure Reason*, 594). On this point, see also Shell's description of the shudder of Kant's sublime as "a life-quickening alternative (despite or even because of its pain) to those 'exhausting' fictional romances against which Kant earlier warns—representations of perfection that both distend and leave us flaccid" (*Embodiment of Reason*, 214); see also the analysis of the role of the sublime in imperialist dis-

course, in Sara Suleri, *The Rhetoric of English India* (Chicago: University of Chicago Press, 1992), 24–48. Robert E. Butts also addresses the issue of Kant as a metaphysical physician in the final chapter of *Kant and the Double Government Methodology: Supersensibility and Method in Kant's Philosophy of Science* (Dordrecht: D. Reidel, 1984), 282–318.

45. John Abernethy, "Lecture VI" (1817), in *Physiological Lectures*, 257–58.

46. See Richard Saumarez, *The Principles of Physiological and Physical Science* (London: T. Egerton, 1812), 21–47. In this context, Shelley's preoccupation with dietary matters, as in his notes to *Queen Mab*, perhaps becomes more interesting and consequential than it is usually taken to be; for the contemporary background to Shelley's vegetarianism, see Virginia Smith, "Physical Puritanism and Sanitary Science: Material and Immaterial Beliefs in Popular Physiology, 1650–1840," in *Medical Fringe and Medical Orthodoxy, 1750–1850*, ed. W. F. Bynum and Roy Porter (London: Croom Helm, 1987), 174–97. For a wide-ranging consideration of this issue, see Steven Shapin, "The Philosopher and the Chicken: On the Dietetics of Disembodied Knowledge," in *Science Incarnate: Historical Embodiments of Natural Knowledge*, ed. Christopher Lawrence and Steven Shapin (Chicago: University of Chicago Press, 1998), 21–50.

47. Attention to such passages has been interestingly pursued, however, in the work of two twentieth-century novelists: Robert Musil and Angela Carter. Musil characterized his "man without qualities," Ulrich, as one who recognizes "that the mucous membrane of the lips is related to the mucous membrane of the intestines" and who argues that the "unreliability of our higher powers" sends us on the way to "man-eating" as much as it does to *"The Critique of Pure Reason"* (Robert Musil, *The Man without Qualities* [1930] [New York: Coward-McCann, 1953], 157, 424). In a statement that captures a central concern of her work, Carter has a character say, "Time and space are the very guts of nature and so, naturally, they undulate in the manner of intestines" (Angela Carter, *The Infernal Desire Machines of Doctor Hoffman* [1972] [New York: Penguin, 1982], 33).

48. Immanuel Kant, *Critique of Practical Reason* (1788), trans. Mary Gregor (Cambridge: Cambridge University Press, 1997), 133.

49. Thomas De Quincey, "Judas Iscariot," in vol. 8 of *Collected Writings*, 196–97.

50. Quoted in *Kiki Smith: Unfolding the Body* (exhibition catalogue) (Waltham, Mass.: Rose Art Museum/Brandeis University, 1992), 35.

51. I give the adage as quoted in Freud, *Civilization and Its Discontents*, in vol. 21 of *Standard Edition*, 106n. In slightly different forms, it was also quoted by Havelock Ellis and others, and a similar line (in French) occurs in the writings

of Voltaire. Erroneously, apparently, it has been attributed to Augustine; the precise origin, if there is one, is unclear.

52. See Immanuel Kant, *Lectures on Ethics*, trans. Louis Infield (New York: Harper and Row, 1963), 169–71.

53. Frantz Fanon, *Peau noire, masques blancs* (1952) (Paris: Éditions du Seuil, 1995), 184.

54. Shell, *Embodiment of Reason*, 400–401n.

55. See "that sublime of crocodiles, *papa*," in "The Spanish Military Nun" (171), and the crocodile associated with the "venerable" coachman, in "The English Mail-Coach" (289), both in vol. 13 of *Collected Writings of Thomas De Quincey*, ed. David Masson, 14 vols. (London: Adam and Charles Black, 1897). See also the commentary on the figure of the crocodile in V. A. De Luca, *Thomas De Quincey: The Prose of Vision* (Toronto: University of Toronto Press, 1980), 102–3. On the broader issue of the social and political tensions in the struggle over the definition of the body in the era during which De Quincey was writing, see *The Making of the Modern Body: Sexuality and Society in the Nineteenth Century,* ed. Catherine Gallagher and Thomas Laqueur (Berkeley: University of California Press, 1987). For the social and political contexts of De Quincey's opium visions in particular, see Alethea Hayter, *Opium and the Romantic Imagination* (Berkeley: University of California Press, 1968), 101–31, 226–54; Virginia Berridge and Griffith Edwards, *Opium and the People: Opium Use in Nineteenth-Century England* (New York: St. Martin's Press, 1981); John Barrell, *The Infection of Thomas De Quincey: A Psychopathology of Imperialism* (New Haven: Yale University Press, 1991), esp. 1–24, 147–81; Josephine McDonagh, *De Quincey's Disciplines* (Oxford: Oxford University Press, 1994), esp. 152–84; and Barry Milligan, *Pleasures and Pains: Opium and the Orient in Nineteenth-Century British Culture* (Charlottesville: University Press of Virginia, 1995), 46–68.

It is notable that Jean-Paul Sartre, in effect, got mired in this moment in De Quincey's visions when he associated "*le visqueux*" with "the primitive clan of lizards"; characterized it as the definitively unsublime "agony of water"; and gendered it as "feminine" and, as such, a "sucking" threat—"sickly-sweet, feminine revenge" (*Being and Nothingness: An Essay on Phenomenological Ontology*, trans. Hazel E. Barnes (New York: Philosophical Library, 1956), 606–9). For a view of slime somewhat closer to my own, see Slavoj Zizek's reference to "the slimy substance of *jouissance*," in *Tarrying with the Negative: Kant, Hegel, and the Critique of Ideology* (Durham: Duke University Press, 1993), 62. See also his comment on the "formless, mucous slime without proper ontological consistency" to which the *femme fatale* is reduced when rejected by the hero of the *film noir* (187).

56. William Beckford, *Vathek,* ed. Roger Lonsdale (London: Oxford University Press, 1970), 15.

57. See John Milton, *Paradise Lost,* 3.362–64.

58. For a different approach to De Quincey's conception of the sublime, which sees it as opposed to embodiment, see Charles J. Rzepka, *Sacramental Commodities: Gift, Text, and the Sublime in De Quincey* (Amherst: University of Massachusetts Press, 1995).

59. On this subject see Norbert Elias, *The Civilizing Process: The History of Manners and State Formation and Civilization* (1939), trans. Edmund Jephcott (Oxford: Basil Blackwell, 1994).

60. Thomas De Quincey, "Conversation," in vol. 10 of *Collected Writings,* 264–65.

61. See, e. g., the ceremony of initiation into the secret Masonic society in D. A. F. de Sade, *L'histoire de Juliette, ou, Les prospérités du vice* (1797), in vols. 8 and 9 of *Oeuvres complètes,* 16 vols. (Paris: Cercle du Livre Précieux, 1966), 9:269–70. For the folklore about the devil's preference in kisses, see, e. g., the account in *Auto da fe celebrado en la ciudad de Logroño en los dias 7 y 8 de Noviembre del año de 1610* (Madrid: De Collado, 1820), 29.

62. See Kant, *Conflict of the Faculties,* 209: "Why do I prolong a feeble life to an extraordinary age by self-denial, and by my example confuse the obituary list, which is based on the average of those who are more frail by nature and calculated on their life expectancy? Why submit to my own firm resolution what we used to call fate (to which we submitted humbly and piously)—a resolution which, in any case, will hardly be adopted as a universal rule of regimen by which reason exercises direct healing power, and which will never replace the prescriptions the pharmacist dispenses?" It is noteworthy that these questions are the last words of this book save for a postscript that complains about harassments and disturbances of his organs of vision; it is noteworthy as well that Kant regularly studied tables of mortality that he had arranged to have sent to him by the local police.

63. Thomas De Quincey, "Kant in His Miscellaneous Writings," in vol. 8 of *Collected Writings,* 85.

64. De Quincey also came to have other reservations about Kant—notably in regard to what he took to be the destructive tendency of his system toward orthodox Christianity. See Robert Lance Snyder, "'The Loom of *Palingenesis*': De Quincey's Cosmology in 'System of the Heavens,'" in *Thomas De Quincey: Bicentenary Studies,* ed. Robert Lance Snyder (Norman: University of Oklahoma, 1985), 338–59.

65. De Quincey, "Coleridge and Opium-Eating," 198n.

66. See Grevel Lindop, *The Opium-Eater: A Life of Thomas De Quincey* (New York: Taplinger, 1981), 241, 207.

67. See Barrell, *Infection of Thomas De Quincey*, esp. 27–32, for his analysis of the relation of this kiss to De Quincey's memory of kissing his dead sister, Elizabeth.

68. Robert Southey, *The Life of Nelson* (New York: A. L. Fowle, 1900), 260.

69. Of course, in reference to the work of Smith and others, much has been made of "abject art" in recent years; here the most significant reference would be to Julia Kristeva's influential formulation of the abject in terms of "guts sprawling" and as the "linings of the sublime," in *Powers of Horror: An Essay on Abjection*, trans. Leon S. Roudiez (New York: Columbia University Press, 1982), 3, 11.

70. See Edmund Burke, *A Philosophical Inquiry into the Origin of Our Ideas of the Sublime and Beautiful* (1757), in vol. 1 of *The Works of the Right Honourable Edmund Burke*, 12 vols. (London: John C. Nimmo, 1899), 185: "How different is the satisfaction of an anatomist, who discovers the use of the muscles and of the skin, the excellent contrivance of the one for the various movements of the body, and the wonderful texture of the other, at once a general covering, and at once a general outlet as well as inlet; how different is this from the affection which possesses an ordinary man at the sight of a delicate, smooth skin, and all the other parts of beauty, which require no investigation to be perceived! In the former case, while we look up to the Maker with admiration and praise, the object which causes it may be odious and distasteful; the latter very often so touches us by its power on the imagination, that we examine but little into the artifice of its contrivance; and we have need of a strong effort of reason to disentangle our minds from the allurements of the object, to a consideration of that wisdom which invented so powerful a machine."

Index

Abernethy, John, 198
abstract expressionism, 38
Account of Some New Microscopical Discoveries, An, 85
Acker, Kathy, 200
Adorno, Theodor, 97
Adventures of Peregrine Pickle, The, 113, 163–64
aesthetics, xiv, xviii, 4, 85, 94, 160, 201, 207; and geometry, 44, 62; and science, 73, 96–98, 116, 119–20, 128–30; and sublimity, 189, 196, 203
Against Nature, 19
À l'heure de l'observatoire: Les amoureux, 194
Aline and Valcour, 137, 171. *See also* Sade, D.A.F.
Alvarado, Pedro de, 156
Analytic Essay on Faculties of the Soul, 83
anatomy, xiii, 82; and Descartes, 42, 53; and the senses, 4, 12–13, 88–89
Anstey, Christopher, xvii, 105–8, 110, 116, 119, 123–24
anthropology, 4, 80, 160, 172; and relativism, xvi–xvii, 112–13; twentieth-century, 145–46, 150–51, 166, 169, 178–79
Anthropology, 192. *See also* Kant, Immanuel

Apocalypse Now, 144
Arens, William, 145, 151
Aristotle, 4
Art of the Eighteenth Century, The, 59. *See also* Goncourt, Edmund and Jules de
atheism, 18, 28, 73
Atkins, John, 138–39, 145, 165–66
Attali, Jacques, 140
Attributes of the Arts, 44. *See also* Chardin, Jean-Siméon
Auden, W. H., 110
Augustine, 181
Austen, Jane, xvii, 99, 132; and city of Bath, 100, 104–5, 110, 114, 117–18, 122
Authentic Narrative of the Death of Lord Nelson, 190

Bacon, Francis, 46
Bakhtin, Mikhail, xi
Bal, Mieke, 61
Bath, The, 113
Bath Characters, 121
Bath Unmask'd, The, 114, 124
Baudrillard, Jean, 133
Baxandall, Michael, 37, 54
Bayle, Pierre, 22–23, 76
Beatty, William, 190
Beckford, William, 202

Index

Index

Index

Index

Index